**This book is to be returned on or before
the last date stamped below.**

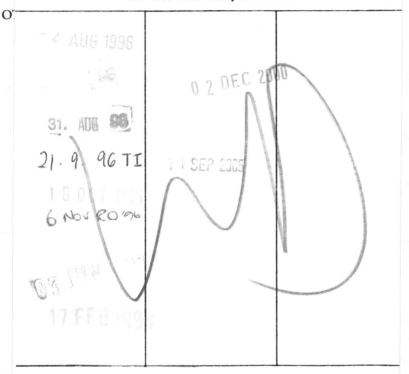

- 2 AUG 1996

31. AUG 96

21. 9. 96 TI

6 Nov RO '96

0 2 DEC 2000

1 1 SEP 2005

17 FEB 1998

SUTTON LEISURE SERVICES

RENEWALS   Please quote: date of return, your ticket number
and computer label number for each item.

OTHER BRITAIN, OTHER BRITISH

Contemporary Multicultural Fiction

Edited by
A. ROBERT LEE

Pluto  Press
LONDON • EAST HAVEN, CT

First published 1995 by Pluto Press
345 Archway Road, London N6 5AA and
140 Commerce Street, East Haven, CT 06512, USA

Copyright © A. Robert Lee 1995
The right of the contributors to be identified as the authors
of their work has been asserted by them in accordance with
the Copyright, Designs and Patents Act 1988

British Library Cataloguing in Publication Data
A catalogue record for this book is available from the British Library

ISBN 0 7453 0645 4 hbk

Library of Congress Cataloging in Publication Data
A catalog record for this book is available from the Library of Congress

Designed, typeset and produced for Pluto Press by
Chase Production Services, Chipping Norton, OX7 5QR
Printed in the EC by T J Press, Padstow, England

Contents

Introduction

Ever since I had begun to identify my subjects I had hoped to arrive, in a book, at a synthesis of the worlds and cultures that had made me.

V.S. Naipaul, *The Enigma of Arrival* (1987)

And we pursued English roses as we pursued England; by possessing these prizes, this kindness and beauty, we stared defiantly into the eye of Empire and all its self-regard ... We became part of England and yet proudly stood outside it. But to be truly free we had to free ourselves of all bitterness and resentment, too. How was this possible when bitterness and resentment were generated afresh every day?

Hanif Kureishi, *The Buddha of Suburbia* (1990)

Other Britain. Other British. The phrases immediately speak to a sense of process – the changing of the demographic guard, 'the nation' (whether aggregated into Britain or localised into England, Scotland, Wales and Northern Ireland) as less some canonical order than, post-empire for sure, an ever more arriving multiculture. Only, perhaps, the push and pull of Britain's membership in the EU, the Common Market, can be said to have stirred national debate quite so contrarily of late.

In play, then, have been the emotions, not to say the nothing if not volatile politics, of both collective and individual identity. How one, how many, *is* Britain? Are those who speak of threatened heritage, the loss of an 'agreed' way of life, simply prone to Little Englander entrenchment, nostalgia, a kind of self-validating and all too selective memory? Are those, conversely, who call for post-coloniality, an overdue recognition of ethnic and cultural diversity within a changed (and still changing) Britain, guilty of special pleading, some 'liberal' ethos born of only minority interests? How, too, to use the register of 'race', 'ethnicity', 'colour' or 'belief' without the pre-emptive strike, intendedly or not the one thing said inside the other?

1

These, to be sure, offer broad-brush terms. Like all binary readings of politics or culture, a danger immediately arises of reducing so much of the human flux and hybridity of recent Britain into sociological cartoon, a betrayingly ahistoric, either/or account. For just as 'English', 'Scottish', 'Welsh' and 'Irish' themselves pluralise as nomenclature into lines (syndromes?) of class, gender, religion, region or even language, so hybridisations like 'Asian-British', 'Caribbean-British' or 'African-British' (themselves to be particularised into, say, Brixton-Jamaican, Cardiff-Bengali, Liverpool-Nigerian) carry their own internal dynamics of heterogeneity and, often enough, tension. Culture, it will surely bear repeating, whether national or local, communal or individual, was ever so: ongoing, enactive, full of exception to any imagined rule.

To come, then, to the focus of this present collection, has this changing make-up of population and self-expression, this 'new' (yet for some, in a vintage paradox, this 'old') British ethnicity, found voice in literature – and more specifically in literary fiction? Is sufficient covered by the notion of 'The Empire Writes Back', a V.S. Naipaul or Hanif Kureishi as simply the returning voice, or face, of a one-time British *imperium*? Have the post-war years, in fact, not seen a transition from an old coloniality (empire-derived, 'immigrant') to a new coloniality (internal, indigenous), or, again, does neither wholly meet the case? What, too, of yet other shaping ethnicities, among them Jewish, Irish, Chinese, or New Zealand–Australian?

Nor can discussion of these new voices, these new accents, be supposed to be taking place in some literary void. The age has been seized by often attritional canon-wars. The 'post-modern' gets held up as either a prompt to liberation, selves, worlds, reflexively made to their own imaginative behest, or, for some diehards, a kind of Franco-American bane originating like 'theory' in all too distant quarters. Gender-studies, too, predicate new regimes of literary hermeneutics, part of an actually far larger concern with the contested place of ideology in literary–cultural concerns in general.

Accordingly, the measure, the understanding, of what so much British fiction now is also requires its own advance: such, at least, is the editorial assumption behind the essays to hand. In this respect, Abdulrazak Gurnah offers a point-of-departure in his account of V.S. Naipaul and Salman Rushdie, two 'migrant' Englands, two 'migrant' Londons, made subject to shared but always sharply different styles of post-colonial imagining.

C.L. Innes pursues a connected line, the England of Buchi Emecheta, Caryl Phillips and Ravinder Randhawa as a site of displacement and settlement in which 'making a home' signifies an act of both history and psychology. Louis James centres on the novels of George Lamming, the organising vision of the Barbadian-born novelist as one of British coloniality refracted in Caribbean-island storytelling and myth. 'Home-making' again supplies the reference-point for Susheila Nasta's account of Sam Selvon's fiction, a dialectic of Caribbeanism 'in the islands' and Caribbeanism in London.

My own account of Hanif Kureishi, David Dabydeen and Mike Phillips seeks to establish a post-migrant perspective, their respective novels as the articulation – often daringly funny and irreverent – of a multicultural England-now. Similarly, Laura Hall argues that the storytelling of Timothy Mo and Kazuo Ishiguro renegotiates 'Britishness', their call to identities beyond essentialism. In Abdulrazak Gurnah's fiction, whether his 'Africa' or 'England' novels, 'journey', I suggest, serves as an axial metaphor for engaging with colonialities of overlapping if different kinds – a 'coastal' or 'interior' East Africa in one sweep, a London or Canterbury in the other.

Michael Woolf addresses the recent fiction of Jewish Britain, from Bernard Kops to Howard Jacobson, Elaine Feinstein to Bernice Rubens, 'Jewishness' as wryest imaginative fare from Holocaust memory to Yiddish humour and from the sacred to the secular. Eamonn Hughes looks at Irish Britain (his account insists on a hyphen: Irish-Britain), a tradition, a gathering, to be differentiated from 'Irish' Irish work and whose best-known names include, luminously, Edna O'Brien, William Trevor, Robert McLiam Wilson and Ronan Bennett. Two Antipodean perspectives round out the collection: 'England' under New Zealand imaginative auspices in an analysis of Janet Frame by Rod Edmond and 'England' under Australian auspices in an overview by Gay Raines.

It would be hard to imagine any one interpretative synthesis emerging from so eclectic a gallery of writers. 'Britain' itself, as focus, shifts and turns in each telling, each successive enfabulation. Yet the absence of the single template can be a positive. For if multiculture, post-coloniality, indeed do beckon, then why not a novel whose 'Britain' speaks from infinitely beyond Middle-England and as plurally as the histories which actually went into, and continue, its making?

A. *Robert Lee*
The University of Kent at Canterbury

1. Displacement and Transformation in *The Enigma of Arrival* and *The Satanic Verses*

Abdulrazak Gurnah

In V.S. Naipaul's *The Enigma of Arrival* the narrator's vision clari-fies, becomes sharper, through observing the process of decay.[1] The dynamics of this process appear paradoxical at first sight, positing a metaphor in which decline and change deliver more precise knowledge. The 'arrival' of the narrator's journey is to accumulating moments of such precision. The focus of this 'novel in five sections' is an analogy. On the one hand, there is an infinitely extendable metaphor of journey and displacement which is figured as trauma, decay and renewal; on the other, there is the convergence of 'the writer and the man' into a more stable syn-thesis. The narrator's – 'the writer's' – understanding of his com-plex condition intensifies as he (in this case) grasps the 'flux' of decay, change and renewal. In the same way that the point or meaning of the 'flux' is present at any moment of interrogation, the convergence of 'the writer and the man' is anticipated by conceiving them as at first separate.

V.S. Naipaul's novel, then, charts a writing journey and reflects, after the point of resolution, on the meaning of 'arrival'. This reflection is a process of 'purifying the eye',[2] so that the migrant traveller, by looking 'fiercely', now sees what was always there but which his untrained eye could not see.[3] The labour of the Naipaul narrator is to learn to see beyond the 'disorder' – a word which echoes throughout the Naipaul text – which accident and luck had brought his way, and to arrive at a discursive pattern that can accommodate these contingencies. It is a labour (and writing for Naipaul is primarily 'labour') to construct the writer's vision, with its overwhelming desire for order, out of the jumble of the man's fragmented experience.[4]

5

If the Naipaul narrator in *Enigma* arrives at knowledge through an endeavour of slowly sharpening focus, Salman Rushdie's two protagonists in *The Satanic Verses* arrive at their crises with great suddenness and violence.[5] They too are migrant travellers with occluded sight, who have constructed illusions of the self which events will challenge. They are hurled towards England out of the sky, 'two brown men, falling hard, nothing so new about that' (p. 5), and are suddenly and distressingly transformed into the antithesis of their imagined selves. The 'reality' they inhabit is unstable and dangerous, and can only be tenuously grasped once the traveller has acknowledged the implications of 'translation' – a word as resonant in the Rushdie text as 'disorder' is in the Naipaul.[6] In any case, in both novels the traveller, who is constrained and constructed by colonial experience, is transformed through migration and forced to re-envision the world.

Naipaul's narrator, as we have seen, is beyond the point of resolution. His account will relive the knowledge of convergence after it has been realised. Like the story, which the narrator constructs out of de Chirico's painting, of the traveller who finds his way back to the quayside only to discover that the ship has already gone and that his journey is over, the narrative fulfils its complex desire for order by giving an account of its desire. Its strategy is not as complex as the narration itself, which along with its tone of unwavering contemplation also has a free and roving range of references which add layers and dimensions of meaning.

The narrator's initial inability to see is figured in a number of ways. He is unable to see details or, when he can, he cannot figure out their meanings. When the weather clears after four days of continuous rain and mist, for example, the narrator remarks: 'all that I saw – though I had been living in England for twenty years – were flat fields and a narrow river' (p. 11). This inability is stated explicitly in the opening section, in the failure to relate trees and flowers to their seasons, or to notice the passage of one season into another. To the stranger in an alien environment, the landscape and its narratives is 'a blur'. Yet the narrator speaks of himself as someone who 'liked to look', and who 'noticed everything'. He describes his failure in the following way: 'I saw what I saw very clearly. But I didn't know what I was looking at. I had nothing to fit it into. I was still in a kind of limbo' (p. 12). So that knowledge of the flowers when it begins to come was like learning to see, or like learning a second language (p. 32).

'Learning to see' is also figured in the relation of the landscape to its history, a relationship that the stranger has many illusions about. To the narrator the valley felt old: 'The setting felt ancient; the impression was of space, unoccupied land, the beginning of things' (p. 15). But in contrast to Conrad's 'half-made places of the world', where the grip of the wilderness and chaos is apparent in the imaging of the landscape as primeval and over-abundant, here everything is put to use. That first impression was wrong, and what at first appeared ancient and unchanged turns out to have been constructed by human design. The image of 'ancient cultures' as frugal and orderly, where the old and the new are found side by side, is contrasted both here and elsewhere in the Naipaul text, with the wastefulness of 'half-made societies that seemed doomed to remain half-made'.[7] In the Wiltshire valley the past is not discarded, which confirms the place as lived in, immemorially occupied and domesticated. Its relics, like the antiquated farm machinery – 'another piece of the past that no longer had a use but had not been thrown away' (p. 16) – speak of industry and ambition, and the desire for order. In 'Africa', which is a prominent point of reference in the narrator's reflections, the past disappears without ruins and leaves no mark of its passage in the minds of its people.[8]

The anxiety or desire to valorise the setting as significant, to see it as more real than 'my little tropical island', is an expression of what Naipaul's narrator refers to several times as 'nerves', the post-colonial migrant's insecurity in the face of the great weight of imperial history and culture contrasted with the ridiculous and disorderly existence of the 'half-made places of the world'. Though the narrator learns to see the Wiltshire valley in ever-increasing complexity as the text develops, and to describe his own place in it with sensitivity, he sees that other landscape only as 'a place of negations'.[9] He is appalled at the way the 'solitude, emptiness and menace of my Africa' (p. 155) comes to haunt him in this valley where he has retreated to recuperate. The details of the narrator's 'my Africa' sound like Naipaul's own novella *In a Free State* (1971) where the 'menace' of Africa is figured in its unknowable and dangerous stasis, one of whose most memorable metaphors is the image of the two African men who rise mysteriously and inexplicably out of the dying land and then disappear into it again. I cite the description in full here:

It was an old, exhausted land. But it was inhabited.

Two men ran out into the road. But perhaps they were only boys. They were naked, and chalked white from head to toe, white as the rocks, white as the knotted, scaly lower half of the tall cactus plants, white as the dead branches of trees whose

7

roots were loose in the crumbling soil. For four or five seconds, no more, the white figures ran with slow, light steps on the stony edge of the road and then ran back from the road into the field of scrub and stone. (p. 218)

This is the abiding 'Africa', the 'Africa' of magic and violence, and it is to this that the soldiers in that story return in their hunt for the king. Paradoxically, the valley was a fitting place for the writing of this 'African book', because at the time of writing it the narrator found the valley as unknowable – 'the absence of knowledge of where I was' (p. 93) – as 'Africa' congenitally is. The narrator's dislocation in this landscape aided the recall of Africa's no doubt more disturbing disorientation.

The narrator's rejection of both the landscape of 'Africa' and that of 'my little tropical island' is relatively unproblematic. 'Africa', on the one hand, is unevolved and unchanging, as much a dystopia and a malady as the great demoralised land represented in Conrad's description in *Heart of Darkness*; on the other hand, 'my little tropical island' is slovenly, stifling and without purpose, brought into being as an agricultural estate of a European empire and now abandoned – as provincial a 'half-made place' as Africa is unchanging. The landscape of the valley, however, cannot be so simply categorised. The narrator feels sensitive and tender to it. The sensitivity is, in part, explicable as the migrant foreigner's intrusion into this space, and demonstrates an anxious expectation of embarrassing rejection. He is relieved, for example, to find that there is no village in the valley:

I would have been nervous to meet people. After all my time in England I still had that nervousness in a new place, that rawness of response, still felt myself to be in the other man's country, felt my strangeness, my solitude. And every excursion into a new part of the country – what for others might have been adventure – was for me like tearing at an old scab. (p. 13)

He feels himself an 'oddity' in that landscape, 'unanchored and strange', and speaks with some tenderness of how his presence might seem to the people in the valley: 'I felt that my presence in that old valley was part of something like an upheaval', whereas Jack, the farm labourer he sees on his walks, appears as the archetypal native: 'genuine, rooted, fitting'. That is the early view, the anxious foreigner focusing on his strangeness. The later view, also expressed here, is that Jack too is a stranger in the valley. By his industry and orderliness he had created his own land out of the decay of the past. This act is evoked in a prose that is rich with religious echoes:

> It did not occur to me, when I first went walking and saw only the view, took what I saw as things of that walk, things that one might see in the countryside near Salisbury, immemorial, appropriate things, it did not occur to me that Jack was living in the middle of junk, among the ruins of nearly a century; that the past around his cottage might not have been his past; that he might at some stage have been a newcomer to the valley; that his style of life might have been a matter of choice, a conscious act; that out of the little piece of earth which had come to him with his farm worker's cottage ... he had created a special land for himself, a garden where (though surrounded by ruins, reminders of vanished lives) he was more than content to live out his life and where, as in a version of Book of Hours, he celebrated the seasons. (pp. 18–19)

In contrast to the rootless migrant, Jack has a commitment to his surroundings, an investment that is part of his conception of himself. What is so remarkably indulgent about this view of Jack, and later of the big house and its ruined garden, is the ability the people of the valley are given to create themselves, to fashion their lives to an image which contents them. This is in sharp contrast to the unheeding and instinctual life of the dwellers in the 'half-made places in the world'. In fact, Jack is rather fortunate in this respect. Most of the other dwellers in the valley receive the more usual Naipaul treatment of people 'without words' (p. 36) – a phrase which in this English context refers to people who are poorly educated or who do labouring jobs or who are 'the dim sighted' about their condition.

This picture of the valley is part of the narrator's romance of England, a fairytale England nurtured by a colonial education and retained even after 20 years of living with the reality. That colonial image is, at times, more real than what is in front of him: winter, for example, is still imagined differently from the narrator's own experience of it. The narrator's view of the valley is a 'literary' one. He reconstructs it in his narrative as metaphor and fantasy of an essential England, and places himself in it as the stumbling stranger coming to knowledge. This process is figured both in images of seeing, but also in images of childhood: 'my second childhood of seeing and learning' (p. 82); a 'gift of the second life in Wiltshire, the second, happier childhood' (p. 84). The migrant, at first a child, grows to adulthood in a hidden valley which is the ancient heart of England. The narrator indulges this fantasy to the extent of imagining that he was 'a man of those bygone times' (p. 23). It seems strange nostalgia for this outsider in an 'ancient' valley, but in another sense it expresses alienation and a desire to be part of the valorised history. So what is seen by the narrator as a receptiveness to the idea of an 'antique' land also expresses the outsider's longing. The contentment that comes from the landscape is to do with the way that it fulfils the migrant's expectations. The admission of such fantasy, which the narrator self-consciously addresses, is itself an expression of the stranger's desire to figure the landscape as complete and the self as fragmented and distressed:

> I had seen everything as a kind of perfection, perfectly evolved ... And I had fallen back on old ideas, ideas not now so much of decay, as of flux and the constancy of change, to fight the distress I felt at everything – a death, a fence, a departure – that undid or altered or threatened the perfection I had found. (p. 51)

The narrator is fully aware that the 'perfection' in question here, which is the garden of the great house in which he had rented a cottage, was made possible by the empire and expressed the self-confidence and prosperity of a triumphant England, and that, in its context, would have excluded him. In describing his relation to the landlord, for example, he sees that the 'empire' separated them and that it 'at the same time linked us' (p. 174).

The narrator returns to this distance between the landlord and himself, and cites the difference in the landlord's frivolous knowledge of the world: an attitude of empire (p. 253). By implication, the narrator's knowledge of the world, in contrast to the landlord's, is detailed and wide-ranging – the precise and proprietal 'my Africa' is a case in point. The ruined garden and the declining landlord are an aspect of the change that has come over England. And if the 'ruins' of the manor and the garden express the desire for 'perfection', they also give an indication of how debilitating perfection is, because, as the narrator sees, it corrupts with self-regard and does not 'encourage action' (pp. 185–6).[10] This is the paradox of the outsider's longing, as figured in Naipaul's text, both to envy the solidity of the imperial culture and to be alert to its self-indulgences.

The narrator's interest in the landlord expresses the links which he senses exist between them, even if some of these links are paradoxical. The landlord, like the narrator, had withdrawn to the countryside to recuperate. He was once a writer (although his writing is given short shrift in the text). He values privacy and solitude, and, like the narrator, he relishes the garden's decay. The narrator sees decay as the moment before creation. He describes his 'temperament' as to see decay 'even at the moment of creation'. It is significant that this position is put in terms of 'my temperament'. The valorisation of individual sensibility is also an aspect of the writerly persona which suffers mysterious and debilitating moments of over-sensitivity which transform the migrant's discomfort to 'nerves'. The narrator understands his particular sensitivity as a writer at least partly as an ability to explain his individual history in terms of a general one:

> I had thought that because of my insecure past – peasant India, colonial Trinidad, my own family circumstances, the colonial smallness that didn't consort with the grandeur of my ambitions, my uprooting of myself for a writing career, my coming to England with so little, and the very little I still had to fall back on – I had thought that because of this I had been given an especially tender or raw sense of an unaccommodating world. (p. 87)

This positioning of the writer as the imaginative locus of history is an insistent trope in the text and is elaborated as the convergence of the writer and the man. The convergence requires the writer's recognition of his 'subject', so arriving at the point of knowledge of his 'material'. Because this knowledge arrives after a writerly journey, as a result of long labour, a distance exists between 'the man' and 'the man writing', and in that gap anxiety and self-doubt breed (p. 102).

For the narrator in *Enigma*, this anxiety expresses itself in the search for 'material'. The 'material' the narrator identifies as his subject, like the knowledge of life as a journey that the traveller in the story of the painting discovers, is the experience of being a stranger in England from a colonised island in the West Indies. By refusing to acknowledge racial antagonism as 'material' earlier than this, he was expressing an affiliation, rejecting the wounded low esteem of racial contempt for a more noble writerly 'vocation':

> Racial diminution formed no part of the material of the kind of writer I was setting out to be. Thinking of myself as a writer, I was hiding my experience from myself; hiding myself from my experience. And even when I became a writer I was without the means, for many years, to cope with that disturbance. (p. 117)

In Naipaul's own text, the means of coping 'with that disturbance' did not appear until *An Area of Darkness*, in an early account of what it was like to be in London.[11] The writerly vocation in the narrator's mind derives from an English–colonial concept of 'culture'. In this account, the writer was something between the gifted figure 'reflecting in tranquillity' of the nineteenth-century Romantics, and the detached observer of 'inner development' of modernist aestheticism. These, as the narrator comes to understand, were ideas made possible by the prosperity and security which arose out of empire. He could think of himself as this kind of writer only by being false: 'I had to pretend to be other than I was, other than what a man of my background could be' (p. 134). At the resolved end of the narrator's reflections, the impulse to be a writer has become a thing of shame:

> refined by my half-English half-education and ceasing then to be a pure impulse, it [the wish to be a writer] had given me a false idea of the activity of the mind. To be what I wanted to be, I had to cease to be or grow out of what I was ... So the past for me – as colonial and writer – was full of shame and mortification. (p. 221)

It was this 'man who had left his island and community before maturity' (p. 220), and who was overwhelmed by the unexpected 'size' of the world (p. 105), who turns out to be the 'material' which enables the writer to converge with the man. And it is only after 20 years of going 'through a lot' that the writer can express the man's experience with 'simplicity and directness': 'He could not have seen like that, so clearly ... And having seen, he might not have found the words or the tone' (p. 157).

The narrative of journey, then, which is the text's subject, also describes its method. The experiences of the ingenuous young migrant as he travels by plane out of Trinidad for the first time can only be rendered 20 years later by the writer (p. 98); the first experience of London – unseeing, or seeing only in relation to a fantasy which was part of the expectations of the colonised stranger – releases itself only after reflection: 'I had come to London as to a place I knew very well. I found a city that was strange and unknown' (p. 123). In Naipaul's *Enigma* therefore, the traveller's coming-to-knowledge requires that he understand his strangeness and learn to look with sharper vision at the place that has accommodated him.

'London' as a metaphor of the colonial and post-colonial migrant's fantasy of England has figured in the work of a number of writers: Naipaul himself in several texts, Sam Selvon, George

Lamming, and G.V. Desani among many others. In these texts, the migrant experiences the loneliness and 'joylessness' of life in the city, whatever other outcomes also befall him (and in most of these cases the migrant is usually 'him'). In Rushdie's *The Satanic Verses*, the whole exploration of migrancy is sited in 'Ellowen Deeowen', the beloved 'Vilayet' of colonial fantasy – 'proper London' – but also the fluid environment where migrant identity is dissolved and demonised by the power of description. When Salahuddin Chamchawala first arrives in London, for example, he experiences the city as 'nightmare' (p. 42), before he learns the 'paleface masks' which will transform him into 'a goodandproper Englishman' (p. 43), including changing his name to Saladin Chamcha. When the crisis of identity arrives for Saladin, which it does at the opening of the novel, he finds that his fragile 'paleface masks' – like his accent, his face and his new name[12] – are powerless to prevent the dominant imperialist discourse of England from transforming him into a smelly Paki-devil. The crisis of identity is triggered by his return to India – for the first time after 15 years – and is figured as an inability to control the face and the accent it had taken so long to construct. The climax of this first crisis is his demonisation as he approaches England. After miraculously surviving the plane's explosion over the Channel, and falling into the hands of the police as an illegal immigrant, the policemen's description of him speeds his transformation into the horned satan of racist discourse. His incapacity to resist the description's power derives from his abdication of identity, his refusal to acknowledge the 'disturbance' – to use the word of the Naipaul narrator in *Enigma* – of the humiliations of his alienness.

So if the Naipaul migrant slowly comes to see as experience and 'labour' wear away layers of illusion, the Rushdie protagonists have a more unstable and crisis-laden time of it. Salahuddin Chamchawala stubbornly chooses to give up his alienness, in order to avoid the mockery which is deeply embedded in the narrative of Englishness, but instead he turns himself into a clown. Gibreel Farishta, like Salahuddin, changed his name (from Ismail Najmuddin – the star of the faith) and constructed a desperado identity for himself that mirrored in a profound sense the valorised hybridity of Bombay itself. Gibreel plays gods in the 'theologicals' of Bombay cinema with tolerant abandon, all gods are the same to him, yet *his* crisis arrives with his loss of faith. Rushdie effectively captures the sudden uncertainty of identity with the image of Gibreel 'haemorrhaging all over his insides'. The illness which follows this haemorrhaging is his profane 'crisis

13

and conversion', which for this Ismail, as for Melville's 'trimmer' in *Moby Dick*, is to apostasy, to a knowledge of God's absence.[13] When he arrives at this, Gibreel begins to recover. His 'metamorphosis' from tolerant hybridity to an outcast self-assertion, however, is not figured in a stoic act of knowledge, as is Ismail's redemption from the sea, but in a melodramatic and grotesque act of defiance – the consumption of 'forbidden foods' (p. 29). It is after this public display that the fracture in Gibreel's unified vision of self becomes nightmare: 'after he ate the pigs the retribution began, a nocturnal retribution, a punishment of dreams' (p. 32). As his anxiety intensifies, he believes that God is punishing him for his loss of faith (p. 189).

Gibreel's dreams come in a serial form, with himself 'characterized ... as the angel' Gibreel. This both continues the cinema jokes around him, and also gives the dreaming world a greater solidity than the whole waking world, which may only exist as a nightmare in the angel Gibreel's mind. Farishta explains to Saladin: 'Point is ... every time I go to sleep the dream starts up from where it stopped. Same dream in the same place ... As if he's the guy who's awake and this is the bloody nightmare. His bloody dream: us' (p. 83). In this remarkable solipsism, the self-obsessed individual is valorised as the unifying centre of experience, a post-modernist conceit if ever there was one, except that Gibreel's obsession leads to paranoia and destruction.

His sense of himself becomes more unstable as the dreams acquire greater authority over his reality. The act of defiance, the assertion of self, is now coupled with migrancy, and stated explicitly in Gibreel's recurring declaration: *To be born again, first you have to die*.[14] But the dreams are an irresistible expression of originary cultural narratives which return in distorted forms after being denied in the act of apostasy. Gibreel's fantasy of being narrated by the archangel describes his ultimate failure to be 'born again' after his discovery of God's absence, and therefore the potential for transformation with which migrancy is valorised turns into paranoia, culminating in that nightmare vision of the city: 'The city streets coiled around him, writhing like serpents' (p. 320). Gibreel is, in the end, unable to credit his expression of dissent, his act of will in defiance of orthodoxy. His doubts make him unstable and turn his reality into nightmare. The 'illusion' of return to belief is hinted at in the instability of his environment; thus London turns into a nightmarish city at just the moment when he begins to believe himself the archangel Gibreel who has returned to haunt the English (p. 353).

The instabilities of these two protagonists, and the potential of their condition, dramatise the inevitable pressure to transformation which acts on the alien, made more complex here in the post-colonial context. For arrival in the 'Vilayet', the centre of empire and its disfiguring narratives, is a profoundly violent experience for the migrant. *The Satanic Verses* begins with a mid-air explosion which deposits bits of the travellers over England. This fragmentation describes the effect of migration:

> mingling with the remnants of the plane, equally fragmented, equally absurd, there floated the debris of the soul, broken memories, sloughed-off selves, severed mother-tongues, violated privacies, untranslatable jokes, extinguished futures, lost loves, the forgotten meaning of hollow, booming words, *land, belonging, home.* (p. 4)

The consequences of this fragmentation threaten survival, and the migrant's strategy in dealing with this menace contains an urgency which is absent in the Naipaul narrator's long and pained look at experience. Something of that process of self-construction and then reflection on the constructed self which we saw in *Enigma* is also there in the treatment of Saladin Chamcha, albeit luridly dramatised in the latter. Saladin's discomfort with the constructed self is figured in a number of ways, ranging from an ironised uncertainty - *'I'm not myself*, he thought as a faint fluttering feeling began in the vicinity of his heart' (p. 34) - to his full-blown demonisation by 'the power of description': 'They describe us .,. That's all. They have the power of description and we succumb to the pictures they construct' (p. 168). The novel's narrator also offers some thoughts on the matter:

> A man who sets out to make himself up is taking on the Creator's role, according to one way of seeing things; he's un-natural, a blasphemer, an abomination of abominations. From another angle, you could see pathos in him, heroism in his struggle ... Or, consider him sociopolitically: most migrants learn, and can become disguises. Our own false descriptions to counter the falsehoods invented about us. (p. 49)

It is clear, then, that such self-construction is a malady, a transformation too grotesque to have any dynamic potential.

On the other hand, as Zeeny Vakil, the Bombay woman who eventually guides Saladin to safety, tells him, it is dangerous to reclaim 'identity': 'When you have stepped through the looking-glass you step back at your peril. The mirror may cut you to shreds' (p. 58). Zeeny is incensed that Saladin has succumbed so fully to his construction as an alien. When not acting up or 'doing funny voices or acting grand', he looks like a 'blank', she tells him. Her comments are a more blunt echo of the narrator's remarks on the pathos of the *self*-denial of the migrant cited above:

> 'It makes me mad sometimes, I want to slap you. To sting you back into life. But I also get sad about it. Such a fool, you, the big star whose face is the wrong colour for their colour TVs, who has to travel to wogland with some two-bit company, playing the babu part on top of it, just to get into a play. They kick you around and still you stay, you love them, bloody slave mentality, I swear.' (p. 61)

Although this position displays a kind of idealism about what identity means, Zeeny's energy is a model of the response Saladin later adopts to escape his demonisation. It is the 'fearsome concentration of his hate' which humanises Saladin in the end (p. 294), and enables him to defy his description. 'Hate' here means more than just a response to the disfiguring narratives, but something elemental and invigorating, the 'will ... to disagree; not to submit; to dissent' (p. 93).

It is after this liberation from 'the power of description' that Saladin is able, finally, to return to his childhood house, to his name and to a reconciliation with his dying father. Clearly this return symbolises a return to a whole self. Salahuddin has walked through the mirror without cutting himself to shreds, and it is significant that at this moment it is Zeeny Vakil who is with him and leads him away. Because Salahuddin attempted to transform himself in order to cope with his migrant condition, he entered a process of change – 'metamorphosis' – which, in the end, is seen as containing potential and dynamism. Gibreel, on the other hand, resists transformation, as we see in this explicit analysis offered by the narrator:

> Might we not agree that Gibreel, for all his stage-name and performances; in spite of the born-again slogans, new beginnings, metamorphoses; – has wished to remain, to a large degree, *continuous* – that is, joined to and arising from his past ... so that his is still a self which, for our present purposes, we may describe as 'true' ... whereas Saladin Chamcha is a creature of *selected* discontinuities, a *willing* re-invention; his *preferred* revolt against history being what makes him, in our chosen idiom, 'false'? (p. 427)

This is a pronounced celebration of hybridity, valorising above all other strategies available to the post-colonial migrant a voluntary openness to all aspects of his condition.[15] In the novel, it is Hind Sufyan who is the archetypal hybrid figure, self-aware as a daughter of a migrant family, but defiant of the patriarchal constraints of her family (p. 249).

In Salahuddin's case, he is able both to eulogise his experience of England as well as to 'return' to India, while Gibreel is destroyed. The optimism of Rushdie's vision of migrancy contrasts to some extent with Naipaul's in *The Enigma of Arrival*, although in both cases the process of coming to knowledge is given noble dimensions. If in *The Satanic Verses* an accommodating openness to experience is seen as the enabling means of staging a revolt against history, in *Enigma* the migrant arrives at understanding through unwavering 'looking'. In the latter case, what is being looked at is the concrete and complex present, which is desired and figured as order. It is contrasted with a debilitating past – 'my little tropical island' – as well as the dangerous stasis of England's 'other' – in this text, 'Africa'. What is implied here is that the migrant's 'labour' inevitably leads to self-insertion into 'England'. Rushdie's text, on the other hand, contends the possibility of walking back and forth through the mirror, and argues the virtues of the transformation of the self as well as the irresistibility of change in the societies the migrant experiences.

Notes

1. V.S. Naipaul, *The Enigma of Arrival*, (London: Viking, 1987).
2. I borrow the phrase from Martin Turner, 'V.S. Naipaul: the purification of the eye', MA Dissertation, University of Kent, Canterbury, 1988.
3. In an interview with Zöe Heller in the *Independent on Sunday*, 28 March 1993, Naipaul speaks of himself in this way: 'I notice *everything* ... Everything. Everything.'
4. There are many references to the labour of writing in *Enigma*. On page 94, for example, there is a reference to the writing of a book which is then rejected by the publisher who commissioned it, almost certainly *The Loss of Eldorado* (1969) although it is not named here: 'It was a labour. Ten or twelve documents – called up from memory, almost like personal memories – might provide the details for a fairly short and simple paragraph of narrative.' In the interview with Zöe Heller referred to above, Naipaul doubts that writing is a 'talent': 'There is inclination. There is will. There is a capacity for

learning. But I'm not sure there is talent, you know.'
5. Salman Rushdie, *The Satanic Verses* (London: Viking, 1988).
6. The word 'translation' first appears in *Shame* (London: Cape, 1983). A variant of it is the 'borne-across' metaphor which Rushdie elaborates on in his essay on Günter Grass and which is included in his *Imaginary Homelands* (London: Granta, 1991, pp. 276–81). These tropes parallel the metaphors of 'metamorphosis' and 'transformation' in *The Satanic Verses*.
7. Naipaul's elaboration on the Conrad phrase is in 'Conrad's Darkness', *The Return of Eva Perón* (Harmondsworth: Penguin, 1981, p. 207; first published by André Deutsch, 1980). In an essay in the same collection, 'A New King for the Congo', Naipaul describes the Zaire landscape in terms that echo Conrad's description of the journey up the river in *Heart of Darkness* (1899): 'And in 1975, the journey – one thousand miles between green, flat, almost unchanging country – is still like a journey through nothingness ... so complete, simple and repetitive still appears the African life through which the traveller swiftly passes' (p. 175).
   In *A Bend on the River* (1979), his last novel before *Enigma*, the ease with which Africans can grow food in the Congo suggests their oblivious profligacy, in contrast to the frugal industry of the Greek and Indian traders among them.
8. This is one of several examples, from 'A New King for the Congo', of how brief 'history' is in Africa:
   A Batetela boy remembered that his ancestors were slave catchers for the Arabs; they changed sides when the Belgians came and offered them places in their army. But that was long ago. The boy is now a student of psychology, on the lookout, like so many young Zairois, for some foreign scholarship; and the boy's girl friend, of another tribe, people in the past considered enslavable, laughed at this story of slave trading.
   The bush grows fast over what were once great events or great disturbances. (pp. 182–3)
9. The phrase comes from Chinua Achebe's celebrated essay on Conrad's *Heart of Darkness*: 'An Image of Africa', *Hopes and Impediments* (Oxford: Heinemann, 1988), p. 2: 'a place of negations at once remote and vaguely familiar'.
10. Compare the estate house in *The Mimic Men*, where the decline of planter society is also figured through an image of the ruins of a great house: V.S. Naipaul, *The Mimic Men* (London: André Deutsch, 1967; this reference to the 1969 Penguin edition, p. 33). In the *Independent on Sunday* interview referred to above, Naipaul remarks: 'I think people should earn their own regard' – by this he means the imperative on every individual to prove him/herself.

11. Naipaul refines this first account of London in *The Mimic Men* (1967), and also in *The Enigma of Arrival* (1987), but here is an early account of 'that disturbance' referred to in the quotation:
    > I came to London. It had become the centre of my world and I had worked hard to come to it. And I was lost. London was not the centre of my world. I had been misled; but there was no where else to go ... Here I became no more than an inhabitant of a big city, robbed of loyalties, time passing, taking me away from what I was, thrown more and more into myself, fighting to keep my balance and to keep alive the thought of the clear world beyond the brick and asphalt and the chaos of railway lines. All mythical lands faded, and in the big city I was confined to a smaller world than I had ever known. I became my flat, my desk, my name. (*An Area of Darkness*, London: André Deutsch, 1964; this reference to the 1968 Penguin edition, p. 42.)

12. This is a description of Saladin Chamcha on his way to England before the plane crash:
    > [His] face was handsome in a somewhat sour, patrician fashion, with long, thick, downturned lips like those of a disgusted turbot, and thin eye-brows arching sharply over eyes that watched the world with a kind of alert contempt. Mr Saladin Chamcha had constructed this face with care – it had taken him several years to get it just right ... Furthermore, he had shaped himself a voice to go with the face, a voice whose languid, almost lazy vowels contrasted disconcertingly with the sawn-off abruptness of the consonants. (*The Satanic Verses*, p. 33.)

    It is a description that could conceivably fit Naipaul, although this need not mean that Saladin is a dramatisation of Naipaul in other respects. Clearly, Saladin is figured critically here, and his self-construction in the model of an aristocratic Englishman – the contemptuous face, 'the sawn-off abruptness of the consonants' – is implicitly there in the Naipaul narrator's account of *his* self-construction.

13. For Rushdie's interest in Melville's *Moby-Dick* (1851), see his essay 'In Good Faith', *Imaginary Homelands* (1991).

14. The novel opens with this line, which is then repeated as the migrant's coda, implying both optimism about transformation and the necessary pain. For its most optimistic variant see the hymn on 'reincarnation' on p. 84.

15. In a discussion of John Berger's *A Seventh Man* which is also included in *Imaginary Homelands*, Rushdie writes:
    > To migrate is certainly to lose language and home, to be defined by others, to become invisible or, even worse, a target; it is to experience deep changes and wrenches in the soul. But the migrant is not simply transformed by his act; he also transforms

19

his new world. Migrants may well become mutants, but it is out
of such hybridization that newness can emerge. (p. 210)
It is no surprise to discover that the discussion of Berger was written in 1987, when *The Satanic Verses* was almost complete.

2. Wintering: Making a Home in Britain

C.L. Innes

They have got rid of the men,
The blunt clumsy stumblers, the boors,
Winter is for women—
The woman, still at her knitting,
At the cradle of spanish walnut,
Her body a bulb in the cold and too dumb to think.

Sylvia Plath, 'Wintering'

The generation of writers who came from the Caribbean, or Africa, or Asia in the 1950s and 1960s were typically male, typically single and, so they believed, typically transient. As Susheila Nasta points out in her contribution to this book, Sam Selvon's *The Lonely Londoners* (1956) epitomises that period, with its collection of single men, living in single rooms, seeing themselves for ever as visitors, always on the verge of returning to the place they still consider home. Ralph Singh, the protagonist of V.S. Naipaul's 1967 novel, *The Mimic Men*, shares that sense of transience, writing in a hotel room, committed in the end to neither country nor family. Naipaul's later collection, *In a Free State* (1971) also gives voice to the transient, the dislocated and disoriented; single men brought from rural or feudal worlds to the loneliness of cities such as Washington and London. Selvon's and Naipaul's characters reflect that period when London Transport, the National Health Service and the factories of the north actively recruited workers from Asia and the Caribbean during the period of post-war industrial regeneration. It was a time also when attendance at educational institutions in England was seen as essential for the young intellectuals who were to replace the colonial administra-

21

tors and professionals when their nations gained independence in the early 1960s, a brief time when those young intellectuals believed their future lay with what seemed the comparatively bright and hopeful futures of these nations.

Twenty or thirty years after the 1956 publication of *The Lonely Londoners*, a new generation of writers have been concerned with re-creating and reflecting upon the experience of those who came from Asia, Africa and the Caribbean, and the experience of their children. Many of these younger writers were born in Britain or came as young children. Almost all of them recognise that they have made their home, or at least one of their homes, there. A far larger proportion of the writers of this generation are female. The desire of women to seek or make a home, to hold their families together, often becomes the focus of recent fiction by male authors. Abdulrazak Gurnah's *Dottie* (1990) Caryl Phillips' *The Final Passage* (1985), David Simon's *Railton Blues* (1983), Timothy Mo's *Sour Sweet* (1982), are all novels which draw upon their central women characters to explore what it means to decide that England is home, however cold and hostile it may be. The male characters rarely make this decision; as far as they are concerned, home-making in its wider sense is not what they are about. They remain birds of passage, transients, while women seek the 'final passage'. Not surprisingly, one can say the same of many of the novels by women writers that have been published in the last ten or fifteen years, including Joan Riley's *Waiting in the Twilight* (1987) and *Romance* (1988), and Farhana Sheikh's *The Red Box* (1991).

This chapter will focus on three first novels written in the 1970s and 1980s: Buchi Emecheta's *Second-Class Citizen*,[1] published in 1974, Caryl Phillips' *The Final Passage*,[2] published in 1985, and Ravinder Randhawa's *A Wicked Old Woman*,[3] published in 1987. All three explore with varying degrees of complexity and ambivalence the meaning and consequences for young Caribbean, African and Asian women, their husbands, siblings and children, of living in Britain, and coming to terms with the community where they seek to be at home, while acknowledging that community's reluctance to accommodate them. Each of these novels can also be read in part as the writer's search for a mode of fiction and an audience, a reading community, which may authentically respond to the writer's own interaction with and search for a place in the face of a literary tradition and establishment which has generally excluded non-Anglo-Saxon voices.

In this aspect, Caryl Phillips' *The Final Passage* is perhaps transitional between the novels of displacement and the novels of

22

settlement, for the ending of the novel leaves open the possibility
that its heroine, Leila, may yet return to her Caribbean home, if
she does not pass, motherless and husbandless, into madness. The
daughter of a black Caribbean woman and an unknown white
father, Leila's identity is also unresolved, for she is accepted
wholly in neither her birthplace nor in England, being categorised
as a 'white girl' in the former (by Michael's grandmother), and a
'coloured' girl in England. But for the reader, what is most notice-
able about Leila is her voicelessness, her inability to communicate
with either her Caribbean mother or her feckless husband.
Phillips' novel in this and other aspects may also be seen as both
inheriting and responding to the representation of Caribbean
women in Jean Rhys's fiction, particularly *Voyage in the Dark*
(1934) and *Wide Sargasso Sea*, (1966), whose protagonists can
find acceptance, secure identity and mental stability in neither the
Caribbean nor England. Like the Creole mothers and daughters
in Rhys's novels, Leila's mother is the victim of sexual exploitation by a series of older white men, and for both writers, colonial
and sexual exploitation are closely linked. Both novelists make
much of the contrast between the colour, heat and community
(however flawed) of the Caribbean, and the wintry greyness and
isolation which they experience in England. (Unlike Selvon, they
do not qualify this contrast with passages celebrating spring in
Hyde Park or the bright lights of Piccadilly Circus.) But whereas
Rhys's heroines are dependent upon and victimised by English
men and remain childless, Leila is abandoned both by her unknown white father and by her Caribbean husband, Michael, who
also abandons his mistress Beverley and son, Ivor. Both Leila and
Beverley are left, quite literally, holding the baby. On the small
Caribbean island where they were born, friends such as Bradeth
and Millie and the watchful eyes of the community as a whole
can exert pressure so that Michael may, however unwillingly, take
responsibility for his offspring and his wife. However, the very
pressures which encourage Michael finally to leave the Caribbean
and seek a world and life larger than the confines of his poor
birthplace, also encourage him to concentrate single-mindedly on
his own survival, economic and psychic, once he gets to England.
Leila becomes a victim of the very qualities she admired;
Michael's drive for status and refusal to be satisfied with a
'respectable' existence, represented by his motorbike and his marriage to Leila, in England send him in search of business deals
and white women. Leila, like her Caribbean island home, is a
victim both of colonial history and the irresponsibility of the
young men who in turn repeat the pattern of neglect and self-

23

interest bequeathed them by the past. It is worth noting that on
the island there is no middle generation of men, except the sad
figure of Footsie Walters, who fails to serve as a dire enough
warning of what may befall Caribbean immigrants to Britain.

The heroine of Rhys's *Wide Sargasso Sea* is forced against her
will to leave Santa Dominica, and is imprisoned in her husband's
house. In Rhys's novel, the English mansion serves as a model of
English society and patriarchal power, built upon wealth taken
from the colonies. Phillips' heroine, Leila, chooses to leave the
Caribbean in order to join her mother in what she imagines to be
a finer house than the one she inhabits in St Patrick's. England
becomes for Leila her 'motherland'. But the address she has been
given turns out to be a crowded slum building, in which all the
lodgers are transients, its rooms catering uncomfortably for shifts
of sleepers. The West Indian men she first encounters in England
are all characters from *The Lonely Londoners*. Leila finds her
mother not in a house but in a hospital, dying of cancer, unable
to find the healing she sought in coming to England. Thus the
image of the hospital and of England as a welfare state replaces
the earlier grandeur of Charlotte Brontë's, and Jean Rhys's Thorn-
ton Grange. Nor can Leila find solace in substitute mother-figures
such as the patronising social worker, Miss Gordon, a true
descendant of the colonial missionary, or the more sympathetically portrayed Irishwoman, Mary, whose kindness and friendship
and half-glimpsed recognition of a shared colonial history Leila
'drowns in the thought of Miss Gordon' (p. 198) and of the white
blonde women for whom Michael deserts her.

Leila's disillusion with England echoes the disillusion of earlier
immigrants who found not the shining metropolis they had en-
visioned, but a bleak and wintry waste land. The novel not only
cites Eliot for its epigraph, but also quietly alludes to his poetry
in a number of passages. Like J. Alfred Prufrock's reader, Leila is
guided through 'half-deserted morning streets which were deco-
rated with drifting strands of fog'. Her daily journey through
London to visit her dying mother takes her through endless, snak-
ing streets, past rubbish and newspapers 'curled around their feet
like dead vines', to 'the etherised sterility of the hospital foyer'.
London is described again and again in terms of what it lacks,
above all its absence of heat and colour.

The London Caryl Phillips evokes is the London of Eliot's
Prufrock, the 'Preludes', and 'The Waste Land'. Phillips also shares
with Eliot a concern with the meaning of history as it is refracted in
the consciousness of living individuals, and his epitaph from 'Little
Gidding', is surely double-edged in its implications:

A people without history
Is not redeemed from time, for history is a pattern
Of timeless moments. So, while the light fails
On a winter's afternoon, in a secluded chapel
History is now and England.

For Leila, remembering school texts, history indeed seems to belong in England, and to have bypassed the Caribbean island she was born. Her life in the Caribbean is perceived by her, and by the reader, as a series of timeless moments, without a pattern. But she is not to be redeemed in England, in the failing light of winter, for here too her life is a meaningless and patternless series of timeless moments. There will be repetition (her life as a deserted mother will be a repetition of her mother's situation and of Beverley's) with little hope of change or meaning. That sense of her life as a series of timeless moments is reinforced by the structure of the novel, which begins with her long wait for Michael and for the departure of the boat, then moves back in time to other scenes where she awaits Michael, before returning to the moment of departure, the journey to England, the series of bus journeys to visit her mother, the funeral, Michael's brutal physical and verbal assaults.

The absence of history, the lack of a meaningful pattern, is closely related to absence of communication. Leila is characterised by both her silence and her longing to break it. Her mother's motives, her husband's wishes and desires remain unspoken; we know Leila's desires through her actions rather than her words. Leila is the central enigma of the novel, but Michael and her mother also remain largely enigmatic. Leila's frustration at not knowing what Michael really wants, at not being able to communicate with her mother, is shared also by the reader, who also seeks to know the motives of the characters, and to know Leila in some sense beyond her suffering. In this voicelessness, *The Final Passage* differs most markedly from early novels set in London or the Caribbean. Selvon's characters create themselves through speech; Lamming and Rhys also bring to life a Caribbean community which creates itself and defines others through varieties of language. When Leila is with her mother or with Michael, there is almost always silence; questions and feelings remain unvoiced. With the important exception of Millie and Bradeth, the voicelessness of the Caribbean islanders makes them as isolated from one another there as they are in England. The closing lines of the novel re-emphasise that link between lack of any but ritual communication, isolation, estrangement from the self and loss of identity:

They must have looked strangely eerie in the winter's dusk, standing there unmoving, woman, child, child to be. Then the snowflakes began to spin, first one, then tens of them. Leila watched spellbound. Then she sped into the house and locked the door behind her.

A speckled, burnished light crept in off the street, piercing the awful inadequacy of the curtains. Leila caught sight of herself in the mirror. She looked like a yellowing snapshot of an old relative, fading with the years. She turned suddenly and saw that somebody had pushed a Christmas card through the front door. She stooped, with Calvin, and picked it up and read it, but it was from nobody. (pp. 204–5)

A central concern in Phillips' later novels has to do with loss of speech, and distortions of self through borrowed languages. *The Higher Ground*, (1989), *Cambridge* (1991) and *Crossing the River* (1993) all seek to re-fashion and re-enter varieties of voices and written language, and to show characters who struggle to communicate through them, or whose vision is obscured through the language they attempt to use. In Phillips' novels the confidently Caribbean voice which is so much a mark of Selvon's work has fallen silent.

There are few silences, however, in Buchi Emecheta's novel. The narrative voice in *Second-Class Citizen* is direct, often colloquial; it buttonholes the reader and rarely pauses for reflection. This direct speaking voice opens the novel and alters little throughout the text:

It had all begun like a dream. You know the sort of dream which seems to have originated from nowhere, yet one was always aware of its existence. One could feel it, one could be directed it; unconsciously at first, until it became a reality, a Presence.

Adah did not know for sure what gave birth to her dream, when it all started, but the earliest anchor she could pin down in this drift of nothingness was when she was about eight years old. She was not even quite sure that she was exactly eight, because you see, she was a girl. She was a girl who arrived when everyone was expecting and predicting a boy. So, since she was such a disappointment to her parents, to her immediate family, to her tribe, nobody thought of recording her birth. (p. 7)

Whereas the structure of *The Final Passage*, with its interspersing of past and present and its series of 'timeless moments' which leave the characters and the reader awaiting fulfilment, gives the reader plenty of space to pause and meditate, Adah's story hurries us briskly from her childhood to her marriage, her coming to England, her first attempt at writing and her decision to leave her husband. Whereas Phillips is generally distanced from his characters, and there is a marked difference between the speech of his characters and the authorial voice who describes them and their settings, the distinction between Adah and Emecheta is often blurred, and in the end almost completely merged. Emecheta dedicates her novel to her five children, and by the end of the novel Adah's fifth child is on its way. Adah's first attempt at a novel, destroyed by her husband, is called *The Bride Price* and we know that one of Emecheta's early published novels is *The Bride Price*, a novel which retains the adolescent longing for romance which Adah identifies when she re-reads her notebook version.

The briskness of Emecheta's narrative is a fitting vehicle for Adah's energy and determination to claim status as a first-class citizen and to overcome the sexism and racism which would relegate her to the realm of the second class. Although Francis is not unlike Michael in his callous sexual exploitation of his wife, his unwillingness to take responsibility for his children and his attraction to white women, one feels that Emecheta's sympathies and her protagonist have more in common with Michael's individualism than with Leila's passive resignation. As Adah's ambition and drive stem from her dead father, Michael draws upon the memory of his grandfather's words for encouragement to 'be somebody':

> If England was the place that Alphonse Walters had led him to believe it was, then how much energy could he afford to waste patching up this newly repaired but still leaky marriage? The more he thought about it, the more he realized the nurturing and the pretence would have to stop. On the threshold of a new life, he could not afford to fail in fulfilling the wishes of his grandparents.
> ... There was no chance of his leaving his country with nothing, that was certain. How much he left with seemed to depend upon how much he wanted, and how hard he was prepared to try. This being the case Michael would sleep soundly and defend his mind against thoughts of Beverley or Leila or the children. (pp. 169, 170)

Like Michael, Adah is an orphan. Both have learned to survive without support, financial or psychological, from their families.

Both have seen marriage as a means of bettering their position, and both move away from their marriages, with little sympathy or compassion for their less robust partners once they are perceived as impediments to their scramble up the ladder to first-class citizenship. For both characters, the absence of parents is simultaneously a psychological factor and a symbol of their severance from their native communities and their cultural history. Michael and Adah share the belief, without irony or reservation, that 'history is now and England'. For Adah the continuities between her world in Nigeria and her life in England are chiefly negative; it is Igbo influence, she asserts, that reinforces Francis' treatment of her as a second-class citizen and which insists that she is good for nothing but child-bearing and child-rearing, preferably of sons. And it is the continuing rivalry between Yorubas and Igbos which intensifies her suffering in London and forces them out of the accommodation owned by their Yoruba landlord.

Both Michael and Adah react with rage and disgust at the housing in which they are forced to live, and at first blame their spouses rather than the racism of English society for the indignity and humiliation they encounter. Indeed, it is in the search for housing, even more so than in the search for work, that the hostility of the English is most bitterly experienced. Here again, realism and metaphorical significance combine, for, as Susheila Nasta has demonstrated, the basement and attic rooms occupied by Moses, the acquisition of his own house, serve as a metaphor for the relationship between the characters in Selvon's fiction and the larger society. But Selvon's characters *are* accommodated; they are *there*, however marginally, and Moses' room is presented as a permanent focus for a small West Indian group. And although in one sense they establish a relatively small area of familiar territory, bounded by 'the Gate', 'the Arch' and 'the Water', they do roam the city and celebrate its cultural and historical glamour, however tarnished. In contrast, the characters in Phillips' and Emecheta's early novels spend a significant proportion of their time in England searching for and being turned away from accommodation. What accommodation they do find is felt to be even more marginal than in Selvon's fiction (Leila spends her first nights in London sleeping in a locked bathroom), and their stay there is constantly under threat. That this should be so seems paradoxical, given that Emecheta and Phillips are writing 20 or more years later than the publication of Selvon's *The Lonely Londoners* (1956), when a large and permanent Black British community was clearly here to stay. Phillips was brought to England before he was a year old, and grew up in Yorkshire; Emecheta had come to England in 1962, and was firmly established by the time *Second-Class Citizen* was published in 1974. But the paradox seems less striking when one remembers that the Notting Hill and Nottingham race riots, Enoch Powell's notorious 'rivers of blood' speech, and the 1971 Immigration Act preceded by only a few years the writing of Emecheta's novel, and that Phillips' first novel was written in the years following Margaret Thatcher's 1978 demagogic appeal to fears of being 'swamped' by immigrants, the growth of right-wing and fascist racist groups such as the British National Party, the imposition of tighter immigration controls, and the series of race riots in 1981. Although none of these events impinge on the consciousness of their characters, arguably both Emecheta and Phillips express, through their emphasis on the difficulty and tenuousness of being accommodated in London, especially with babies and children, the nation's political, social and cultural refusal to accept even those black people born in Britain as members of the community.

In contrast to Selvon's London novels, one is struck too by the narrowness of the community and worlds encountered by the main characters in these later novels. Selvon incorporates Africans and later Asians into the community that inhabits Moses' world; Adah and Francis appear to meet no West Indians and no Asians. Indeed, the only Africans they get to know, and the only ones even referred to in the novel, are Nigerians. Leila and Michael, on the other hand, meet only West Indians, apparently from their own region, and no Africans or Asians. Their characters experience an even more limited version of London, all of it dirty and bleak, and none of them ever refers to the tourist landmarks, the historical and cultural signifiers which impress Selvon's 1950s immigrants. Paradoxically, again, this lack of wider reference may be produced by a consciousness which can take London for granted, without yet being able to take London as its own, or assign new significance to it. For Selvon's and Naipaul's characters, living in London was felt as part of a wider experience of travel and adventure; for a later generation, England is felt as a place of oppression and restriction.

Yet, however ambivalent they may feel about their identities as Igbo or West Indian, no character in Emecheta's or Phillips' novels dreams of denying it. They may strive to succeed in spite of that identity and the cultural baggage it brings, but their awareness of themselves as Nigerians or West Indians remains unquestioned. Nevertheless, both novels show hostile racial stereotypes impinging on that awareness, creating in Adah as she lies in hospital and in Leila after Michael's desertion, paranoia and willed

isolation. In Francis and Mr Noble it produces a defeated acceptance of their status as second-class citizens, a status partially
alleviated (for Michael too) by sexual relations with white women,
although Emecheta is quick to assure us that these white women
are merely poor white trash.

Ravinder Randhawa's *A Wicked Old Woman* is more centrally
concerned with exploring the difficulty of escaping stereotyped
identities imposed by the dominant white society. Unlike the two
novels previously discussed, this one takes as its central character
a woman who has grown up in England, Kulwant, herself the
daughter of immigrant parents from India. She has few memories
of India, which is for her perhaps a homeland, but not a home.
For this reason the prevailing stereotypes in England are all the
more powerful, and her search for identity and for a way of being
involves her 'trying on' a series of roles and disguises. Clothing
and costume become a dominant motif in Randhawa's novel, and
this motif is closely connected to naming and to imposed and
assumed identities in a multicultural community.

That motif of multiple identities, of exteriors which hide other
layers of inner 'selves', and the problem of creating an Indian
identity, are introduced in the opening childhood memory of an
attempt to transform a Russian doll into one that has a *bindi*, a
red mark, on its forehead. The next two episodes, 'Kuli's Cover-
up' and 'Kuli's Double-up' contrast opposing stereotypes of the
Indian: the first is the poverty-stricken recipient of European
hand-me-downs, the Oxfam Indian, an old and crippled victim;
the second, and older, British image is the oriental princess, the
exotic, mysterious and beautiful maiden who is the focus of desire
for the blond hero, Michael. As a schoolgirl, Kulwant seeks to live
up to this latter image, but her response is produced not only by
his admiration, but also by her anxiety to be accepted and to be
given status in an all-white world, as well as her own adolescent
sexual desire for 'the other', and her rebellion against the protec-
tiveness of her parents and what she sees as their embarrassingly
'un-English' attitudes. But when Michael's insistence on marriage
threatens her confused but deeper sense of being, and her own
dreams of fulfilment through further study and a career, she
breaks away and declares independence. Although the novel is by
no means allegorical in mode, her reaction, which is a whole-
hearted embrace of yet another stereotype of Indianness, as well
as Michael's resentful and often vindictive response, can be read
as a shadowing of the larger history of England's relationship with
India, from its status as 'the jewel in the crown' of the empire
and the laboratory for turning Indians into British subjects

through education (as well as other and blunter means), to India's assertion of independence and emphasis on cultural nationalism.

Kulwant's reaction to her failed relationship with Michael, her unwillingness to accept assimilation on his terms and his inability to acknowledge and value her subjectivity, is to insist on becoming 'the complete Indian woman'. From accepting an identity defined as 'the other', she turns to an identity which asserts her belonging within the Indian community. Despite the puzzlement and misgivings of her parents, she demands an arranged marriage, gives up all attempts to 'fit in' with her English classmates or to pursue an independent life, and seeks to become the good Indian wife and mother. Inevitably, her attempt to conform to that stereotype is also doomed to failure; the stereotype itself is too narrow and confining, her motives for embarking on the marriage too much compounded of resentment, fear and self-denial to allow the relationship to flourish. Her husband begins to seek a reciprocal relationship elsewhere and the marriage falls apart; her sons blame Kulwant for the disintegration of the marriage. Ironically, her very determination to become a good Indian wife and mother, as she believes the role to be defined by others, is the cause of her failure. And only in later life does she begin to understand the paradox that her attempt to become Indian and reject assimilation into Englishness, took as the signifier of Indianness that special feature emphasised by Europeans as the mark of difference and unacceptability, the arranged marriage.

Kulwant's third identity, which she assumes as we encounter her in the novel, and which corresponds to western media images of India in the 1970s and 1980s, is her identity as victim, a needy recipient of Oxfam and welfare state handouts. If she can not become 'English' or 'Indian' on her terms, then she will become the monster they have created, as the episode title 'Frankly Frankenstein' suggests. As such, she need no longer take responsibility for her failures, for her family or for the community. Her only project is to retreat, and become her disguise as a helpless and needy old woman, from whom nothing can be expected. She envisions her future as one of the unaccommodated, so marginalised that she will be able to take refuge as a 'a smelly old hag whose address would be a patch under Charing Cross Bridge' (p. 4). In this novel again, the motif of accommodation as a metaphor or belonging in the larger society becomes significant. Kulwant's quest for identity and a role is linked to her wandering from one building to another, and her own family's desire for her to join them and accept the accommodation they can offer. There are also numerous other images of homelessness; most horrific are

Kulwant's memories of the Indian family burned in their house by racist arsonists. And linked to Kulwant's story as a member of the older generation is the story of Rani, who runs away from home, denies any Indian identity, assumes the name of Rosalind, and finds meagre shelter in hostels, empty houses and squats.

Kulwant envies those of the older generation, like her parents, who, having been born and brought up in India, 'know who they are'. That generation, like Emecheta's Adah, has a singleness of identity. In Kulwant's mind, her mother comments: 'I have known what I am, that has guided me to which I should be. I have never lost my anchor of certainty' (p. 54). But the second and third generation of Asians in Britain are inevitably 'hybrid' or split, and this duality is carried in the names by which they are called. Kulwant is also called Kuli (suggesting coolie labourers, the opposite of the oriental princess), her son is called both Arvind and Arnold, Rani insists on being known as Rosalind. Only the older generation and the English, such as Kulwant's friend Caroline and Arvind's wife Shirley, retain a single name and a clear sense of self throughout the novel. Identities are also complicated by allegiances in terms of class and work; despite their hard-earned wealth, Arvind and Shirley resolutely choose to identify with working-class Londoners and he continues to live beside and work in his garage, although Shirley equally resolutely insists on an Indian identity for her husband and their children. Kulwant's other son, Anup, revels in his status as a 'Buppie' (a black yuppie), and his house proclaims his wealth, while his wife, Pavan, tries to reconcile her life as a successful doctor, her concern for the community, and her 'duties' as a wife. Each character reacts to the conflicting demands of being Asian in England in different ways: Kulwant by assuming the stereotypes, following the advice of the grandfather in Ralph Ellison's *Invisible Man* and 'yessing them to death'; Rani by furiously resisting all imposed identities; Arvind by rejecting the middle-class and professional ambitions of his parents; Rani's mother by assuming blindness; Ammi and her daughters by placing community commitment above personal fulfilment.

Randhawa is by no means uncritical about the artificiality of some aspects of Indian community in England. For Kulwant, the Asian Centre is a 'simulation Sub-Continent'

> patched together with a flotsam of travel posters, batik work, examples of traditional embroidery, cow bells and last but not least woven baskets that you knew were from Oxfam. It was supposed to be inviting, user friendly: a home from home for the Asian woman trapped in the isolation of her house; a help-

ing hand for the Asian man shell-shocked from dealing with the revolving door racism and vagaries of white bureaucracy. (pp. 30–1)

Kulwant wonders if it provides work merely for 'professional coolies', 'making a profession of their nationality'. Randhawa is also sceptical of writers and media workers who seek to write 'ethnic novels' or to represent the community on stage and screen, and there is mingled sympathy and satire for Maya, who has embarked on research for a television programme on 'Madness in the Indian Community'.

Nevertheless it is through community and storytelling that healing and some sense of wholeness can be found. Ammi's nightmare of fire and holocaust can be quieted only by her involvement in providing food and other assistance for the Greenham Common women, and she is joined in this enterprise by her daughters and by other members of the community. But it is above all in the common purpose of finding and rescuing Rani that Kulwant sheds her isolation and her chosen identity as a cripple. She joins her daughter-in-law, Rani's mother, her old schoolfriend Caroline, West-Indian Angie, Maya and others in a marathon of storytelling, which gradually draws Rani back from semi-consciousness and the abyss of madness. Storytelling can heal the individual whose mind has been nearly destroyed by the seeming contradictions of being Asian, English and female. Communication can in turn create a community and heal divisions within it. But storytelling and communication are not enough, for it requires action by members of that community to counteract the mad and vicious accusations of older English men like Michael, who are unwilling to hear or sympathise with either Kulwant's or Rani's stories.

Ravinder Randhawa's novel does not conceal the complexities and difficulties that confront Asians who seek to be productive members of the larger community, to live in England rather than merely survive on the margins. Assimilation is shown to be neither desirable nor possible, but neither is it desirable to retreat into an artificial Indianness. In her novel's movement from a series of isolated and maimed characters towards a mingled community of different races, classes and generations, in which women take the lead as healers and storytellers, however, this first novel by Randhawa suggests less pessimism than do either Phillips or Emecheta for the future of a multicultural community (as opposed to the success of individuals) in Britain. But in all three novels, the metaphor of marriage, of making a home and of finding psychological being and identity in England is central. The parting words between Kulwant and her husband might speak for all three of the central couples:

'I never thought my life would be split like this. I didn't marry in order to separate.'
'Another one of England's gifts.'
'It's not England. It's what's wrong between us.'
'How can you tell the difference?'

Notes

1. Buchi Emecheta, *Second-Class Citizen* (London, Fontana, 1977). All page references are to this edition. It was originally published in 1974 by Allison and Busby, two years after *In the Ditch* (London, Allison and Busby, 1972). However, *In the Ditch* takes up Adah's story where *Second-Class Citizen* leaves off and might be seen as forming a sequel to it.
2. Caryl Phillips. *The Final Passage* (London, Faber, 1985). All references are to this edition.
3. Ravinder Randhawa, *A Wicked Old Woman* (London: Women's Press, 1987). All references are to this edition.

3. The Disturbing Vision of George Lamming

Louis James

On 22 June, 1948, the *Empire Windrush* landed 492 Jamaicans at Tilbury. In the decade that followed, they were joined by a quarter of a million West Indians escaping massive unemployment in the islands, moving into jobs which poor pay and conditions had made unattractive to British workers. Among these was George Lamming, a Barbadian who had been working in Trinidad, who arrived in 1950 on the same boat as another Caribbean writer, Samuel Selvon.

The black immigration created, improbably, a literary movement. The immigrants came largely from poor agricultural societies still marked by centuries of slavery and the repression of colonialism. The Caribbean islands were small. The largest English-speaking island, Jamaica, had some two million inhabitants, but this was an exception; Barbados had but a quarter of a million. The island cultures were predominantly oral in expression, and with the exception of the privileged elite, West Indians lacked the educational advantages of metropolitan countries.

Many of the immigrant writers came from the less privileged classes in the Caribbean. Wilson Harris from Guyana had begun life as a government land surveyor. Samuel Selvon's parents could barely afford his high school education in Trinidad, and when he arrived in London, he scraped a frugal living as a freelance journalist and junior civil servant at the Indian Embassy. Lamming, like V.S. Naipaul, was a scholarship boy from a humble village family, and he wrote his first novel while working in various factories. Yet in the three decades following the Second World War, it was West Indians in England who established the fastest growing branch of the 'new literatures in English' that were developing out of the old Commonwealth nations. In the 15 years from 1952 to 1967 alone, West Indians published some 137 novels besides a considerable volume of short stories, poems and plays.[1]

35

These writers were paradoxically both intimate with, and alienated from, British culture. Their education in the Caribbean had been an intensively British experience. At school, their poets were Wordsworth and Keats; their novelists Dickens and Charlotte Brontë. Their history and geography were those of Europe. Yet they lived in a tropical world, and they were nurtured by an emotional and cultural milieu that their intellects were taught to deny. England was a world in which Piccadilly Circus, Trafalgar Square and Marble Arch were as exotic as the Taj Mahal or the Acropolis might have been to British imaginations.[2]

Arrival in England brought a further shock, for their imaginative worlds came into sharp conflict with the grey reality of Britain after the war. It was out of this fractured vision that West Indian writers saw the British experience afresh. Their writing was marked by creative dislocation and experimentation.

This is well illustrated in the fiction of George Lamming. Through his six major novels, he has uncompromisingly searched for artistic forms to embody his vision both of Britain and his native Caribbean. His work has been continually innovative. His first novel, *In the Castle of My Skin* (1953), touched into being a whole sub-genre of novels about childhood in the Caribbean.[3]

The Emigrants (1954) was the first in a line of novels about what Caryl Phillips has called 'the Final Passage' of the Caribbean peoples in the triangular trade routes from Africa to the Caribbean, the Caribbean to Europe. *Of Age and Innocence* (1958) explored the final evolution towards Caribbean national independence; *Season of Adventure* (1970) portrayed the struggle between traditional and contemporary forces in the post-colonial West Indies; while *Water with Berries* (1971) and *Natives of My Person* (1972) investigated the psychic and mythological roots of the Caribbean identity. Each work was a new artistic departure.

Partly because of the difficulty of his work, only Lamming's first novel has achieved wide popularity. Mervyn Morris has suggested that Lamming is essentially a poet writing novels; Lamming himself has strongly rejected this, declaring 'This is a cross I carried with me a long time, that I was only a poet trying to write prose.'[4] His complexity of vision and form, Lamming argues, lies deeper than his choice of a medium.

From its opening, *In the Castle of My Skin* introduces a magic world. The evocation of growing up in a small Barbadian village, the relationship between the young 'G.' and his mother (no fathers figure in the community), and the mother's cohesive role in the village itself, are done with affectionate precision. It was the authenticity not only of experience, but of the language, which startled early readers and liberated young Caribbean writers. Edward Kamau Brathwaite, whose own writing has enabled scores of younger writers to find their native idiom, wrote of the impact of reading Lamming's *Castle*: 'Here breathing to me from every pore of line and page, was the Barbados I had lived. The words, the rhythms, the cadences, the scenes, the people, their predicament. They all came back. They all were possible.'[5] It was from reading Lamming that Brathwaite dated his own creative rebirth as poet of Caribbean 'nation language'.

Yet the power comes not just from its ability to evoke intimate experience, but from the precarious equipoise of its vision. The village is built on sandstone marl. In the rains that open the novel the water brings both life and decay, as the village is threatened with being literally washed away. It is the mother's song, and the answering chorus of the villagers, that holds the community together in the stormy night. The village both enriches and threatens. The villagers crowd round to watch the boy being washed, a close community; the fence collapses, breaking the pumpkin vine, and sharing becomes intrusion.

When 'G.' returns at the end to make his farewell, Lamming describes, with intimate detail, his mother cooking a 'last supper' of cuckoo and flying fish. The detail re-creates the sensuous richness, the precise cultural ritual of food, which nourished his childhood. But it is a world which he is now losing. The work is a Barbadian *Portrait of the Artist as a Young Man* and, like Stephen Dedalus in the subsequent *Ulysses*, 'G.' ends in a tower, isolated from the community. Here, the artist is black, and the tower is not ivory, but ebony.

The lucid evocation of 'G.'s' experience forms only one element of the book, one which is deliberately fragmented as the boy grows up and becomes a young intellectual. The individual experience of 'G.' turns to reportage as he becomes one of a group of schoolboys debating the nature of life, community and language on the beach, in counterpoint to the antics of the scurrying crabs; both boys and crustaceans crouch within their 'castles'. The island becomes objectified into a scene in moonlight, drenched with eldritch light and sexuality. The voices of the villagers are dramatised into individual voices – those of the village shoemaker or Mr Foster – or focused into the chorus-like speeches of the village elders 'Ma' and 'Pa'. By the end of the book, 'G.'s' account of village life has become a sporadic journal, as he comes to say 'in a sense more deep than simple departure ... farewell, farewell to the land' (p. 303).

The political import of this novel has been much discussed.[6] At a time when Caribbean novels tended to avoid political issues,

Castle confronted head-on the trauma of the colonial hegemony. The plantation overseers control the village; behind them stands the plantation owner, Mr Creighton; and beyond this, potent but intangible, the 'Shadow King' of British imperialism. The school-children, regimented into squads for the King's birthday, are as tightly packed and depersonalised as their forebears were on the middle passage slave ships. Barbados is claimed not just as ruled by England, but as a mimetic copy of the metropolitan isle itself: 'Barbados is truly Little England!' (p. 39).[7]

The history of slavery is erased through a process of educational amnesia. 'Thank God nobody in Barbados was ever a slave' think the school children. 'It didn't sound cruel. It was simply unreal' (p. 57). Reading the text itself becomes perilous for the English reader. In an early episode the village boys show a white visitor their cockerel, and it voids shit in his face. Underlying the nostalgic vision of childhood in a poor black community is an edgy anger against the white world, whose exploitation had drained the village of its communal life. Lamming intimates this resentment is directed towards the white readers of his book, who may have a voyeuristic interest in the village's disintegration.

The colonial trauma is placed within still larger issues. Towards the end, searching for the self that lies within the 'castle of his skin', 'G.' is contrasted with Trumper, his boyhood friend. Trumper has travelled to the United States and discovered Black Power. 'But you'll become a Negro like me an' all the rest in the States an' all over the world', he declares, ''cause it ain't have nothin' to do with where you born. 'Tis what you is, a different kind o' creature.' Trumper only needs to assert his blackness to become one with the universal Negro race (p. 299). But 'G.' cannot feel easy about this: 'Suppose I didn't find [my black identity]. This was worse, *the thought of becoming what you could not become.*' The question is unresolved.

The crisis lies as deep as the words used to write the novel. As children, 'G.' and his friends inhabited a world of inchoate feelings.

> With the sea simmering, and the sand and the wind in the trees, we received so many strange feelings. And in the village in the cellar, at the school, at this corner or that corner of the house, something was always happening. We didn't notice it then, but when something bigger appeared like the sea and the sand, it brought with it a big, big feeling, and the big feeling pushed up all the little feelings we had received in other places. We weren't ashamed. Perhaps we would do better if we had good big words like the educated people. But we didn't. (p. 153)

Language was an escape.

> You could say what you liked if you knew how to say it. It
> didn't matter whether you felt everything you said ... You had
> language to safeguard you. And if you were beginning to feel
> too strongly, you could kill the feeling, you could get it out of
> the way by fetching the words that couldn't understand what
> the feeling was about. It was like a knife. (p. 154)

How can one dissect human experience in a literary work, and
preserve the emotions out of which that experience arose?

If *Castle* ended with 'G.' leaving his island, Lamming's second
novel, *The Emigrants*, picks up the experience of a group of West
Indians travelling to Britain. Lamming has declared that the
emigrants 'can be seen as the extensions of the boys of *In the Castle
of My Skin*", and the narrator of the opening has obvious affinities
with 'G.'. However, they do not share the same identities; rather
they explore the same questions about the post-colonial Caribbean
posed by the earlier novel. The emigrants are from different
countries across the Caribbean, including Venezuela, and Lamming
uses the passage of the ship, *The Golden Image*, past the French
islands of Guadeloupe and Martinique, to broaden the context of
emigration beyond the Anglophone area. As the story develops in
Britain, the stories of the Caribbean immigrants, including that of
Higgins, a cook from Grenada, join with those of Frederick, an
Englishman once employed in Trinidad, and Azi, an African living
in Britain.

The long first section of the book establishes the characters
and the common denominators of their journey. 'Torpedo' and
'the Governor' have both been to England before, in the RAF,
and have no illusions about what they will find. Yet as the name
of the ship, *The Golden Image*, indicates, they are all still seeking
a status and sense of purpose they find lacking in their home
islands. Some know that, outside the cage of the ship, there is a
void. 'Beyond their enclosure was NO-THING. NO-THING that mattered' (p. 105).[8] Yet within the space there was the possibility of
new creation. Preparing to disembark, Higgins feels 'It mattered
to be in England. Yes. It did matter. Wherever there was life
there was something, other than NO-THING' (p. 106).

The section ends with a long dramatised coda, a railway
journey taken by the emigrants from Plymouth to Paddington,
interweaving the voices of emigrants and Britishers with railway
instructions ('WILL PASSENGERS KEEP THEIR HEADS WITHIN THE
TRAIN'). The section begins with a search for El Dorado in

Britain, the infinite promise of a New World, and ends with an ominous premonition of the *Heart of Darkness*:

Tell me, Tornado, Tell me.
What, man, what?
When we get outta this smoke
When we get outta this smoke, w'at happen next?
More smoke. (p. 124)

This is taken up in the central sections which take place in the darkened cellar that serves as a barber's shop, and in the secretive women's hairdressers where the women congregate. Underlying the encounters and manoeuvres of the immigrants, the recurring theme is that of failure to make contact with the England they had come to find. As Tornado explains, the emigrants had the legitimate hopes of children coming to the mother country. The English

'never seem to understan' that these people in these places got an affection for them that is greater than that of any allies in war time. ... An' that's why, if ever there's any fightin' in our parts of the world, we'd be nastier to the English than to any one, because we'd be remembering that for generations an' generations we'd be offerin' them a love they never even try to return. (p. 186)

A key figure is Frederick, an Englishman employed in Trinidad as a gamekeeper. He seduces and rejects a West Indian girl, Miss Bis, who as a consequence loses all self-esteem to the point where, when Frederick later meets her, he does not recognise her. In an attempted expiation for this betrayal, he marries Una, also from Trinidad, but he does not love her, and the relationship fails. Frederick is impotent, sexually and morally, a white corpse searching for resurrection. The book ends with violence, as a new group of emigrants claim shelter in the Mombasa Club run by one of the first wave, 'the Governor'. But he slips off into the night, leaving the African Azi to take charge. The one element of hope, as Sandra Paquet points out,[9] lies in the writer Collis. Collis is to some extent an extension of Lamming himself, who comes to a more sympathetic understanding of his fellow-emigrants. It is with Collis that the book ends: 'And Collis returned to the window and watched the night slip by between the light and the trees' (p. 271).

As noted, *The Emigrants* was a pioneering novel, the first in a

series on immigrant life which which ran from Samuel Selvon's
The Lonely Londoners (1956) to novels by second-generation
migrants, such as Caryl Phillips' *The Final Passage* (1985). Yet
although it is shot through with moments of brilliance, as a whole
it remains curiously unrealised, lacking imaginative cohesion.
Lamming had not found a sufficiently compelling central image
round which to organise his theme.

There is a tighter form in his two subsequent works, *Of Age
and Innocence* (1958) and *Season of Adventure* (1970). These have
never received popular recognition, but they mark the summit of
Lamming's artistic achievement. These novels return to the Caribbean, creating the imagined island of San Christobal. It is at once
West Indian – the ambience and social organisation is immediately recognisable to those who know the Caribbean – yet it
brings together aspects from a number of different islands to
represent the whole Caribbean area. San Christobal is given a
history going back to pre-colonial times. The heroic conflicts
between the Caribs and the first colonisers are told in the story
of 'the Tribe Boys and the Bandit Kings'.[10] A history of slavery
has created a society split between the westernised capital city,
and the inland Forest Reserve with its tribal roots, its drumming
and its potential for revolution. The two novels cover the period
immediately before and following independence from the British.

The 'age' and 'innocence' of the title of the earlier novel indicate
the consciousness of the two generations of an island on the brink
of independence. The older is divided between the reactionary
forces of the white Chief of Police and his minions, and the representative of the black peoples, Ma Shephard. Ma Shephard is
portrayed with sympathy; she has dignity, courage and a deep sense
of the black spiritual traditions. Yet in the end these roots in the
past also prevent her from understanding the potential of a new
society. The 'innocence' is the group of boys – reminiscent of those
in *Castle* – whose racial ties mirror those of the conflicting adult
world: – the Indian Singh, the European Rowley, the African Bob
and the Chinese Lee. These lack the racial consciousness of the
adults, and join in a sworn blood-brotherhood as 'the society'.

At the centre of the conflicts is Ma Shephard's son, a revolutionary leader. In the opening scene, set in a plane approaching San
Christobal, Shephard produces a gun and violently threatens the
passengers, in particular Marcia, who as a young white woman
awakens a sexual love–hate relationship created by white women
who have humiliated him in the past. By one view, Shephard is
mentally unbalanced but, as the book progresses, Lamming
questions the very nature of madness. Shephard's violent behaviour

41

can be seen as the inevitable reaction of the colonised to the colonial trauma.

Fanon is in the backgound here, and Lamming has explicitly discussed the possible need for those traumatised by colonialism to purge themselves with violence.[11] For all his moral and political shortcomings, then, it is Shephard who holds the key to political change on the island, and different elements on the island seek his death: the police officer Crabbe, the Englishmen Bill and Mark seeking vengeance for the death of a white woman, the Indian policeman Baboo. When he is killed, the novel turns into a political murder story, with the question, 'Who killed Shephard?' becoming an examination of the conflicts in the way of the island's independence.

Set against the adult conflicts, the boys live out their loyalties to each other. When the islanders boycott Crabbe's family, they smuggle oil for lighting to Crabbe's son, Rowley. In a tragic accident, Rowley dies in a fire which also destroys a mental hospital and many of its inhabitants. The gap between the boys and even the more sympathic members of the older generation is underlined when Ma Shephard (wrongly) implicates the boys in the fire, breaking their bond of admiration and trust for her. Accused, they become the new 'Tribe Boys' against the post-colonial 'Robber Kings', and the novel ends with the group watching through the night together, waiting for what the new day will bring.

Season of Adventure also explores the interface between different levels of social consciousness in a country now in the aftermath of independence. If the preceding novel used a mystery – who killed Shephard? – this novel is organised around the quest by Fola, an intelligent and well-provided-for San Christobal girl, to discover her father. In 1956, on a visit to Haiti, Lamming had watched the Ceremony of the Souls in which the celebrants recover contact with the spirits of the ancestral dead. It was an experience to which Lamming was to return in several works, as a potent image of cultural healing. The compelling opening scene is set in the *tonelle*, the Ceremony of the Souls. Fola has been brought there out of curiosity by her (British) history lecturer, and finds herself catapulted into a troubled questioning of her own identity. She knows she is the illegitimate daughter of Agnes, beautiful but temperamentally vulgar, who has now married Piggott, the Chief Commissioner of Police. The identity of her real father has never been revealed. Fola's search brings her into violent conflict with her parents. She turns to look for her father first through the self-taught artist Chika, who promises to paint her father; but her search is for more than a single individual, and she is increasingly drawn to the world of the Forest Reserve, to the common people led by the revolutionary Powell, to their rituals of ancestors, and their drum-based common culture inspired by the drummer Gort, whose music is the spiritual life of the community. In her quest, Fola becomes trapped in the conflict between a drum-based culture going back to Africa, and the European rule of law.

Piggott is killed, and the question surrounding Fola's father is implicated in the mystery; who murdered the Chief Commissioner? In the resulting fracas, the soldiers puncture the drum, destroying the spirit of the people. Fola has to discover the ambivalence of her blood – we learn she may have been fathered either by a black or a white man, as both impregnated her mother Agnes on the same day – and Powell reacts violently to her attempt to help in the struggle of the black folk, turning his hate murderously against her. The themes of love and hate intermingle throughout the novel, echoed in the song that becomes its motif: *'But when I hate you/ It's 'cause I love you.'*

Lamming is working out deeply-felt personal issues here, and introduces himself in an interpolated chapter in which he claims half-brotherhood with Powell. As Mervyn Morris has noted,[12] the novel's ending is unsatisfactory. Having pursued Fola's search for her father through the San Christobal society, Lamming finds no resolution to the mystery of the cultural identity sensed in the *tonelle*. Fola's experience in the *tonelle* of links with the past reverberates through the novel, but it is not fulfilled.

In his last two novels to date, Lamming returns to the theme of exile, and to the predicament of the expatriate West Indian. No one in *Water with Berries* (1971) sees a future in returning to San Christobal. The novel takes its title from Caliban's speech to Prospero in Shakespeare's *The Tempest*:

> when thou cam'st first,
> Thou strok'st me and made much of me, wouldst give me
> Water with berries in't ...

Lamming, in *The Pleasures of Exile* (1960), had already discussed parallels between the Prospero/Caliban myth and the colonial experience,[13] and here he develops the theme in an allegorical form. At the outset the main character, Teeton, a black artist from San Christobal, is planning to break loose from the comfortable, stifling relationship with his London landlady, the Dowager. This reverses the situation in *The Tempest*, where it was Prospero who was exiled on Caliban's island; now Caliban has come to England. For Teeton is one aspect of Caliban, now in

43

England as the tenant of Prospero's wife. (Prospero here is Gore-Britain, a West Indian plantation owner.) Fernando is 'Prospero's' brother. He murders Gore-Britain in revenge for the spoliation of the island, before escaping to England.

Lamming offers no simple retelling of Shakespeare's story. Another apect of Caliban is seen in the East Indian Roger, cut off from his roots, and driven to destroy those around him in a self-hating sado-masochism. He violently rejects the love of Nicole who, as a white American, stands outside the Caribbean/British conflict. Nicole is killed. Another mentally disturbed Caliban figure is Derek, who as a black actor can only find work on the British stage playing Othello. In a tragicomic comment on his inner death, he turns to specialising in acting corpses on stage.

Miranda appears in two guises. Her innocent side appears as Myra, a tragic figure raped in San Christobal by common people seeking revenge against the way they have been exploited. It is Myra who, in a moment of insight on Hampstead Heath, shares with Teeton an intimation of the Ceremony of the Souls, but this promise of spiritual healing is interrupted and leads nowhere. The other side of Miranda is imaged in Randa, who sells her body to the American ambassador to save Teeton in San Christobal. Teeton callously rejects her, disgusted by her action, and she commits suicide. Both are victims of the traumas of colonialism.

Psychic disturbance and violence permeates the novel. At the end, Teeton rids himself of his inseparable love and hate for the Dowager by murdering her and burning her body. Roger reacts to his loss of Nicole by going on an orgy of pyromania. Derek horrifies the audience by coming alive on stage and raping the heroine of *A Summer's Error in Albion*, a character also called Miranda. The tentative search for a solution in the earlier novels has gone; *Water with Berries* reveals only the psychic trauma of colonisation, and the open-ended violence to which it leads.

The circle is completed by Lamming's last-published novel, *Natives of My Person* (1972). If *Water with Berries* explores the rage of Caliban, this novel re-creates the quest of Prospero during the colonial expansion in the sixteenth and seventeenth centuries. Wilson Harris has written of the intermingled idealism and greed of the colonial adventure:

> The religious and economic thirst for exploration was true of the Spanish conquistador, of the Portuguese, French, Dutch and English, or Raleigh, or Fawcett ... an instinctive idealism associated with this adventure was overpowered within individual and collective by enormous greed, cruelty and exploration.[14]

In *Natives of My Person*, a complex work, Lamming explores the failure of the colonial exploit, which began with the violence of plunder and murder, but then attempted to colonise and 'develop' native populations that were left.

The Commandant captains the ship *Reconnaissance* in a seventeenth-century voyage to the isles of Black Rock. The colonisers of Lime Stone, the imaginary country Lamming uses to denote Europe, had christened the island San Christobal. It is now impoverished, and the natives decimated. The Commandant's mission is a secret one, subverting the mercenary wishes of the Lime Stone House of Trade and Justice. Challenged by his mistress, the Commandant wishes to make amends for a career of plunder by instead setting up a model society. 'Now my ambition is in reverse; and I reckon it is a more noble preference to plant some portion of Lime Stone in the virgin territories of San Christobal. This purpose I declare to be absolute and true' (p. 17). Yet his idealism is tainted by the same unyielding will that directed his earlier predatory exploits. His crew, also, are seeking freedom from their own guilt, but are trapped by their moral inadequacy, and only perpetuate more violence. The Boatswain, humiliated by the Lady of the House who uses him sexually in exchange for false hopes of advancement, longs to free himself by her murder. When the Surgeon's moral failure is recognised by his wife, he ruthlessly drives her to insanity and the madhouse. The common sailors in the crew cannot escape their greed for gold.

There is a mutiny. The Commandant is shot before the *Reconnaissance* reaches San Christobal, and the ship is left to an enigmatic outsider, the Pilot Pinteados. In the brief coda that closes the novel, three women, embodying the humane values the Commandant and his crew lack, wait on the island, hoping for the creation of the new community which so far has eluded them.

The novel explores the colonial adventure in metaphorical terms. The various nationalities in the crew point to the way the whole of Europe was involved in the exploition of the Caribbean, and Lamming has said that the ship images both the colonial quest and the authoritarian structures of African and the Caribbean colonial society that they construct.[15] The novel reaches beyond this into the essential failure of national and international politics in the Third World, to the 'underdevelopment' created by colonialism. The novel stimulates enquiry and thought beyond the bounds of its own plot.

Of the writers who laid the foundations of modern Caribbean literature – Wilson Harris, George Lamming, V.S. Naipaul, Samuel Selvon, Derek Walcott and Edward Kamau Brathwaite –

Lamming is the least read today. This is partly due to his difficulty. Yet, although Wilson Harris is arguably harder to read, he
has an ever-expanding reputation. One reason for Lamming's
comparative eclipse may be his political stance. While the racial
implications of Selvon's work, for instance, are softened by his
humour, the vision of *Water with Berries* is as uncompromising,
and uncomfortable, as the latest race riot on television.

This is not simply a matter of the reader's discomfort. As Wilson Harris declared as early as 1964, Lamming's restless vision
can be at odds with the basic requirements of fiction, for his
intellectual intentions undermine the imaginative coherence of his
characters and plot. 'This over-elaboration is one danger which
confronts Lamming', wrote Harris. 'He must school himself ... to
work for the continuous development of a main individual character ... '16 As literary form, Lamming's novels are flawed.

Yet Lamming has never made literary form his first objective.
He has followed his disturbing imagination wherever it took him,
and subverted any neat solution to his troubled vision. His work
is interwoven with passages whose intelligence, insight and poetic
power give his fiction a unique and enduring stature.

Notes

1. These figures are taken from Kenneth Ramchand, *The West Indian
   Novel and its Background* (London: Faber, 1970), pp. 274–89.
2. A vivid description of this cultural experience can be found in, for
   example, Shiva Naipaul's 'The Writer Without a Society', in Anna
   Rutherford, (ed.), *Common Wealth* (Aarhus: Dangaroo Press, 1972),
   pp. 114–15.
3. See my paper, 'The Sad Initiation of Lamming's "G."', in Rutherford
   (ed.), *Common Wealth*, pp. 135–43.
4. Mervyn Morris, 'The Poet as Novelist', in Louis James (ed.), *The
   Islands in Between* (London: Oxford University Press, 1968), p. 73;
   Ian Munro and Reinhard Sander (eds), *Kas-Kas* (Austin: University
   of Texas Press, 1972), p. 10.
5. E.K. Brathwaite, 'Timehri', *Savacou*, no. 2 (September 1970), p. 38.
6. See, for example, Wilfred Cartey, 'George Lamming and the Search
   for Freedom', *New World: Barbados Independence Issue* no. 3
   (1966–67), pp. 121–8; Ian Munro, 'The Theme of Exile in George
   Lamming's *In The Castle of My Skin*', *World Literature Written in
   English* no. 20 (November 1971), pp. 51–60; Ngugi wa Thiongo,
   'George Lamming's *In the Castle of My Skin*', in *Homecoming* (New
   York: Lawrence Hill, 1972), pp. 110–26.

7. George Lamming, *In the Castle of My Skin* (1953; London: Longman, 1970).
8. George Lamming, *The Emigrants* (London: Longman, 1954).
9. Sandra Paquet, *The Novels of George Lamming* (London: Heinemann, 1982), p. 44.
10. George Lamming, *Of Age and Innocence* (London: Michael Joseph, 1958), pp. 94–9.
11. 'Interview with George Lamming', in Ian Monro and Reinhard Sander (eds), *Kas-Kas: Interviews with Three Caribbean Writers in Texas* (University of Texas at Austin, African, Afro-American Research Institute, 1972), pp. 5–12.
12. Morris, 'The Poet as Novelist', pp. 82–3.
13. George Lamming, *The Pleasures of Exile* (London: Michael Joseph, 1960), pp. 95–159.
14. Wilson Harris, *Tradition, the Writer and Society* (London: New Beacon Books, 1967), p. 72.
15. George E. Kent, 'A Conversation with George Lamming', *Black World*, 22, no. 5 (March 1973), p. 96; quoted in Paquet, *The Novels of George Lamming*, p. 114.
16. Quoted in Harris, *Tradition*, p. 38.

4. Setting Up Home in a City of Words: Sam Selvon's London Novels

Susheila Nasta

Wat a joyful news, Miss Mattie,
I feel like me heart gwine burs'
Jamaica people colonizin
Englan' in reverse
  Louise Bennett, 'Colonisation in Reverse', in *Jamaica Labrish* (1966)

No Barbadian, no Trinidadian, no St Lucian, no islander from the West Indies sees himself as a West Indian until he encounters another islander in a foreign country ... In this sense most West Indians of my generation were born in England.
  George Lamming, *The Pleasures of Exile* (1960)

Although a sense of the need to migrate clearly affected early writers born in the Caribbean, such as the Jamaican Claude McKay who left in 1912 for the United States, the period immediately following the Second World War was particularly important for the arrival in London of a number of talented young West Indian artists. London, as Henry Swanzy, producer of the influential BBC Radio programme 'Caribbean Voices' once aptly observed, became a literary headquarters, a centre where writers from the various islands were meeting for the first time. Paradoxically perhaps, after departure from the islands they attempted to establish a firm West Indian cultural identity.

Over 40,000 West Indians emigrated to Britain in search of employment. Originally invited to the 'mother-country' by the labour government in an attempt to solve the immediate labour crisis following the Second World War, and commonly known as the 'Windrush' generation', these islanders moved to Britain expecting to improve their standard of living. But the streets of London were not paved with gold and the journey from island to city was in many cases one of disappointment and disillusion. Moses, the 'hero' of Sam Selvon's well-known group of novels on the immigrant experience in Britain – *The Lonely Londoners* (1956), *Moses Ascending* (1975) and *Moses Migrating* (1983) – makes the following satiric observations on the plight of black Londoners:

> The alarms of all the black people in Brit'n are timed to ring before the rest of the population. It is their destiny to be up and about at the crack o'dawn. In these days of pollution en environment, he is very lucky, for he can breathe the freshest air of the new day before anybody else. He does not know how fortunate he is. He does not know how privileged he is to be in charge of the city whilst the rest of Brit'n is still abed. He strides the streets, he is Manager of all the offices in Threadaneedle Street, he is Chief Executive of London Transport and British Railways, he is superintendent of all the hospitals, he is landlord of all the mansions in Park Lane and Hampstead ... He ain't reach the stage yet of scrubbing the floors of Buckingham Palace ... There is a scramble amongst the rest of the loyal population for these royal jobs, but with time, he too might be exalted to these ranks – who knows? Instead of moaning and groaning about his sorrows, he should stop and think and count these blessings reserved solely for him. He should realise that if it wasn't for him the city would go on sleeping forever.[1]

The black man is therefore the backbone of the city, but we see him only at night. Many fictional and non-fictional accounts document this period of West Indian cultural history. While Selvon's pioneering work *The Lonely Londoners* was emblematic in its creation of a black colony in the heart of the city, there are many other works, such as George Lamming's *The Emigrants* (1954) and his well-known collection of essays, *The Pleasures of Exile* (1960), Andrew Salkey's *Escape to an Autumn Pavement* (1960) and V.S. Naipaul's *The Mimic Men* (1967), which also deal with the loneliness and disillusion of the early immigrant experience. Interestingly, few women writers, apart from Jean Rhys whose work spanned the pre-war period, were published at this time, largely due to the fact that the first wave of immigration to Britain was predominantly male. Other women writing during this period, such as the poets Una Marson or Louise Bennett, gained

49

little recognition in the publishing world. This imbalance between the sexes is often reflected in the subject-matter of these early works where there is a notable absence of successful love relationships, children or any organic family life.

Jean Rhys's *Voyage in the Dark* (1934), for instance, portrays a familiar sense of dislocation and cultural confusion as Anna Morgan, her white Creole heroine, attempts to feel her way in an unwelcoming city. Her England is a world where no home life is experienced and Anna, like many of Rhys's later heroines, survives on the edges of society in an almost surreal metropolis which is frequently reduced to nothing more than colourless rooms in sordid boarding-houses. The characters, like V.S. Naipaul's Ralph Singh in *The Mimic Men* or even the 'boys' in Selvon's *The Lonely Londoners*, remain adrift whatever their situation:

> It was as if a curtain had fallen, hiding everything I had ever known. It was almost like being born again. The colours were different, the smells different, the feeling things gave you right down inside yourself was different. Not just the difference between heat; light; darkness; grey. But a difference in the way I was frightened and the way I was happy ... Sometimes it was as if I were back there and England were a dream. At other times England was the real thing and out there was the dream, but I could never fit them together.[2]

This early representation in Rhys of a kind of cultural schizophrenia points to several fundamental issues which are still major preoccupations in the works of many contemporary second-generation writers; writers who are giving voice to the experiences of their own generation of people, often born in the United Kingdom but still without a clear sense of home either in Britain or back in the islands. Writers such as Caryl Phillips, Grace Nichols, Fred d'Aguiar, Joan Riley, Merle Collins, David Dabydeen and Linton Kwesi Johnson, to name but a few, all reflect a concern with these issues. For the experience of Britain does not create a simple antithesis between tropical exoticism and darkness in a cold clime, nor is the meeting of the two worlds in the imagination easily reduced to a nostalgic vision of a lost paradisiacal childhood and an alien world which replaced it. The problem is, more centrally, one of different ways of seeing, of different modes of apprehending reality which have to be accommodated within a new context. Even for Jean Rhys in the 1930s (she is commonly categorised a white West Indian), the main difficulty was in coming to terms with the idea of London as an illusion, as a dream built on the foundations of the colonial myth; a myth which has to be demythologised in the mind of the artist who comes from a previously colonised world.

Yet, ironically, it was London that created the possibility, in many cases, of a bridge between the past – a history of racial admixture, cultural disorientation and economic exploitation – and the present, which posited a strong need to establish a West Indian 'cultural pedigree'. As Donald Hinds noted in *Journey to an Illusion* (1966), escape from the islands was frequently a stage on the route to self-discovery:

> Deep down I knew I loved my persecutors. Our Caribbean background was shaped by English things ... but at last I was coming to terms with myself ... I am indeed grateful to the English. Grateful for forgetting me in order to discover myself.[3]

The birth of a Caribbean consciousness by confrontation with the 'mother-country', and the re-definition created by the juxta-position of the two worlds, are central themes in a great deal of West Indian expatriate fiction. Frequently, as in Lamming's work *The Pleasures of Exile*, identity can only be found by facing this dilemma within the context of the Old World, by confrontation with the 'other'; the meeting between island and metropolis, Cali-ban and Prospero, must occur and is a necessary prerequisite to the flowering of a real West Indian identity. Moreover, combined with the physical and psychological realities of survival in the alien city, the majority of writers also faced the problem of over-coming the divisive effects of a colonial educational background, an education which had repeatedly told them that 'real' places were 'cold' places and these were elsewhere:

> Everything seemed to conspire against us. The faces we saw in advertisements were not our faces; the places seen in films were not our places ... he books we had to read were not our books ... Writing began and ended with Charles Dickens. He it was who determined what style ought to be and through whose eyes we saw more vividly than the tropic rain beating against our windows, the nagging London drizzle and old men warming hands over fires in musty rooms.[4]

This craving for fantasy, or a desire to create an alternative world based on the masquerade of the colonial myth, had far-reaching effects on the voices of this first generation of Caribbean writers. They searched, often in vain, for the solid world of a metropolis, a world which had grown up in their imaginations on dubious and artificial literary foundations. In V.S. Naipaul's *The Mimic Men*, Ralph Singh's inability to possess the heart of the city reflects the pain of the necessary process of demythologisation:

> Here was the city ... *the world*. The trams on the Embankment sparked blue ... Excitement! Its heart must have lain somewhere ... *I would play with famous names* as I walked the empty streets and stood on bridges. But the *magic of names* soon faded ... my incantation of names remained unanswered. In the great city, so solid in its light – to me as colourless as rotten wooden fences and new corrugated iron roofs – in this solid city *life was two-dimensional*. (My italics)[5]

Similarly, Sorbert, in Andrew Salkey's *Escape to an Autumn Pavement*, comes to the realisation that he has not inherited a language and culture from his British colonial education but rather a sense of the lack of it:

> I walk around London and I see statues of this one and the other ... There's even Stonehenge. And do you know how I feel deep down? ... I feel nothing ... We've been fed on the Mother Country myths. Its language. Its literature. Its Civics ... What happened to me between African bondage and British hypocrisy? What?[6]

This sense of something missing, the sense of a cultural and historical void beneath the excitement that a group identity in the 'metropolis' can bring, is exacerbated by the whole question of a language acquired but not possessed. As was evident from Ralph Singh's reverential incantation of names, the naming of a thing and the knowledge, understanding or possession of it can be very different things. Societies, like the individuals of which they are composed, need their own areas of privacy, areas into which they can retreat and refresh themselves. For the West Indian writer abroad for whom the language, as V.S. Naipaul said 'was mine' but 'the tradition was not',[7] this cycle of disillusion and cynicism is a crucial stage in the process of decolonisation, for it is only through this process and the reclamation of an authentic language for identity that the writer can begin to rescue his/her community from the illusory myths of the imperial centre. And it is in this area of language – a language *for* rather than *against* identity – that Sam Selvon's writing holds such an important and influential position.

* * *

Sam Selvon's fiction, set in London between 1950 and the mid-1980s (he left Britain after 28 years to live in Canada), is a crucial milestone in the history and development of Caribbean writing. Recently described as the 'father of Black Literature in Britain'[8] by Maya Angelou, the African-American writer, Selvon's London works – the short stories collected in *Ways of Sunlight* (1957); *The Housing Lark* (1965), a novel, as its title suggests, concerned with the housing problem; and the 'Moses' novels, *The Lonely Londoners* (1956), *Moses Ascending* (1975) and *Moses Migrating* (1983) – span a crucial period in the growth of black writing in Britain. With the use of a modified form of 'dialect' or what we should describe as a consciously chosen Caribbean literary English, for both the language of the narrator and that of the characters, *The Lonely Londoners* was a pioneering work as it moved towards bridging the difficult gap of perspective between the teller of the tale and the tale itself. As one of the first full-length novels to be written in this language form, it also reflected an innovative departure from the more standard modes of portraying unlettered characters in traditional fiction. In style and content, therefore, it represented a major step forward in the process of decolonisation.

Selvon's sojourn in London from 1950 to 1978 acted as a creative catalyst in the development of his art, enabling links to be drawn between the two preoccupations of his fiction: Trinidad and London. Through the encounter with London, it became possible to move, on the one hand, towards a more fully realised picture of the world back home and, on the other, to define and establish a Caribbean consciousness within a British context. Only in London, says Selvon, 'did my life find its purpose'.[9]

The settings of Trinidad and London have formed the major focus of Selvon's work to date. However, while the Indian cane community is carefully observed in the best-known Trinidad novels, *A Brighter Sun* (1952) and *Turn Again Tiger* (1957), Selvon did not come from a rural background himself nor was he 'Indianised' in any sense. Born in 1923 of East Indian parents, his father was a Madrassi, Selvon related from an early age primarily to the multicultural world of modern Trinidad. Speaking of the Hindi language, he has said; 'I just ignored it ... I grew up so Creolized among the Trinidadians ... Not as an Indian, but as a Creolized West Indian as we say.'[10]

The tensions and conflicts implicit in the idea of creolisation are a frequent theme in Selvon's art, whether his subject is the East Indian peasantry, the urban middle classes, the rootless trickster figures of his London fiction or the calypsonian characters in the short stories set in Port-of-Spain. Indeed, in the black London that Selvon creates in *The Lonely Londoners*, we are unaware of the 'boys' particular cultural identities. So powerful is the shared dynamic of the group at this stage that even Cap, the Nigerian, begins to behave like a West Indian.

Like many other immigrants of his generation, Selvon came to London to find work. Describing himself as largely self-educated, he had begun his literary career as a journalist with the *Trinidad Guardian*. Soon after his arrival in London, his first novel, *A Brighter Sun*, was published, gaining him international recognition and enabling him to become a full-time writer.

The Lonely Londoners is the first of three works dealing with the central figure of Moses Aloetta, a 'veteran' black Londoner, and his experiences with a group of ordinary and unlettered immigrants, 'black immigrants ... among whom I [Selvon] lived for a few years when I first arrived in London'.[11] As in his collection of radio plays, *El Dorado West One* (adapted from *The Lonely Londoners*), the novel represents a comi-tragic attempt to subvert and demythologise the colonial dream of a bountiful city. Characteristically, Selvon's reversal of the original myth in the plays – a myth linked of course to the European voyages of discovery in the sixteenth and seventeenth centuries of seeking a golden land – has several important reverberations as far as the economic base of nineteenth-century imperialism and Caribbean colonial history are concerned. But Selvon's political commentary is always implicit and the world of his Londoners is not gold, but grey; his questers may be led and supported by the sage figure Moses but they are limited to the bleak reality of surviving in the wilderness of an alien and alienating 'mother-country'.

At the beginning of *The Lonely Londoners*, the atmosphere of Selvon's city is described: 'as if it is not London at all but some strange place on another planet' (p. 7).[12] Typically, the narrator subverts standard English in the novel's opening: 'One grim winter evening, when it had a kind of unrealness about London, with a fog sleeping restlessly over the city' (p. 7). Selvon, controlling the narration and using a modified form of Caribbean English, creates a distance between the narrative voice and the city while establishing an intimacy between the reader and the storyteller. The unemployment office 'is a kind of place where hate and disgust and avarice and malice and sympathy and sorrow and pity all mix up. Is a place where everyone is your enemy and your friend' (p. 22). More generally:

it have people living in London who don't know what happen-

ing in the room next to them, far more the street or how other
people living ... It divide up in little worlds ... and you don't
know anything about what happening in the other ones except
what you read in the papers. (p. 74)

We meet few white characters, enter few homes and topographi-
cal description is scarce, yet the boundaries of Selvon's black
enclave are carefully defined and always made accessible to new
arrivals, who need careful initiation into the games of survival.
Black London is thus domesticated by the rituralistic repetition of
the names not only of important and viable areas – it is bounded for
instance in the west by 'the Gate' (Notting Hill), in the east by 'the
Arch' (Marble) and in the north by 'the Water' (Bayswater) – but
also by the stories of the 'boys' who return with exciting 'ballads' to
relate after venturing out into uncharted areas of experience in the
city, 'ballads' which strengthen and reinforce the fragile identity of
the group's own mythology. Selvon has himself pointed out that the
London these immigrants inhabited lacked any of the normal pillars
of security or cohesion. His characters may see the sights or taste
the bitter-sweet attractions of the metropolis, but they ultimately
live in a restrictive, two-dimensional world.

With its apparently unstructured episodic style and the comic
dexterity of Selvon's use of a modified form of 'dialect', or what
Kamau Brathwaite has more recently termed 'nation language',
the novel when it first appeared was often mistakenly regarded as
an amusing social documentary of West Indian manners. As such,
its primary intention was to reveal with pathos and compassionate
irony the humorous *faux pas* of the black innocent abroad. The
surface textures of the loosely-knit sketches or 'ballads' recounted
through the ambivalent voice of the third-person narrator seemed
to support his view. As readers we are swiftly drawn into the pace
of the narrative and the initiation rites for the 'desperate hustlers'
as they 'land up' on Moses' doorstep with 'one set of luggage, no
place to sleep, no place to go' (p. 8). Similarly, the idiosyncrasies
and eccentricities of Selvon's various characters, known collec-
tively as 'the boys', are clearly delineated. We witness the first
shocks of arrival at Waterloo in the almost surrealistic opening to
the novel as Moses journeys to the station through the fog of a
London winter, the endless and usually abortive search for employment and the constant hunt for the forbidden fruits of 'white
pussy'. The boys (the term itself suggests the almost primeval
innocence of the immigrants), picaresque and calypsonian rogues
from a variety of islands, circle like vultures around their sage and
liaison officer Moses, who attempts at times to offer solace.

However, from a very early stage in the novel, the romance of the city is counterpointed by a frightening sense of dislocation. Sir Galahad's (known on arrival as Henry Oliver) initial buoyancy is fractured when he ventures out alone for the first time. The 'sun shining but Galahad never see the sun look like how it looking now. No heat from it, it just there in the sky like a force-ripe orange. When he look up, the colour of the sky so desolate it make him frighten' (p. 26). Selvon's descriptions of Galahad's reactions to a different climate are fresh and enlightening, using terms of reference from a tropical world to describe the incongruities. The psychologically disorientating effects of the alien surroundings on the newcomer are implicit in the way the language is used. Most strikingly perhaps, the collision of the two worlds of Trinidad and London in Galahad's mind, with the dreamlike image of the 'force-ripe orange', enables the reader to experience the extremity of Galahad's fear. Similarly, by imposing the language of his subjects on the city, Selvon remakes it in their own image. At times, as Gordon Rohlehr has pointed out, they shrink it by the new use of reductive analogies: the walls of Paddington slums, for example, crack like the 'last days of Pompeii'.[13]

Moses' developing scepticism about the resources of this community, and his urgent need to discover a private identity, provide one of the major tensions in the novel as the voice of the third-person narrator mediates between the consciousness of the group and the predicament of Moses himself. After a visit from Big City, who has ambitions to be a world-wide traveller, we are shown Moses' growing awareness of the futility of his existence:

> after Big City leave him Moses used to think bout ... money, how it would solve all the problems in the world. He used to see all his years in London pile up one on top of the other, and he getting no place in a hurry. (p. 82)

Moses' sense of a pointless repetition here is significantly reflective of a voice that becomes more articulate as the novel proceeds. Set apart from the others as the sage figure, with the knowledge of years of ballads behind him, he also has to come to terms with a sense of loss. This is dramatised most clearly in his relationship with Galahad; from the opening pages at Waterloo Station, Moses tries to persuade the newcomers to return 'back home' immediately. His words reveal the pain of a superior irony. While Galahad's dreams of the city may be fulfilled, like those of V.S. Naipaul's Ralph Singh in *The Mimic Men*, by the phrase 'Charing Cross' or by the magnetism of Piccadilly Circus, Moses' consciousness becomes increasingly disturbed. Although he attempts to relive his own past through Galahad's love affair with the city, he has already reached a point of stasis. As he says to Galahad, 'All them places is like nothing to me now' (p. 69). As Galahad's persona becomes increasingly inflated – he begins to feel more and more 'like a king living in London' – Moses is drawn further and further into his introspective reflections and desire to 'draw apart'. And the boys' protective self-caricatures and nicknames become identifiable as only a transport form of camouflage within the black colony. Moreover, the nature of the language itself in the city of words they have created, with its reliance on repetition, drama and anecdote, can also become a regressive force, a form of restriction with disturbing implications for the possibility of growth within or outside the community.

Selvon's 'ballad' style in *The Lonely Londoners* shifts easily between an oral and a literary tone and bears many correspondences with the native tradition of Trinidadian calypso. The oral calypsonian ballad is well known for its use of a subversive irony, the melodramatic exaggeration of farcical anecdotes, racial stereotyping, repetition for dramatic effect and the inclusion of topical political material. Also, as John Thieme has recently shown, there are close parallels with Trinidad Carnival, a form that is essentially 'parodic, egalitarian and subversive' but constantly offers the possibility for renewal and regeneration. As such, *The Lonely Londoners*, he says, is a central Carnival text;[14] furthermore, Carnival as a system of discourse enables a creolisation of language and form that brings together the marketplace culture of Carnival and the world of the printed book. Thus Selvon's attempts at literary decolonisation both colonise Englan' in reverse and look forward to the later works of Caribbean writers such as Michael Smith, Earl Lovelace, Grace Nichols and Linton Kwesi Johnson, who combine the literary and the oral without privileging either.

Selvon's 'boys', then, originate in many ways from a world of language, 'a world of words through which they grope for clarity'.[15] Sexual themes are almost always present but from a male viewpoint (for which he has been criticised in recent years), though they conform to and parallel in many respects the classically chauvinistic attitudes of the urban trickster figures of calypso. Rather like the ultimately reductive and self-denigratory effects of their nicknames, their view of women as 'pretty pieces of skin' reflects ultimately the boy's uncertainty and insecure sense of self.

It is partly because the inherited values of white society reduce their own stature that they must adopt these postures. This technique of 'naming' or 'labelling' as a means of self-defence is evident when Sir Galahad sets off 'cool as a lord' to meet his white date and confronts the colour problem. Never easily deflated, Galahad is left talking to the colour black as if it is a person, telling it that 'is not *he* who causing botheration in the place, but *Black*, who is a worthless thing' (p. 72).

There is no beginning or end to the experiences of 'the boys' in *The Lonely Londoners*. Although details about Moses accumulate – we know he is tiring of Britain and frequently dreams of a return to Trinidad – they are unobtrusive and are fitting to his development as the novel proceeds. The surface fragmentation or conscious disorganisation of the novel's structure therefore becomes part of its main purpose, that 'beneath the kiff-kiff laughter, behind the ballad and the episode, the what-happening, the summer-is-hearts ... is a great aimlessness, a great restless swaying movement that leaving you standing in the same spot' (p. 125). By the end of the novel Moses is aware of a meaningless repetition and circularity in the group's existence.

The phrase 'what happening', which echoes throughout and is the fundamental rationale of its numerous episodes, comes to imply less a resilience in the face of complicated experience than a painful sense of futility and incoherence. Moses' basement room which acts as a kind of surrogate religious centre is where 'the boys' congregate every Sunday morning to swap ballads and talk about this and that. But the stories are never finished and the breathless narration of this section (pp. 122–5) emphasises it lack of direction. The repartee of the community has become a self-undermining rhetoric; as the boys attempt to swap well-worn anecdotes, we witness Moses' detachment as he becomes almost a mythical repository, a Tiresias figure who can never escape the constant 'moaning and groaning and sighing and crying'. The oral and rhythmic nature of the prose adds weight to this as the synchronisation of voices degenerates into a deflationary climax which then subsides to the original theme: 'So what happening these days?' Significantly, the questions are not addressed to any particular subject; they ring out like voices in the wilderness.

Only Moses, who has almost merged in consciousness with the narrating voice, seems to be moving forward and can perceive the need to discover a new language for existence. The black London of Selvon's 'boys' has become by the close only a city of words: there are no firm foundations (apart from Moses' basement room), and the surface security provided by this shared code, which has reduced the vast metropolis to a manageable West Indian colony within the city, will only perpetuate their isolation as they have no desire for integration. We leave Moses looking down into the River Thames and articulating this sense of a void: 'when you go down a little you bounce up a misery and pathos and a kind of frightening-what? He don't have the right word but he have the right feeling in his heart' (p. 126). This search for the 'right word' or an appropriate and individual voice to define a new reality for the Caribbean writer in London is central to an understanding of Selvon's first experimentations in *The Lonely Londoners* and becomes the main preoccupation of a new Moses who is still in Britain 20 years later in *Moses Ascending* (1975).

* * *

In *The Lonely Londoners*, Selvon faced the problem of both dealing with an early and exploratory response to the creation of a black London as well as discovering a suitable literary frame in which to express this experience. The slight area of narrative uncertainty in *The Lonely Londoners* is clarified in *Moses Ascending* (1975), where Moses becomes very much the self-conscious narrator. In this novel we meet a Moses who is actively trying to draw apart from all the hustling of the early days. He is now endeavouring to construct a fully-realised individual persona at an important level; in the changed social and political climate of the 1970s, a world where oppressive immigration laws affect entry and departure, Moses' development is explored metaphorically. He buys his own, admittedly dilapidated, house (due for demolition in three years); he is no longer a tenant but a landlord. Furthermore, he wants to be a writer and sets out to write his memoirs in the uppermost room with a large view of the city, his 'castle';

> After all these years paying rent, I had the ambition to own my own property in London, no matter how ruinous or dilapidated it was. If you are a tenant, you catch your arse forever, but if you are a landlord, it is a horse of a different colour. (p. 8)

Or, as Moses says to Sir Galahad (now a fervent representative of the Black Power movement); 'I just want to live in peace, and reap the harvest of the years of slavery I put in Brit'n. I don't want people like you around, to upset the applecart' (p. 9).

Moses ascends only for a brief spell to live in the attic or 'penthouse' of his own house which, as the novel proceeds, becomes increasingly crowded with Bob (his illiterate white Man Friday from the 'Black Country'), Jeannie (Bob's girlfriend and Moses' sometime mistress), Brenda, and the Black Power group as well as some 'Pakis' who enact a sheep slaughter in his back yard. His ambitions, to be 'Master' of his own house and an erudite black man of letters, suggest the possibility, in fantasy at least, of gaining security and moving away from the stasis of the old days, the days of the 'what happening' and the 'kiff-kiff laughter' we saw in *The Lonely Londoners*. Moreover, the image Moses evokes at the opening, of gaining a 'bird's eye view' of life, is indicative of his intention to achieve some distance from his community. But the preservation of such a sanctuary, a literary haven in Shepherd's Bush, is not shown to be a viable proposition, and Moses' 'castle' (p. 46) is progressively undermined as the novel proceeds.

The atmosphere of *Moses Ascending*, like that of Selvon's earlier work, is initially congenial and suggests an innocently mocking comedy concerned with the idiosyncrasies of the new generation of 'Third World immigrants' in the city. But Moses' attempts to separate himself from his own community in order to make an investment in 'truth', as he calls it, are barbed throughout by a subtly ironic method which attacks both the aspirations of the budding black writer with his recently acquired social graces, as well as those new political radicals who make up the Black Brit'n he now lives in. The tensions which were developing by the close of *The Lonely Londoners* have culminated in an almost total dissipation of the original group. The supposed security of the West Indian island in the metropolis, the strength created by the 'boys' shared sense of dislocation and cultural identity have collapsed. Tolroy and family are returning to Jamaica, Big City has gone mad (he 'walks about the streets muttering to himself, ill-kempt and unshaven ... as if the whole city of London collapse on him'); others, we hear, have gone up north and some simply 'down in the underground' (p. 16) never to emerge.

Of the original group, only Galahad and Moses remain and Moses has lost much of his faith in the idea of black unity:

> I will tell you one thing that I have learnt in this life. It is that the black man cannot unite. I have seen various causes taken up and dropped like hot coals. I have seen them come together and then scatter ... in all directions. (p. 49)

Moses' attempts to shield himself from the suffering of his people, however, are not taken seriously and Galahad, as we shall see later, becomes a major factor contributing to his old friend's steady descent from his newly-won attic freedom.

Moses' developing scepticism concerning the question of commitment to an ever-continuing series of futile causes can be compared once again to V.S. Naipaul's *The Mimic Men*, in which Ralph Singh strives through his writing of a personal history to move beyond those sequences of false behaviour in his past which led only to a barren cycle of events. Both Selvon and Naipaul have frequently commented on the dangers for the post-colonial artist in becoming over-involved in what Naipaul has termed the 'corruption of causes',[16] and Selvon too has voiced a need to develop his art further than what he regards as the ultimately limiting strictures and preoccupations of a literature committed in the main to the assertion of a literary nationalism. In addition, his desire is to break through certain narrow interpretative categories – of 'protest', 'hardship' or 'slavery' – often assigned by certain metropolitan critics to the supposed naturalistic work of writers such as himself.[17] Although Selvon does not indicate that he wants to withdraw from the black writer's struggle for acceptance in an established literary world, or that he is retreating from his responsibilities to that world 'where I belong' (which now includes the whole of the Third World as well as Trinidad), he does suggest the need for an expansion of consciousness, a widening of horizons in the new literatures of the world to include grounds of more universal applicability and significance.

Interestingly, Selvon made those observations in 1979 just after his departure from Britain where he had lived for 28 years, a period which also spans the creation of the Moses figure. Moses, however, does not simply present autobiography; as a representative voice of the old generation of immigrants, he typifies to Selvon 'all that happened (during that phase)... he also spoke in the idiom of the people which was the only way that he could ... express himself'. Based on a 'true-life' character, Moses, in spite of all his 'presumptions to be English ... remains basically a man from the Caribbean'.[18] Yet by the close of *Moses Ascending*, with the growth of a new generation of Black Britons, the Black Power movement, the festering hostility between Asian immigrants and blacks, we become aware of the impossibility for Moses of forming an organic relationship either with his own community or the white world outside. He is outdated, a misfit, a black colonial adrift in the city, straddling or attempting to straddle both worlds.

From an early stage we are shown how Moses, with the status of a black landlord, attracts exactly those types he is attempting to avoid. Being 'unprejudiced', his only stipulation regarding tenants is that none of the old group lives in his house and he leaves all the house management in the incapable hands of his white Man Friday, Bob, an even-tempered, illiterate Midlands white. But the house becomes an illegal centre for the smuggling of Pakistanis into Britain and the headquarters for the local Black Power movement. Moses only becomes conscious of the real 'goings-on' in the house when he witnesses the assembly of a Black Power demonstration in the street below. Similarly, his attention is first drawn to the mysterious Faizull Farouk when he hears the bleating of a sheep – a victim for a Muslim sacrifice – in his back yard.

While Moses' lack of awareness is treated humorously, his predicament has several disturbing implications. The episode of the sheep-slaughter, for instance, is representative of the seriousness of Moses' new situation. On one level, the description of this scene is a successfully comical account of an absurd event which is symptomatic of the confused clash of cultural values affecting the new generation of immigrants in Britain. Moses is interested in the episode only because Galahad has pressurised him to research topical material for his writing. The 'Pakis' are religiose about the whole affair and attempt to adhere strictly to Muslim rituals. In contrast, Bob, watching from a window upstairs, reacts with horror:

> A solitary shriek of horror rent the atmosphere. It was so unexpected and piercing that Faizull lose his grip and slip off the sheep ... I was the onlyest one to keep my cool: I look up to the penthouse and see Bob leaning out of the window as if he vomiting.
> 'I will get the RSPCA to arrest you!' He shout, 'You too, Moses!'
> Everything was going nice and smooth until this white man run amok. (p. 63)

The position of Moses in relation to Bob compares interestingly here with that of Moses and Galahad in *The Lonely Londoners* when Galahad tells Moses the 'ballad' of his attempt to catch a pigeon for his supper in Kensington Gardens. There is obviously one major cultural difference between the two episodes and that is Bob's conventional English attitude concerning cruelty to animals and Galahad's perspective as a man who is starving in a strange world where animals (even pigeons) grow fat while human beings starve. Bob's lack of familiarity with the cultural context of what he sees curiously parallels that of Galahad when confronted with a universe of cosseted dogs and protected pigeons; a world with different emphases of value. But, most importantly, this parallel involves a further contrast: that between Moses as confidant or fellow-West Indian in *The Lonely Londoners* and Moses as landlord having to accommodate the sensibilities of a native Englishman in *Moses Ascending*. From being simply an outsider listening to those similar to himself, Moses has moved to the more complicated position of attempting to be an insider with responsibilities both to his tenants and his neighbours which require him to mediate between the black and white worlds. He therefore cannot remain the easy-going black radical of the early days; he is now a man with vested interests who desires to fit in and to find a place in British society. This desire is emphasised by the exaggerated adoption of certain British customs which he considers to be proper to his class, such as a drinks cupboard and a white manservant. This different is further exaggerated by the language he speaks.

Moses' literary ambition is gently parodied by Selvon, his faith in his ability to write 'Queen's English' is shown to be not that dissimilar to his recent rise in social status, and the language he uses further reflects the hybrid nature of his personality. The first-person narration modulates between the formality of nineteenth-century English, Trinidadian proverbs, Greek myth, American films, contemporary advertising jingles and the banter of the old days. Selvon's linguistic resourcefulness, his subversion of the 'Standard' and his iconoclastic methods which unite both calypso with western literature, only serve to heighten our awareness that Moses can not yet fully inhabit a 'home'; he is not yet master of his own house or of the language with which he wants to compose his memoirs. Furthermore, his partial misunderstanding of many of the terms he is trying to appropriate reflects once again the divisive effects of the acquisition of a second-hand language – a language used but not possessed. Moses is not trying to own the 'magical' heart of the city but he is attempting to become a writer and in doing so needs to discover an appropriate voice.

Selvon's portrayal of Moses' attempts to find a voice is one of total confusion: a confusion of notions of order and reality, and the creation of a conglomeration which one reviewer called a 'verbal salad of ungrammatical wit and literary and biblical references'.[19] However, while the inconoclastic effects of this hybrid language may be inspired, as in the following extract describing the sheep slaughter –

> Kay sir rah, sir rah, as the Japanese say. It was a motley trio Faizull shepherd into the house. I have seen bewildered adventurers land in Waterloo from the Caribbean with all their incongruous paraphernalia and myriad expressions of amazement and shock, but this Asian threesome beat them hands down. (p. 74)

– the result is ultimately one of pathos. Similarly, in Moses' inno-

vative, highly ironic and lyrical 'essay' which he composes to the
black man early in the novel (pp. 11–15), the only coherent piece
he manages to complete before Galahad's Black Power pressure
disturbs him, we see the means by which Moses' potentially
serious and political subject-matter is parodied by Selvon and
rendered absurd by his literary style.

The essay deals with the plight of black workers in a hostile
white urban society (quoted on page 49), a position of depriva-
tion and inequality, and an issue that might have most naturally
found expression in a polemical attack. Yet Selvon's technique
and the quality of the pathos that results moves beyond the basic
facts of the issue itself. In its wide range of 'literary' effects and
the eccentric use of a mixture of 'literary' terms, the piece, which
is too long to quote in full here, mirrors the growth of Moses'
linguistic affectations since his retirement. Moses' range incorporates nation language, standard English, the Shakespearian 'Fie'
or 'God's blood things have come to a pretty pass', as well as
allusions to historic moments such as the 'Black Watch'. At times,
Moses even uses a modified form of Caribbean English to
describe the white man's predicament. This conglomeration of
linguistic modes and Moses' very sincere attempt to write in the
argumentative style of the traditional essay form, an attempt
which achieves precisely the opposite effect, are typical of the
novel as a whole. While Moses sets out to present us with all the
advantages of the black worker's position, he establishes with
innocent elegance a very different picture.

Moses Ascending is very much a novelist's novel. There are
explicit references by Moses, the fictional author, to other real
Caribbean writers living in London – George Lamming and
Andrew Salkey for instance – but more significantly, the predomi-
nant tension in the book stems from Moses' attempts to become
a black writer and to establish an authentic voice that his own
people will listen to. The novel therefore dramatises the difficulties Moses faces as a black post-colonial writer in Britain. After
careful study of the pros and cons of the writing process, Moses
begins to feel that he ought to be able to write a book with a
proper plot and theme. Furthermore, he must reveal the breadth
of his education and knowledge by using a language that can
incorporate classical myth, legend, the Bible and oral folklore. The
result is, as Michel Fabre has pointed out, the 'sophisticated
appropriation' by 'colonial writing' of a literary style 'formerly
reserved for the British born'. Moses' voice reflects almost a car-
nivalisation of language as he blends outdated, jerky phrases with
Trinidadian syntactical shifts and turns. Through Moses as a

64

'writer-of-memoirs, Selvon as a novelist claims the right to depart from the naturalistic ways of using English usually prescribed to non-British writers ... [he] does not assimilate into the ... mainstream, he explodes it'.[20]

Moses' relationship with Sir Galahad and the Black Power movement is also instructive. Throughout the novel, the development of Moses' private identity is threatened by the public and political world of Brenda and Galahad and the avidly supported Black Power group. Moses does not withdraw completely from them (it is he in fact who acts when the 'Party' does not have enough money to rescue two of its innocent brethren gaoled after an unfortunate encounter with the police). Yet, paradoxically, Moses' remaining sense of incompleteness and a doubting of his selfhood are created most strongly by the pressures his own people impose on him. It is because he is a *black* writer that the conflict between his personal wish to write his memoirs and the demands made upon him by a fast-developing political situation are exaggerated. As Moses becomes increasingly plagued by what his 'proper' subject should be, his private work is gradually stultified, and he through conscience becomes involved in events which do not really concern him. Furthermore, the possibility of further withdrawal is no longer a viable alternative.

Galahad and Brenda will not accept Moses' refusal to be involved in what he calls the 'bandwagon' of Black Power. Moses regards the new movement only as an alternative to more 'ballads' and 'episodes', 'liming' or roaming the streets. Galahad, the political activist, is ridiculed by the narrator's wider vision which penetrates beneath his Black Power 'glad rags' and the use of the latest political jargon to expose a still profoundly vulnerable awareness of self. Selvon gently exposes the corruption at the centre of the party but it is in Galahad's harsh criticisms of Moses' writing that Selvon pinpoints the serious damage which Galahad's unconscious self-contempt reveals. Furthermore, it undermines Moses himself who begins to feel like a traitor. Galahad says to him:

'What shit is that you writing?'
'I am composing my Memoirs', I say stiffly ...
'You don't know one fucking thing about what's happening, Moses.'
'Memoirs are personal and intimate' ...
'That's no ... use ... nobody ain't going to be interested in anything you have to say. If you was writing about the scene today, and the struggle, I might of got the Party to back you. In any case, who tell you you could write?'

'I am not an ignoramus like you', I say beginning to lose my cool.

'You think writing book is like kissing hand? You should leave that to people like Lamming and Salkey.'

'Who?'

'... You see what I mean? Man, Moses you are still living in the Dark Ages. You don't even know we have created a Black Literature.' (pp. 49–50)

This confrontation between Galahad and Moses is perhaps the most explicit demonstration in the novel of Selvon's concern to explore the difficulties facing the writer who remains abroad. *Moses Ascending* does not present the reader with any comfortable resolutions but a sense of continuity is created by Selvon's demonstration of the impossibility for the post-colonial writer in Moses' circumstances to achieve such an end. Selvon repeatedly emphasises the absurdity of the whole situation and Moses' movements in the novel (whether upwards or sideways) create a cyclical ironic pattern framed by the 'goings-on' in the house and culminating in Moses' final return to live in his own basement room. At one level Moses seems only to have moved from basement to attic and back again during his 20-odd years in Britain; he is still living an underground existence and his fall from power at the close of the novel almost verges on the tragic. But Selvon's ambiguous ironic tone holds good even in this final moment of humiliation when Bob, Brenda and 'Paki' have all turned against him to further their own interests: 'Thus are the mighty fallen, empires totter, monarchs dethrone and the walls of Pompeii bite the dust. Humiliated and degraded I took up abode in Bob's erstwhile room while he and Jeannie moved in to the Penthouse' (p. 143).

Having failed to set up home in a city of words, Moses resolves to sell up and return to Trinidad. The gauntlet that he flings at his former tenants in the form of an 'epilogue up his sleeve' becomes the central theme of *Moses Migrating* (1983) in which Moses finally decides to leave London and return home for Carnival. The novel opens with the reality of departure and is illustrative of Selvon's continuing preoccupation with the theme of the exile's displacement and the lack of a firm centre. Moses writes a concerned letter to Enoch Powell thanking him for his generosity in helping black Londoners to return to their native lands: 'Dear Mr Powell, though Black I am writing you to express my support for your campaigns to keep Brit'n White ... I have always tried to integrate successfully in spite of discriminations and prejudices according to race etc.' (p. 1).[21]

The comic-grotesque reversals of the colonial encounter are developed as Moses, travelling third class in a liner – Selvon mock-seriously invokes the trials of the Middle Passage – ends up in the 'upside-down' world of the Trinidad Hilton, a tourist, in other words, in his own country. The metaphorical possibilities of rooms and houses as a correlative or frame for the lack of a firm cultural identity are thus extended; but it is neither basement nor attic but hotel room which bears the weight of significance. The quintessential transitoriness, artificiality and unreality of the hotel room (under ground too) image the special hollowness and disorientations of Moses' post-colonial identity. Moses seems fated to find no true home in either Britain or Trinidad. No more than in *The Lonely Londoners* or *Moses Ascending* does Selvon's character arrive at a promised land. The lack of a resolution, and perhaps the lack of a possible resolution, is demonstrated in the open-ended quality of the novel's final episode, with Moses in a kind of suspended state, just outside the doors of Heathrow Airport, 'like I was still playing charades' (p. 179).

Notes

1. Sam Selvon, *Moses Ascending* (London: Davis-Poynter, 1975), p. 11.
2. Jean Rhys, *Voyage in the Dark* (1934; London: Penguin, 1975), p. 7.
3. Donald Hinds, *Journey to an Illusion: A Study of West Indian Migration* (London: Macmillan, 1966), p. 4.
4. Shiva Naipaul, 'The Writer Without a Society', in Anna Rutherford (ed.) *Commonwealth* (Aarhus: Dangaroo Press, 1971), pp. 115–16.
5. V.S. Naipaul, *The Mimic Men* (London: André Deutsch, 1967; Penguin, 1972), pp. 18–19.
6. Andrew Salkey, *Escape to an Autumn Pavement* (London: Hutchinson, 1960), p. 46.
7. V.S. Naipaul, 'Words on Their Own', *The Times Literary Supplement*, 4 June 1964, p. 472.
8. Maya Angelou, informal conversation with Sam Selvon at literary prize-giving 1988.
9. Peter Nazareth, 'Interview with Sam Selvon', *World Literature Written in English*, vol. 18, no. 2 (1979), p. 422.
10. Gerald Moore, 'The English Novel Abroad', BBC Broadcast, 4 January 1974.
11. Nazareth, 'Interview with Sam Selvon', p. 421.
12. Sam Selvon, *The Lonely Londoners* (London: Alan Wingate, 1956), p. 7.
13. Gordon Rohlehr, 'The Folk in Caribbean Literature', *Tapia*, December 1972, p. 7.

14. John Thieme, 'The World Turn Upside Down: Carnival Patterns in *The Lonely Londoners'*, *Toronto South-Asian Review*, vol. 5, no. 1 (1980), p. 202.

15. This notion of a city of words has also interestingly been used in relation to the African-American Ralph Ellison's classic novel of exile, *Invisible Man*.

16. V.S. Naipaul, 'The Regional Barrier', *The Times Literary Supplement*, 15 August 1958, p. 37.

17. Nazareth, 'Interview with Sam Selvon', pp. 430–1.

18. Susheila Nasta, 'The Moses Trilogy: Sam Selvon Discusses his London Novels', *Wasafiri*, vol. 1, no. 2 (1985), p. 5.

19. Jill Neville, *Sunday Times* (Review section), 24 August 1975, p. 25.

20. Michel Fabre, 'Sam Selvon', in Bruce King (ed.), *West Indian Literature* (London: Macmillan, 1979), p. 123.

21. Samuel Selvon, *Moses Migrating* (London: Hutchinson, 1983; Washington: Three Continents Press, 1991), p. 1.

5. Changing the Script: Sex, Lies and Videotapes in Hanif Kureishi, David Dabydeen and Mike Phillips

A. Robert Lee

People think I'm caught between two cultures, but I'm not. I'm British; I can make it in England. It's my father who's caught.

Hanif Kureishi, interview (1986)[1]

A hierarchy of power relationships is being revealed: the superior white (superior in social and human terms) is surrounded by inferior creatures, the black and the dog, who share more or less the same status.

David Dabydeen, Analysis of David Monier's 'Henry, 10th Earl of Pembroke' (1985)[2]

I suspect anyone who reads contemporary fiction must gravitate towards thrillers, because certainly in the UK, contemporary novels aren't very interesting. They don't give you a picture of the society you live in. I can't get a feeling of when they were written or where. One thing I get from thrillers is a sense that anything can happen, that life is unpredictable and always menacing. In a way my whole experience parallels that.

Mike Phillips (1989)[3]

In summer 1991 the magazine supplement of the *Independent On Sunday* ran a feature highlighting the absence of Black British faces in media images of the countryside.[4] Whether in Tourist Board or British Rail posters, TV documentaries or Post Office stamps, the myth of pastoral England (with its customary aggregation of Scotland, Wales and Ireland) as a white-populated, and at least nominally Christian, island garden, it concluded, largely continues to hold sway.

So much, so familiar. The article made a nice piece of journalistic reprise: despite a rising multiculturalism, the vestigial Anglo-Saxonism of those seen to patrol the English – the British – green. The same, had the point been extended, might more or less equally have been said of the *written* landscape. For there, too, whether the Garden-of-England Kent of Chaucer's *Canterbury Tales*, the 'this England' of Shakespeare's *Richard II*, the village bailiwicks of Agatha Christie's Miss Marple, or the moorlands of *All Creatures Great and Small*, the topography has been much the same, a white, and thereby effortlessly assumed 'raceless', order of things.

On most appearances, a black or Asian cricket team from the present-day city doing a country tour, a Brixton or Bradford school outing, or the occasional black or Asian 'New Age' traveller, may have been as far as things have gone. Accordingly, when in 1992 the constituency Tories of Cheltenham rejected the black barrister, John Taylor, as their by-election candidate, did not the smack of racism in part derive from some viscerally felt transgression of white rural England?

Is not a similar sub-text in play in the reaction of the white villagers of Letchmore Heath to the Hare Krishnas of the Bhaktivedanta Temple? A Victorian mock-Tudor manorhouse it may have been. An unwelcome touch of hippiedom there may have been in George Harrison as benefactor. But the real egregiousness (and which no doubt led to a large part of the original village moving out) lies in the sight of multifarious Hindu worshippers in an English rural setting, a panorama of non-Christian monks and festival, shaven heads, dark skins. Once again 'agreed' England, pastoral England at any rate, seems under challenge. In this respect, and to come to the main focus of this essay, has not 'colour', like 'ethnicity' or 'race', again historically been thought more the domain of the city than the country and, as a kind of epilogue, of the suburbs? Not that, even with the written *city*, matters have been especially more straightforward.

For a belief has arisen that most necessary business has been taken care of under the mantra 'The Empire Writes Back'. Certainly, 'British' post-colonialism looks to a stellar litany, to V.S. Naipaul, Sam Selvon, Wilson Harris, George Lamming, Salman Rushdie, Anita Desai, Timothy Mo, Ravinder Randhawa and Buchi Emecheta. Can it, then, be doubted that in their different storytellings 'immigrant' Britain has not been given its due treatment: the imaginative coming-to-bear of each interwoven colonial legacy of Africa, India, the Caribbean or Hong Kong, and throughout, the shared reference-back into 'middle-passage' slavery, plantation labour, indenture or subalternism?[5]

Well, yes, in fact, it can. Without setting up arbitrary divides of generation or subject-matter, none of these writers loses when it is pointed out, diplomatically, but firmly if required, that whole areas of cross- and multiracial England/Britain thereafter still remain. It may be one thing to take on the grand themes of coloniality, a once-imperial history on the turn, the shadow of pasts shared and yet not, 'England' as itself refracted not only through its own one-time empire but through other cultural regimens – America in the pages of a Clancy Segal or Paul Theroux, or even Japan, courtesy of a Kazuo Ishiguro. It becomes, however, quite another, whatever the overlaps, to write, and in turn to read, indigenous lives 'of colour' pursued and articulated wholly, or almost wholly, as from inside the very grain of British society.[6]

One consequence, on the page and in theatre and music, has been the rise of new, hybrid styles, whether in the form of a Jatinder Verma 'Indian' version of Molière's *Tartuffe* or *Le Bourgeois Gentilhomme* for Tara Arts, a Benjamin Zephaniah or Linton Kwesi Johnson 'reading', a novel at once 'English', 'African' and diasporic like Caryl Phillips' *Crossing the River* (1993), or a pop tradition embracing east-west Beatles lyrics and groups from The Two Tones to Steven Kapur's Apache Indian.

All of these, however obliquely, underline the changing regimes of race and culture in British society, without, to be sure, seeking to evade the continuing racism of 'sus' laws, 'anti-immigrant' clamour, terrace behaviour at a Millwall or Aston Villa football-ground, or at another level of class, behind the subterfuges of suburban prejudice. For Asian–British or Caribbean–British cultural formations have been quite as various in their own right as any other.

Ethnic politics, once thought to mean largely defensive anti-racism, so produces a spectrum which includes Asian Toryism, black Labour Party MPs, Rasta Garveyism, Caribbean–British radicalism. Ethnic intercommunalism can flourish, as in Moss Side or Brent, or turn divisive, as between Sikhs and Muslims in Slough and Southall. Further cross-currents lie in black-on-black crime, Asian youth gangs, intergenerational tension, controversies over women's gender roles and separate religious schooling, or the push and pull behind the often rancorous talk of 'coconuts' (brown outside, white inside) and the like.

None of which is to suggest that the pathways of British ethnicity yet equate with those of America. Scales, histories, population densities all differ, a multiculturalism drawn from Euro-America, Afro-America, 'Latino' America (whether *chicano*, *cubano-americano* or *puertorriqueño*), Asian America (the best-known the Chinatowns, Little Tokyos, Manilatowns, Koreatowns or new-immigrant Vietnamese or Hmong communities), or, re-emerging, tribal or Native America.[7] Even so, willingly or not and at whatever speed, Britain heads in the same general direction, be the demography Asian or black, or of an older provenance, Jewish, Irish, or variously Greek- and Turkish-Cypriot, Italian, Polish, Maltese, Armenian or Australian–New Zealand. An ever-gathering literary voice for this ethnicity can anything but surprise.

'The Empire Writes Back', however, even 'with a vengeance' as Salman Rushdie exulted in 1982,[8] has somewhat too often had the effect of laying down a pre-emptive configuration, that of post-independence, first-generation immigration, with a kind of internal colonialism to follow. But a 'black presence' (the phrase, perhaps unsurprisingly, incorporated into a David Dabydeen title) has indeed had a far more long-standing part in British life and culture.[9]

The roll-call has been as lively as various: Elizabethan 'moors', Augustan house and body servants, ex-slaves, exiled African and Caribbean intellectuals, black GIs and jazzmen, a one-time Indian middle class bound upon education and/or gentility, a first-ever Asian born MP, West Indian professional cricketers, a post-war generation of Caribbean nurses and transport workers, Asians from across the sub-continent and Kenya.[10]

In their wake, Britain's multicultural demography stands as plain fact, whether native-born or renewed by yet other tiers of immigration and voyage. Englishness or Britishness, furthermore, if defined without these currents past or present would not merely be selective but wilful. Nor is it merely 'symbolic ethnicity', the quaint or passing display of cultural wares in 'Asian' Leicester, 'Bengali' Whitechapel, 'Chinese' Liverpool or 'Arab' Kensington. A necessary, and always deeply threaded, historicity underwrites each. The markers, many in kind, bear some re-emphasis.

In religion one thinks of an Afro-Caribbean church, Hindu/Sikh temple or Muslim mosque, and all the cultural ground-breaking, residency, language history and community relations involved. In foodways, Indian or Chinese especially, the cuisine of empire has again become agreed British fare (a point turned to subtle good purpose in Timothy Mo's *Sour Sweet*),[11] restaurants and take-aways, too, as often as not having moved from side street to High Street. Pop music would be unthinkable without reggae, ska, rap, hip-hop and dub, bhangra or other forms of 'Asian' rock fusion, and to be heard as much on 'Top of the Pops' or CD as in a once-a-year Notting Hill or like carnival.

Sport, inevitably, carries another signature, whether a Haringey or Edinburgh track-meet, virtually any boxing event (with Frank Bruno as heir to the affection for Henry Cooper), a city/suburban netball or hockey league, or the kinds of athlete now representing the UK at cricket, rugby or soccer (currently 30 per cent of all professional soccer players are black, though with well-taken concern for likely attack, less than 2 per cent of spectators are black). Is a doubt still to be entertained, three decades on from the Basil D'Oliveira controversies, and against their own sense of nationality, that (to cite current names) a Linford Christie or Tessa Sanderson, Mark Ramprakash or Gowri Retchiku, *still* do not quite make it – being 'British' when winning but something other when off the track or playing-field? Others, Lennox Lewis, for instance, of Caribbean parents, British-born and Canadian-raised, may pose a more legitimate doubt, though rarely in the context of a linked and hitherto far too under-attended process, that of the black-British diaspora.

School populations bear similar signs of mix and change. Classrooms, once white British in the main, now inevitably draw upon Caribbean-British and Indo-Pakistani-British catchments, each with an impact on school talk and custom, each with a spoken English different from that of its parent generation, each with a youth culture syncretically both mainstream and ethnic. In the case of Caribbean England, the story of first-into-second-generation has its own symptomatic lineage in E.R. Braithwaite's classic white–black 'classroom' novel, *To Sir, With Love* (1959), C.L.R. James' anatomy of British race and culture, *Beyond a Boundary* (1963), and John Western's interview collection, *A Passage to England* (1992).[12]

Who, moreover, turning on the television, does not 'see' as no more than everyday British reality black or Asian newsreaders like Trevor McDonald, Moira Stuart and Zeinab Badawi, or black or Asian programming (recently *Empire Road* to *Desmond's*, *Asian Eye* to *All Black*) with black and Asian character-parts, to take up the *Independent*'s argument, even given profile in 'rural' TV light comedies from *Lovejoy* to *Chef!*? None of which is to say that editorial evasion or timidity does not still apply, but it would be absurd to deny advances.

Certainly, from the 1950s on, the point had not been missed by white political alarmists, from the Enoch Powell of his 1968 'rivers of blood' hysteria (by 1976 he was speaking of 'unassimilated and unassimilable populations ... alien wedges in the heartland of the state') to the Norman Tebbit of his 1980s 'cricket-test' Little Englandism. Both found themselves, one is enjoined to believe to their surprise, eagerly underwritten by the NF and BNP (later followed by groups such as Combat 18, The Third Way, the Nazi rock bands who make up 'Blood and Honour' and sundry columns of Union Jack-toting skinheads). A genteel *Daily Telegraph* or populist *Sun* or *Daily Sport* could also be relied upon to supply further coded warnings.[13]

So-called 'race' happenings, too, be it Notting Hill or Moss Side in the 1960s, or thereafter Docklands, Toxteth, Bristol St Pauls or Broadwater Farm, have traditionally led to calls for tougher statutes, a halt by quotas and other regulation to 'immigrant' Britain. The usual telegraphese of 'Enough' or 'Send Them Home', however, typically excises the thought that the UK might indeed, *be* 'their' home, albeit of a kind newly made over and styled. Under this construing, and the similarity with resistance to EU membership or, of late, the local spitefulness towards Croatian refugees in Essex, supply analogies, 'England' remains better the enclave than a society called upon to evolve (as if the evolution were not in fact happening) into a new, even welcome, further plait of cultures and traditions.

At the level of High Culture the impact of rearguard nostalgia for a supposedly classical 'England' has been patent, whether 'heritage' TV, the cult of Trollope by John Major and his like, or Prince Charles and architecture. The attempted time-calling of F.R. and Q.D. Leavis in the 1970s especially serves, the former in his phase of 'Nor Shall My Sword' apocalypse, and the latter, despite her own Jewish immigrant roots, fearful of 'unassimilated multi-racial minorities'.[14] No less than in the Powell–Tebbit continuum, white Englishness again acts as the norm, the essentialised touchstone for the nation at large.

In turn, a down-the-middle post-war literary circuit of, typically, William Golding, Angus Wilson, Iris Murdoch, Antonia Byatt, Margaret Drabble, Anita Brookner, Faye Weldon, David Lodge, Malcolm Bradbury, John Mortimer, or the Amises, *père et fils*, gives off an Englishness of generally comforting familiarity – 'liberal' (despite Kingsley Amis in his role of curmudgeon), morally about business, rooted in English ways and irony. The choice of necessity always theirs to make, rarely has any of them tackled multicultural Britain with any degree of appetite. One has to wonder why.

The upshot may well be an 'Englishness' ostensibly given over to society, class manners, the changing regimes of marriage, family or gender, or even, in a larger sense, the politics of end-of-empire. But it remains, somehow, a selective and 'our' English-ness/Britishness, one overwhelmingly of white middle-England with only the occasional foray (as in the case of Martin Amis) into the black or Asian hinterland – the nation's inlaid 'other' and yet endemically own history.

Little wonder that to step outside this social pale still invites talk of the maverick, the once-off, as, amid the shapings of modernism, once happened to *Ulysses*, or, of late, could be said to have happened in part to Julian Barnes' *Flaubert's Parrot* on the dual grounds of its Europeanism and its intellectuality. Better, as immediate best-seller status and TV adaptation readily bore out, the easeful England-abroad of Peter Mayle's *A Year in Provence*.

Nor can it surprise that Jeannette Winterson or Adam Mars-Jones, virtually by rote, are taken to write Gay, and so non-mainstream, fiction. Again, Caryl Phillips is said to write less British than African-diasporic novels, a category, however, which did not arise in the case of Barry Unsworth's slave-narrative (and Booker prize-winner) *Sacred Hunger* (1992). As to Hanif Kureishi, David Dabydeen and Mike Phillips, their writing routinely is called immigrant, and not least, paradoxically, when attracting the plaudits of the reviewers ('We badly need good novels about the immigrant experience in Britain', wrote a well-intending, but custodial, Penelope Lively, of David Dabydeen's *The Intended*).[15] The then 'fact' of this non-Englishness, this 'immigrant' racialness, helps situate their novel-writing more towards the edge than centre.

* * *

A distinct counter-view, however, lies at the heart of the present account. The fiction of Kureishi, Dabydeen and Phillips, all early novels to be sure, in fact speaks out of, and to, the absolute centre of 'England'. That is, whatever their author's literal place of birth, they proceed from, and inscribe, a quite ineradicable and historic multicultural Englishness or Britishness.

For Kureishi that also includes his theatre and film writing, whether his well-named and self-positioning *Outskirts* (1981), filmscripts as all-colour and panoramic as *My Beautiful Laundrette* (1985), *Sammy and Rosie Get Laid* (1987) and *London Kills Me* (1991), or an Anglo-Pakistan novella like *With Your Tongue Down My Throat* (1987). For Dabydeen it extends to vernacular poetry collections like *Slave Song* (1984) and *Coolie Odyssey* (1988), his timely, excavatory anthology, *The Black Presence in English Literature* (1983), and his two art-historical studies on racial iconography, *Hogarth, Walpole and Commercial Britain* (1985) and *Hogarth's Blacks: Images of Blacks in Eighteenth Century English*

Art (1987). For Phillips, it involves his frequent past *Guardian* and other reportage and broadcasting.[16]

None of which is to seek any special dispensation as to their respective imaginative strengths and weaknesses; rather it is to seek recognition of changed working terms for 'England' or 'Britain'. Theirs, also, are British novels, however differently arrived at (in all the phrase's implication) the Britain they inscribe. A further irony may also be that each, too, possesses his own 'British' or 'English' shaping irony, whether the carnivalesque of Kureishi's *The Buddha of Suburbia* (1990), the dialogues of memory in Dabydeen's *The Intended* (1991) and *Disappearance* (1993), or the *film noir* laconicism of Mike Phillips' mysteries, *Blood Rights* (1989) and *The Late Candidate* (1990); his third novel, *Point of Darkness* (1994), perhaps inevitably, situates itself in an America of the Bronx and California.[17] If the notion of margin has any further utility, it has to be as the margin at the centre.

For in writing from inside the 'racial' dialectic, they each give voice to what being 'British' has come to mean, and from an angle no longer one of immigrant periphery but of post-immigrant frontline and beyond. Francis Mulhern's recent account of Raymond Williams in Homi K. Bhabha's *Nation and Narration* (1990) supplies a well-taken overall pointer:

> One of the most radical works of literary criticism produced in England in recent decades is Raymond Williams's *The Country and The City*, and one of its most radical elements is precisely its refusal of that familiar condensation of a nationality, a state and a language in the spellbinding notion of 'English'. It was by refusing it that Williams could begin to reread 'English literature' in its real formative conditions, and to read the words of the classes and populations, at home and on other continents, that it marginalized or silenced.[18]

* * *

In 'The Rainbow Sign' (1986), his autobiographical meditation on British-Pakistani 'Englishness' and on the course of white racism from empire to the skinhead culture of widespread 'Paki-bashing' (with its smacks not only at the political Right but at the Labour Party for its failure to confront the racism in its own ranks and practices), Hanif Kureishi puts the call for a changed recognition of 'nation' in clear, unrefusable terms.

The tone, as the title of the piece, also perfectly echoes the moral urgency of James Baldwin and Richard Wright whose essays and fiction, as he remembers, 'I read ... all the time':

It is the British, the white British, who have to learn that being British isn't what it was. Now it is a more complex thing, involving new elements. So there must be a fresh way of seeing Britain and the choices it faces: and a new way of being British after all this time. Much thought, discussion and self-examination must go into seeing the necessity for this, what this 'new way of being British' involves and how difficult it might be to attain.

The failure to grasp this opportunity for a revitalized and broader self-definition in the face of a failure to be human, will be more insularity, schism, bitterness and catastrophe.[19]

To say of Kureishi's own writing that it addresses the issue of 'being British isn't what it was' and of 'a new way of being British' could not better suit.

Among the many pleasures of *The Buddha of Suburbia* (1990) – the buoyancy of tease and wit, the ability to orchestrate in the manner of *My Beautiful Laundrette* or *Sammie and Rosie Get Laid* a fast-moving, much populated 'script' – has to be Kureishi's sense of a 1970s quintessential suburb, Bromley, and of London (with New York to follow by way of contrast) as a form of gallery, of carnival.

The note is struck, and then sustained, from the outset: 'My name is Karim Amir, and I am an Englishman born and bred, almost. I am often considered to be a funny kind of Englishman, a new breed as it were, having emerged from two old histories.' As the novel works through its two-part story ('In the Suburbs', 'In The City'), Karim's Holden Caulfieldish, teenager line in self-deprecation ('Perhaps in the future I would live more deeply'), not to say his eager androgyny and sense of dressing for, and in due course, of literally stage-acting a part, does just the right service. It enables him to play the participant-observer for each local tableau of a Britain facing, in terms of race, politics and sex, every seeming and contradictory way at once.

This is a Britain dimly still something on the world stage yet shot through with provincialism, righteous yet out for a sex-and-drugs romp, civil yet edging into a latest racist and punk violence, and above all, given to exoticising its citizenry of 'colour' even as it fears them and wishes them gone. Invoking the arrival of his father, Haroun, and his equally 'aristocratically useless' friend, Anwar, from Bombay in the 1950s or so, Kureishi's notation of an England anything but the 'gentlemanly' civilisation each seeks comically deflates both empire and those who seek to emulate the supposed manners of empire:

77

London, the Old Kent Road, was a freezing shock to both of them. It was wet and foggy; people called you 'Sunny Jim'; there was never enough to eat ... Rationing was still on ... Dad was amazed and heartened by the sight of the British in England, though. He'd never seen the English in poverty, as road-sweepers, dustmen, shopkeepers and barmen ... no one had told him the English didn't wash regularly because the water was so cold – if they had water at all.

And when Dad tried to discuss Byron in local pubs no one warned him that not every Englishman could read or that they didn't want tutoring by an Indian on the poetry of a pervert and a madman.

Who better than Karim, too, to observe the rise of this same father, pink-towelled, big-chested but otherwise diminutive, the offspring of servanted Brahmins, as indeed 'The Buddha of Suburbia', 'God' as his son dubs him, unable to work out the London bus routes yet pledged to deliver the path to true enlightenment? 'They are looking forward to me all over Orpington', he is heard to boast, as he reads from among a wondrous clutter of 'Eastern' books (of which *Yoga For Women* with its 'pictures of healthy women in black leotards' heads the list). Who if not Karim as Bromley's almost-Candide to relish and yet decry the fakery of this 'spiritual' paterfamilias – the Muslim turned Buddhist, the bottom-of-the-ladder civil servant married to the Walnut Whip consuming, *Steptoe*-watching 'Mum', Margaret? Transcendence for this Buddha, apparently, as much lies in copious sex with the one-breasted interior designer Eva Kay, as in yogic meditation and clearing of the mind.

Karim readily acknowledges his own paradox, the anti-Typhoo-tea-making faddist, the would-be body beautiful always conscious of his smallness, the dedicated follower of fashion never quite certain whether to dress up or down. 'Coolness' vacillates with easy embarrassment, just the mix to make him the nicely compromised arbiter of his own father as 'the only man in southern England ... wearing a red and gold waistcoat and Indian pyjamas'. 'I really wanted to be the first Indian centre-forward for England', he confides, only to meet Little Englander racist abuse from a white girlfriend's irate father ('Hairy Back') and, in a teasing further twist, just as the latter's guard-dog lovingly mounts him. His love-envy of Charlie Kay (Charlie Hero as will be), Bromley's 'other' Bowie, catches punk-glitz in close-up, Karim as admirer of the bravura yet also obliged to acknowledge the ennui, the rising desperation, behind the mask.

Who, to extend the list, but 'Indian' Karim, to play the anything but innocent witness role in the Anwar–Jeeta–Jamila imbroglio? The 'Paradise Stores' grocery becomes for him the perfect backdrop for a mix of farce and pathos: Anwar's starvation in the name of patriarchy, Jeeta's killing silences, the fate of the arranged bridegroom, Changez. The latter especially scores as a portrait. If Changez is denied conjugal rights with Jamila, doubly 'impersonated' by Karim both in the theatre and in bed, and, all gut, slapstick and erotic experiment with his Japanese prostitute Shinko, and made to talk Peter Sellers 'Indian', he still achieves his own kind of dignity. Even so, as a suitably deadpan Karim then reports, he manages to cause the death of his father-in-law when he hits him with a sex-aid. Matchingly, who can be better placed than 'English' Karim to give the measure of his Uncle Ted and Auntie Jean ('Gin and Tonic'), the former who gives up DIY and double-glazing for meditation and the latter all drink and acerbity at the galling unrespectability of Haroun's rise to suburban guru ('Why has Eva brought this brown Indian here?')?

The wheel turns again as Haroun and Eva move into London-as-capital, 'God' as ever more the self-willed stereotype (with a re-instituted Bombay accent), Ted as William Morris artisan, 'Mum' as recovering divorcee replete with new boyfriend, Karim's brother, Allie, as gay designer–clubber, and Karim en route to his own pending if uncertain avatardom as TV soap opera star. Each acts out his or her part in a series of deftly observed close encounters, not least those involving theatre types (Karim launches a career playing Mowgli in a stage adaptation of Kipling's *The Jungle Book* – truly a cartoon of a cartoon), in all the city as playfield, at once vanity fair and sex shop.

A required episode of group-grope under 'living theatre' rules and a *socialiste de salon* AC/DC director, Pyke, with the all-for-experience Eleanor and jaded wife Marlene in tow, edges as much towards gymnastics as love. Commune-living, with Jamila as a main player, becomes a roundabout of who cooks, who sleeps with whom and where, who rules. Trotskyism appears in the person of the working-class Terry Tapley who, all-protesting, paradoxically acquires salary and public affection as that class-enemy of the proletariat, 'Sergeant Monty', a TV policeman. Gender-bending takes the form of Jamila as lesbian and Changez as increasingly feminised proxy-mother to her child, Leila Kollontai. Kureishi's narration tracks each transformation to perfection: 'chattering class' cocktail-party gives way to punk or street happening, boutiqueland to council highrise, arts-talk to a racist litany of wog, Paki, nigger.

The city panorama fills out, too, in period detail, the pop music (Dylan to Pink Floyd, The Stones to The Doors), dress-styles (headbands, saris, velvet, late-Hippie flairs), foodways (pulses, vegetables, quiche), the ambiance of incense, joss-sticks and drugs-of-choice from pot to cocaine, amphetamines to acid, and Eva's inexorable move across all the going venues of fashionability in SW3, W8 and NW3. A closing New York sequence pits Charlie's glam-rock, sexually anything-goes 'celebrity' Manhattan against a London in which Haroun and Eva announce, if none too certainly, their contrastingly provincial intention to marry. Karim, veteran of all aspects of 'the scene' and 'in the centre of this old city that I loved', remains (how otherwise?) both 'happy and miserable at the same time'.

Like the suburbs and city which bred him, he also finds himself, wryly, self-awakeningly, bound (whatever, once again, his own genial confessions of uncertainty) upon a quest for new balance. Is his to be the politics of 'the street' or the Labour Party, both of which, self-absorbed and in pursuit of other ends and pleasures, he has failed to honour with quite winning fallibility? For all that he can look to India by inheritance and to England by upbringing, does not his own equipoise lie as much in the workings of gender or of career or of his own creativity as of ethnicity? How, indeed, is an 'Englishman born and bred, almost' to find his own best centre, his fulcrum, and elude definition by any one, all-purpose, determinant, be it 'colour' or anything else?

The hallmark of Kureishi's writing is to make accelerated serio-comedy of the whole, a state of the nation told with rare particularity in the voice of Karim Amir as one of London's utter, though ostensibly new-made and new-found, own. *The Buddha of Suburbia* as Pilgrim's Progress so becomes the unlikely amalgam of Kama Sutra and Bromley-to-Kensington upward mobility, nothing if not a latter-day, exhilaratingly styled 'take' on England-now.

* * *

David Dabydeen's *The Intended* (1991) and *Disappearance* (1993) may well fall short of Kureishi's sheer virtuosity. But they nevertheless show their own perfectly inventive readiness to take on the making of multicultural Britain. Both novels entail a historical reckoning of sorts, the one set in Balham under the street-rules of South London, and the other in a village near to the Hastings of consecrated English myth behind whose gentility lies a power-play both domestic and colonial and in all ways at odds with appearances.

Both, further, deploy narrators of Guyanese origin, enabling Dabydeen to keep in play a double-schema of place and memory,

two complementary sites of being. The former, 'Indian West Indian ... the most mixed-up of the lot', left in adolescence to fend
for himself in a rented room south of the Thames and on a
monthly Social Security cheque, bookish and sex-curious in equal
parts, eventually embarks on a second leavetaking to study English at Oxford. The latter, 'black West-Indian of African ancestry,
but ... trained in the science and technology of Great Britain', in
his thirties, has been sequestered to coastal Kent as engineer in
the construction of a sea-wall meant to hold back a crumbling
land's edge. His will be a double kind of leavetaking, from belief
in England as still the imperium and from his own inherited colonial deference.

More than a hint of Dickens lies in Dabydeen's image of England in *The Intended*. Social Services hostel or rented room, this is
London as lower middle class making-do and a labyrinth of racist
threat. Well may the narrator show his paces at 'lit crit', his
alertness to image or play of viewpoint, in each out-of-school
book session. But he cannot, too, avoid seeing in the Chaucer or
Conrad of his A-level the silhouette of an England past which
domestically and colonially has helped both to make, and unmake,
him personally. If, too, his is the path to Oxford, most of his
Asian–black coterie will head vengefully into a future of pimping,
drugs, sex-videos and theft.

For good or ill, he increasingly begins to see, England's outposts have become inroads, its peripheries mainlands. The point
gains further emphasis when, on a summer job at Battersea Fun
Fair, he has to clean the 'world' murals in a tunnel-of-love. The
human difference and variety they pictorialise offer him the very
touchstones of a changing perspective.

The Intended no doubt occasionally veers too close to an autobiographical grain, to sources in Dabydeen's own life. But the
novel's cast ensures a lively turn of events and encounter: Shaz,
English-born of a Pakistani family, knowing before his time,
tough-tender, destined to play pimp; 'Pocket' Patel, Gujarati-
speaking, an eventual crack and porn-video dealer; Nasim, a
Muslim believer, moved by his family to Sheffield after being
wounded in a racist attack, and whose hospitalisation embarrasses
the narrator as an image of Asian weakness ('his wounds were
meant for all of us'); and Joseph, the emotionally damaged rastaman, a kind of untutored word-poet ('black people must have
black words') whose 'crazy exegesis' and 'broken' would-be film
montage hints of 'a complete statement of the condition of England'. Others equally add their mark, whether Mr Ali, initially all
landlord, but who eventually seeks from his tenant a 'human'

epigraph for the sister who left India, became ill and must be buried in Balham, or Nasim's sister, Rashida, at once close by age yet distant by religion and caste, or Shaz's feckless, for hire street-girl, Monica, as against the narrator's kindly, up-from-the-village, Janet.

London thus implicates him in competing and overlapping regimes. He seeks to distance himself both 'from all the noisy West-Indian-ness' and black and Asian 'victim' media images. Yet he also relishes the black/Asian diaspora faces he sees on the tube, fellow Indo-Afro-Caribbean-English 'undergrounders' as it were. Shaz gives him a night with Monica as a parting gift; Nazim's mother, by suitable contrast, a Koran. He thinks England variously a going-away and yet an arrival, a place of now 'uncertain citizenship' yet whose literary canon he will go to university to study. Little wonder, at the novel's conclusion, he speaks, not a little reflexively, of at last emerging from invisibility into his own complex visibility.

Underwriting the England of his adolescence, too, is the Guyana of his childhood, a past, however, as shrewdly conflicted as anything in his London present. 'The boy goin England', the narrator recalls in the Creole of the grandmother with whom he spends holidays in Albion Village, Berbice, Guyana, and who takes him over at the break-up of his own parents. Albion Village so yields to Albion itself, two worlds by history, conquest, language, coloniality, each entwined within the other, and, as he more and more recognises, in process of producing a yet subsequent cultural regime drawn from both.

Despite his grandmother's injunction 'Go and don't look back ... or else Albion ghosts go follow you all the way to Englan'', his own mix of ancestry compels him. He recalls the figure of Juncha who 'came from India in a boat with a dhoti wrapped round his waist and a sack of belongings on his back', who then made good but whose offspring squandered the gains. In his fisherman great-uncle, Richilo, he looks back to a wastrel-shaman, an artist of sorts lost in 'drunken vulgarity'. When his own grandfather slaughters a stolen lamb, the hint of Old Testament sacrifice nicely gives an echo to his own life. His friend Peter, simpleton, Holy Fool, dreams of Rohan Kanhai and cricket glory, a search for grace amid childlike play and confusion.

Of the women, Aunt Pakul inverts the assumed passivity of Asian (albeit Caribbean-Asian) womanhood, seeking out and physically punishing his wife-beating father. Another vintage matriarch, Gladys, causes him to summon up a scene of voodoo, even as Independence in 1973 launches Guyana into modernity.

'You is me', a well-intending, vernacular Aunt Clarice, inveterate Bible-lover, tells him. It strikes just the right note of doubleness, contrariety, for *The Intended*'s journey-story through the border-lands of self and history, race and nation.

Disappearance attempts something more ambitious, a kind of highly imagised England parable. Midway into the novel, Mrs Rutherford, the dissident Englishwoman in her sixties who has long returned to Kent from a stint as wife and teacher in Africa and who rents a room to the engineer-narrator, delivers her verdict on empire. 'The history of England is a nasty sickness,' she gives witness, 'We carried it all over the world. Boatload of ivory or boatload of black bodies, it was all the same.'

To the Guyanan, protégé of the white expatriate Professor Fenwick, this comes as deeply unexpected. But it stands at one with other unexpectedness. African masks, full of colour and animism, hang incongruously on the walls of Mrs Rutherford's 'venerable' cottage. If, an Englishwoman to the core, she cultivates her garden, it is to relish the violence built into the names of English flowers. Behind her seeming composure (the home-made wine and the like) lies a history of sexual promiscuity; her husband's a taste for pubescent black flesh in colonial Africa and her own the need to shock and subvert the colonial England which made him.

For his part, the narrator finds himself called upon to acknowledge deceits and concealments of his own. He thinks back to the emblematic darkness he once created by destroying the lights on an American-donated basketball court. His bad faith in an affair with a village woman still pursues him. Above all, he thinks with uncertainty on his part in the 'engineering' – the modernisation through land-irrigation and levelling – of rural Guyana, so much of it at the expense of a regard for its natural and human costs and for which he has been chastised by 'Swami', a Creole Indo-Guyanese worker.

If *Disappearance* becomes somewhat over-diagrammatic in its use of crumbling cliffs and seawalls, historical tides and erosions, its play of mystery remains well pitched. Who, really, is Mrs Rutherford? Who, really, is the narrator? How to link Mrs Rutherford's African masks, the 'white-washed' English cottage domain, the crumbling Dunsmere Cliff, and the black engineer from Guyana? How, also, to work out the connections between Mrs Rutherford's past in Africa in the company of a husband fixated on child-rape and her liaison with a local patriot-hero in the form of Mr Curtis who fights to battle both the sea and the sea-change bringing an end to empire? Has she, or has she not, had a fling with the also colonial, if 'Paddy-playing', Irishman, Mr Christie?

Does not all this have its echoes in the narrator's own 'sense of darkness'?

Dabydeen no doubt overdoes the signposting, his resort to the schematic. But as an inquest on selves shaped, or just as likely mis-shaped, by coloniality, the mirror it holds to the interplay of the national and personal histories involved does timeliest service. It seeks to reflect how, at home or abroad, and at both ends of the equation, one is indeed to live post-colonially.

* * *

I woke up late with a feeling of frustration. I had dreamed about a political meeting, where I'd been standing by the platform waiting to deliver an important speech about being black in Britain.

But though I put my hand up and waved and argued with the people sitting near me, I wasn't called.

The voice to hand from *Blood Rights* belongs to Samson Dean, black Londoner, journalist-turned-gumshoe, a longtime adept (not least on account of having separated from his white wife and their young son) in the racial dispensations of contemporary Britain. In invoking 'frustration', 'an important speech about being black in Britain', not being 'called', the implications of the metaphor inside Dean's dream and the laconic manner of its telling suit perfectly, a theme, and an idiom, to take on new ground.

It may have been simply a question of time before a black-written English thriller series made its bow. If literary kin were needed, as commentary has been quick to point out, it can likely best be found across the Atlantic, either in Chester Himes' gallows-humour 'Harlem domestic tales', as Himes himself liked to call them, and featuring Coffin Ed and Gravedigger or, though written in the 1980s, in the immediate post-war black Los Angeles chronicles of Walter Mosley as pursued by his Private Investigator, Easy Rawlins.[20]

Yet quite as much as Himes or Mosley (with Chandler or Hammett also in the frame), Phillips shows his own command of the working rules. Behind the ostensible crime lurks a vortex of others. The command of locale, whether 'street' London north and south of the river or Manchester from Piccadilly to Moss Side, is not to be doubted. Wrong and right trails teasingly overlap. The suspense is finely calibrated. Above all, and without seeking more of his genre than would be fair, each of his thrillers, much to immediate purposes, also confirms a yet further and more compelling aim: nothing less than a shy at the unravelment, the detection, of latter-day 'racial' Britain.

As a plot-line *Blood Rights* immediately engages – the request from a wealthy, Lambeth-based MP, Grenville Baker, for Dean to find their art-college daughter, Virginia, who has drifted into drugs. From there the story circles outward to Baker's unacknowledged son, Roy Akimole/Baker, 'educated' in Moss Side and Risley Remand and who, with his Tysonesque sidekick, Winston, embarks on would-be blackmail of (and retribution against) his white absentee father. The cast-list extends to Shirley Akimole, Dean's old Manchester flame, Detective Sergeant Borelli, an Italian-British former schoolmate elevated to tough local copper, Boss, ska-singer and inveterate punter, and Goonay, the 'anglicized Tamil' and middleman in a Nigerian money-laundering scam.

The human centre, however, of *Blood Rights* lies in Roy, 'mixed-race' offspring, Mancunian to the Bakers as Londoners, from the gang and Reform School side of the class-divide as against the monied establishment, and above all, at once white British and black British. He it is, racially obliged like the investigator's own son to face both ways at once, a kind of concealed harlequin at the very heart of Britain as a multiculture, who most of all (and literally) embodies the 'mystery' Dean must really solve.

The Late Candidate, a novel given an even more explicit London political donnée, has Dean investigating the fatal stabbing of his old sidekick, Aston Edwards, a black Labour Party councillor and leader of the Housing Committee. Phillips again impressively builds a picture of British society, from inner-city London to Handsworth in the racially mixed East Midlands, and involving the Parkers, a mean Irish-London dynasty in the building trade, Walter Davis, a black would-be MP, Vijay Prashad, an Indian-British politico, Maman Nightingale, from the French-speaking Caribbean and Tony Waites, the wrongly accused young black for whom police and other racism have become standard British fare. Yet deftly as the plot turns upon a corrupt local government and housing caper, so once again an obliquer, altogether more pervasive, mystery increasingly becomes evident: the phenomenon of Britain as racial maze, conundrum, hall of mirrors.

Dean himself, however, is fleshed out in more substantial profile, as are his guilts over his son and ex-wife, his affair with the bisexual Sophie, his Argentinian-born lover who teaches photography in a local college, and again, his guarded, arm's length relationship with Detective Sergeant Borelli. In Dalton Taylor, too, Phillips supplies a London Jamaican to contrast with a non-immigrant black generation of whom Maman Nightingale's tough, helpful son Aubrey is typical. But what the Aston Edwards case, at base, most opens up is the issue of Britain as indeed a contested national home and of the need for a new, and much fuller, appreciation of who is constructing what across changed, and changing, lines of race and citizenry.

Put another way, the novel seeks to ask how England or Britain has failed to build for its own increasing eclecticism. In detection of this order, and without any intruding loss of pace or vernacular, *The Late Candidate*, like its predecessor, takes a popular-culture literary form into far more consequential terrain than might have been expected. For no less than Kureishi or Dabydeen, Mike Phillips, too, can be said to have understood the changing script in British history – and written accordingly.

Notes

1. Marcia Pally, 'Kureishi Like A Fox', Interview with Hanif Kureishi, *Film Comment*, vol. 22 (September–October 1986), pp. 50–5.
2. David Dabydeen, *Hogarth's Blacks: Images of Blacks in Eighteenth-Century English Art* (Aarhus: Dangaroo Press, 1985), p.26.
3. John Williams, 'Moving Out Of The Ghetto: Mike Phillips and Gar Haywood', *Independent*, 9 August 1989, p. 9.
4. *Independent on Sunday*, 26 August 1991.
5. The seminal text in this respect has to be Bill Ashcroft, Gareth Griffiths and Helen Tiffin (eds), *The Empire Writes Back: Theory and Practice in Post-Colonial Literatures* (London and New York: Routledge, 1989). See also, Paul Gilroy, *'There Ain't No Black in the Union Jack': The Cultural Politics of Race and Nation* (London: Hutchinson, 1987).
6. General histories include G. Bennett, *The Concept of Empire from Burke to Attlee* (London: A. and C. Black, 2nd edn, 1962); and J.M. Mackenzie, *Propaganda and Empire* (Manchester University Press, 1984). The classic analysis of the historical–cultural implications of empire remains Edward Said, *Orientalism* (New York: Random House, Vintage Books, 1979).
7. Relevant accounts (and anthologies) of American multiculturalism as a literary tradition include Wolfgang Sollers, *Beyond Ethnicity: Consent and Descent in American Culture* (New York: Oxford University Press, 1986); Ron Takaki, *Strangers from a Different Shore* (Boston: Little Brown, 1989); Cordelia Candelaria (ed.), *Multiethnic Literature of the United States* (Boulder: University of Colorado Press, 1989); 'Special Multiculturalism Issue', *Mother Jones*, vol. 16, no. 5, (September–October 1991); Ishmael Reed, Kathryn Trueblood and Shawn Wong (eds), *The Before Columbus Foundation Fiction Anthology* (New York:

Changing the Script

W.W. Norton, 1992); J.J. Phillips, Ishmael Reed, Gundar Strads and Shawn Wong (eds), *The Before Columbus Foundation Poetry Anthology* (New York: W.W. Norton, 1992); and Hans Bak (ed.), *Multiculturalism and the Canon of American Culture* (University of Amsterdam Press, 1992). My own attempts to map this efflorescence can be found in A. Robert Lee, 'Ethnic Renaissance: Rudolfo Anaya, Louise Erdrich and Maxine Hong Kingston', in Graham Clarke (ed.), *The New American Writing: Essays on American Literature Since 1970* (London: Vision Press, 1990), pp. 139–64; 'Ethnic America: The Non-European Voice', *The British American*, vol. 3, no. 1, (June 1991) pp. 9–10; 'Decolonizing America: The Ethnicity of Ernest Gaines, José Antonio Villarreal, Leslie Marmon Silko and Shawn Wong', in Theo d'Haen and Cedric Barfoot (eds), *Shades of Empire: Studies in Colonial and Post-Colonial Literatures* (Amsterdam: Rodopi, 1992), pp. 271–84; 'Acts of Remembrance: America as Multicultural Past in Ralph Ellison, Nicholasa Mohr, James Welch and Monica Sone' in Hans Bak (ed.), *Multiculturalism*, pp. 81–103; 'Self-inscriptions: James Baldwin, Tomás Rivera, Gerald Vizenor and Amy Tan and the Writing-in of America's Non-European Ethnicities', in A. Robert Lee (ed.), *A Permanent Etcetera: Cross-Cultural Perspectives on Post-War America* (London: Pluto, 1993); 'Afro-America, The Before Columbus Foundation and The Literary Multiculturalization of America', *Journal of American Studies*, vol. 28, part 3, (December 1994), pp. 433–50.

8. 'The Empire Writes Back With a Vengeance', *The Times*, 3 July 1982, p. 8.

9. David Dabydeen (ed.), *The Black Presence in English Literature* (Manchester University Press, 1985).

10. See G.C.L. Bertram, *West Indian Immigration* (London: Eugenics Society, 1958); Paul Foot, *Immigration and Race in British Politics* (London: Penguin, 1965); Dilop Hiro, *Black British White British* (London: Eyre and Spottiswoode, 1971); James L. Watson (ed.), *Between Two Cultures: Migrants and Minorities in England* (Oxford: Blackwell, 1977); E. Cashmore, *Rastaman; The Rastafarian Movement in England* (London: Allen and Unwin, 1979); Nigel File and Chris Power, *Black Settlers in Britain 1555–1958* (London, Heinemann, 1981); Peter Fryer, *Staying Power: The History of Black People in Britain* (London: Pluto, 1984); R. Visram, *Ayahs, Lascars and Princes: Indians in Britain 1700–1947* (London; Pluto, 1986); Gilroy, *'There Ain't No Black in the Union Jack'* (see note 5); Harry Goulsbourne, *Ethnicity and Nationalism in Post-Imperial Britain* (Cambridge University Press, 1992); Nick Merriman (ed.), *The Peopling of London: Fifteen Thousand Years of Settlement From Overseas* (Museum of London, 1993); Winston James and Clive Harris (eds), *Inside Babylon* (London: Verso, 1994).

87

11. Timothy Mo, *Sour Sweet* (London: André Deutsch, 1982).
12. E.R. Braithwaite, *To Sir, With Love* (London: Bodley Head, 1959); C.L.R. James, *Beyond a Boundary* (London: Stanley Paul, 1963); and John Western, *A Passage to England: Barbadian Londoners Speak of Home* (London: UCL Press, 1992).
13. See, especially, T.R. Lee, *Race and Resistance: The Concentration and Dispersal of Immigrants in London* (Oxford: Clarendon Press, 1977); C. Brown, *Black and White Britain: The Third Policy Studies Institute Survey* (Aldershot: Gower, 1984); Gilroy, *'There Ain't No Black in The Union Jack'* (see note 5); E. Pilkington, *Beyond The Mother Country: West Indians and the Notting Hill White Riots* (London: I.B. Tauris, 1988); and S. Smith, *The Politics of 'Race' and Residence: Citizenship, Segregation, and White Supremacy in Britain* (Cambridge: Polity Press, 1990).
14. F.R. Leavis, *Nor Shall My Sword: Discourses on Pluralism, Compassion and Social Hope* (London: Chatto and Windus, 1972); Q.D. Leavis, *The Englishness of the English Novel* (Cambridge University Press, 1983), p. 325.
15. Cited as 'advance praise' on the jacket of David Dabydeen, *The Intended* (London: Secker and Warburg, 1991).
16. Hanif Kureishi, *Outskirts, The King and Me, Tomorrow-Today!* (London: John Calder, 1983); *My Beautiful Laundrette* and *The Rainbow Sign* (London: Faber, 1986); *Sammy and Rosie Get Laid* (London: Faber, 1987), and *London Kills Me* (London: Faber and Faber, 1992); *With Your Tongue Down My Throat*, in *Granta*, vol. 22, (Autumn 1987). David Dabydeen, *Slave Song* (Aarhus: Dangaroo Press, 1984); *Coolie Odyssey* (London: Hansib Press and Aarhus: Dangaroo Press, 1988); *The Black Presence in English Literature* (Wolverhampton, 1983); *Hogarth, Walpole and Commercial Britain* (London: Hansib Press, 1987); and *Hogarth's Blacks: Images of Blacks in Eighteenth-Century English Art* (Aarhus, Dangaroo Press, 1985).
17. Hanif Kureishi, *The Buddha of Suburbia* (London: Faber, 1990); David Dabydeen, *The Intended* (London; Secker and Warburg, 1991) and *Disappearance* (London: Secker and Warburg, 1993); Mike Phillips, *Blood Rights* (London: Michael Joseph, 1989; Penguin, 1990), *The Late Candidate* (London: Michael Joseph, 1990; Penguin, 1990) and *Point of Darkness* (London: Michael Joseph, 1994).
18. Francis Mulhern, 'English Reading', in Homi K. Bhabha (ed.), *Nation and Narration* (London: Routledge, 1990).
19. 'The Rainbow Sign' (London: Faber 1986).
20. For a complete bibliographical reference to Chester Himes, see A. Robert Lee, 'Hurts, Aburdities and Violence: The Contrary Dimensions of Chester Himes', *Journal of American Studies*, vol. 12, no. 1

(April 1978), pp. 99–114. Walter Mosley, *Devil in a Blue Dress* (New York: Norton, 1990); *A Red Death* (New York: Norton, 1991); *White Butterfly* (New York: Norton, 1992); *Black Betty* (New York: Norton, 1994).

6. New Nations, New Selves: The Novels of Timothy Mo and Kazuo Ishiguro

Laura Hall

> The nation fills the void left in the uprooting of communities and kin and turns that loss into the language of metaphor.
>
> Homi Bhabha: *Nation and Narration* [1]

Colonialism and, in its wake, post-colonialism have not only inscribed and re-inscribed borders and nations but at the same time those who actually live under the sway of empire. But after the mapmakers and politicians finished their tasks and returned home to the nation at the centre of the British Empire, they found a new 'gathering' of post-colonials and emigrés re-inscribing that very nation from within in what Homi Bhabha calls 'a hybrid national narrative'.[2] The post-colonial writer, located 'within and between two worlds',[3] is ideally situated to create a new fictional and imaginative terrain. This is the literary space inhabited by Timothy Mo and Kazuo Ishiguro whose novels reflect the complexities of their origins and experiences. Post-coloniality, in the writing of both these British authors, is a mediation of multiple layers of cross-cultural and 'hybridised' identities assembled out of the remains of the British Empire and in the shadows of the Chinese and Japanese Empires. The new nation that they write out of is a post-war Britain where the old assumptions about class and race relations no longer hold. The working class is no longer deferential, the aristocracy appears to be an endangered species and the subjects of the rapidly crumbling British Empire are not only 'there' in some pink coloured spot on the globe but 'here', in London, Bradford and other parts of Britain.

The project of writing 'within and between two worlds' is further obfuscated by the realisation that those 'two worlds' cannot be separated into discrete entities but are inextricably interwoven. Writers from that vast undifferentiated area called the 'Orient' find that they have been textually anticipated and that they must write to a public already 'informed' by a European orientalist discourse.[4] Writers such as Mo and Ishiguro not only have to deal with commonly-held stereotypes of Chineseness of Japaneseness, but scholarly constructs of the same thing. This is a discourse that casts the 'other' in a past that is perceived to be more authentic and pure than the all too real present which has been contaminated by the *realpolitik* of colonialism and nationalism. The point made by critic Rey Chow that the experience of being Chinese is 'the experience precisely of being impure'[5] can be extended to almost any culture touched by the forces of modernity. She criticises the sinologist's 'idealistic preoccupation with "authentic" originariness', asking how this can be achieved given the past century and a half of disruptive contacts with the West. Westernisation 'as an indelible, subjective part of modern Chinese people's response to their own "ethnic" identity is consistently disregarded'.[6] This very cross-culturality, however, provides fertile ground for the imagination of post-colonial writers.

Cross-culturality and hybridity mark the beginning of new and better inventions than those that proceed them from history and the social sciences. Post-colonial culture, note the authors of *The Empire Writes Back*, 'is inevitably a hybridized phenomenon involving a dialectical relationship between the "grafted" European cultural systems and an indigenous ontology'.[7] Wherever Mo and Ishiguro's characters invoke tradition, whether for the purposes of survival or as a trope of power, the results are either comic or pitiable. In neither case does their work yield itself to the orientalist quest to understand 'Chineseness' or 'Japaneseness'.

Nevertheless, for many reviewers, this is the only context in which they can be placed in order to be understood. While recognising that the outsider view of other societies may be one of exotic spectacle, they still hold on to the reverse notion that writing from the inside must therefore be representative of 'authenticity' without questioning the concept itself. Mo's credentials as Hong Kong insider are cited by Michael Neve in a review of *The Monkey King* when he declares that Mo, 'writes from within, from real acquaintance with the feeling that sweeps the local population as a typhoon draws across the South China Sea'.[8] In other words he is reassured that Mo is delivering the 'real thing', not the synthetic stuff of *tai pan* novels. Having established the author's status as insider, the review ends by praising one of his 'best insights' that 'in the proper Chinese fashion' there is an 'absence of sex'. Buried within this statement are some assumption about Chinese attitudes towards sex and what it means to write about sex. The 'absence of sex' in the novel, i.e. graphic sexual description, is taken to be a signifier of the Chineseness of the novel rather than a narrative strategy.

Similarly, Gabriele Annan in a review of Ishiguro's work, interprets his three novels as comments on 'Japaneseness'.[9] Although only the first two novels refer to Japan or contain Japanese characters, Annan nevertheless considers all of the novels to be 'explanations, even indictments, of Japaneseness ... Characters who place too high – too Japanese – a price on these values are punished for it.' Even the *The Remains of the Day* which is set firmly in England without a Japanese character in sight, becomes a commentary on Japaneseness. The jolly English villagers are each 'an argument for spontaneity, openness, and democracy, and against Japaneseness'. The message of *Remains of the Day* for Annan is: 'Be less Japanese, less bent on dignity, less false to yourself and others, less restrained and controlled.' In other words, Englishness means spontaneity, openness and democracy; Japaneseness means too much dignity, too much self-sacrifice, too much restraint and control. Annan misses the point that in two nations going through an identity crisis, what is 'Japanese' and what is 'English' is no longer as certain as it used to be. The same can be said for concepts of what is 'Chinese'.

The binary of primordial notions of ethnicity and 'cultural authenticity' on the one hand and the modern and thus assimilated and alienated native on the other are rendered banal by the innovativeness of writers such as Ishiguro and Mo. To read them either as cultural informants or as deracinated cosmopolitans misses the point that these two writers are not only re-imagining what it means to be Chinese or Japanese but, more significantly, what it means to be 'British'.

* * *

Timothy Mo, born in Hong Kong to an English mother and Cantonese father and living in England, writes about people who are on the fringes of several empires. Hong Kong, which was ceded to Britain in 1843 and is due to be returned to the People's Republic of China in 1997, serves as the setting for his first novel *The Monkey King* (1978). His second novel, *Sour Sweet* (1985), follows the fortunes of a family of Hong Kong immigrants as they struggle to succeed in London. These first two novels present the apparent diasporic dilemma of reconciling the ideology of continuity with the practice of change within the domain of the family. Mo does not draw his characters as hapless victims of circumstance but as pioneers who learn to improvise under distinctly untraditional circumstances. Gradually the reader is let in on the sly joke – that 'tradition' itself has been invented or is at best a half-remembered thing.

By contrast, the second two novels are set in the global arena of historical events. The protagonists, caught in these power games of nations and empires, can hope to establish only some small realm of personal autonomy. *An Insular Possession* (1986), addresses the historic acquisition of Hong Kong by Britain during the Opium Wars. The most recent novel, *The Redundancy of Courage* (1992), takes the contemporary predicament of someone born into the Chinese diaspora of Southeast Asia where one form of insecurity has been exchanged for another in the era of nationalist struggles for independence. Post-colonial liberation becomes the perfect ironical setting in which Mo can critically explore the broad themes of loyalty, freedom and heroism as well as the political and personal ramifications of 'being Chinese'.

In *The Monkey King*,[10] Mo takes up the personal implications of Chinese identity through the critical eye of his mixed-blood protagonist, Wallace Nolasco. From the outset, Nolasco prefers to identify with his exotic Portuguese ancestor rather than his more immediate Cantonese forebears whom he regards as an 'arrogant and devious' people. Nevertheless, he honours the arrangement his late father has made with Mr Poon, a wealthy Hong Kong businessman, to marry him to May Ling, the daughter of Poon's concubine. For Mr Poon's part, marrying May Ling to a respectable Cantonese family has been out of the question and marrying lower would decrease the esteem of the Poon family; therefore, 'a poor Portuguese was a creative solution ... Compromise was at the center of Mr Poon's political system' (p. 16). He hopes that the marriage will at least ensure the continuity of the family empire.

Despite his marriage, Nolasco remains on the outside of the tightly-knit family and its daily round of petty domestic politics – on the whole he sees his exclusion as a mark of status. He struggles to maintain this edge of superiority but his only real trump card over Mr Poon is his refusal to fulfil his only apparent function in life, namely the production of an heir. Otherwise, the distinctiveness of his Portuguese blood remains a frail assertion and not evident from his passive existence in the household.

Only when Nolasco and May Ling are thrown on their own resources in a small village in the New Territories does he begin to discover his own potential. Nolasco, freed from the preordained path mapped out for him by the family patriarchs, finally becomes an innovator and a useful member of a community. Under his tutelage, the entire village economy shifts from the subsistence agriculture that the peasants had practised for centuries to a thriving tourist enterprise complete with boating lake and food and souvenir stalls. They embrace his ideas wholeheartedly and out here in the margins Nolasco becomes a 'somebody' in his own right, not because of his family connections. In the contrast between life with the Poons and life in the New Territory, Mo comments not only on the stifling nature of family relationships but also on tradition.

On the surface the New Territories would appear to be a backwater of unchanging 'traditional' Chinese peasant life, but like Mr Poon, the peasants have found compromise and pragmatism to be the sensible thing, even in matters of tradition. For instance, when squatters move on to the villagers' land during a period of civil war, the two groups come to a face-saving concession, manipulating genealogies to locate 'a focal but mythical ancestor in the tenth generation: a sensible compromise'. 'Tradition', like history, is subjected to manipulation and invention to suit the political exigencies of the time.

When Nolasco is recalled to the Poon household, he finds that he – rather than Poon's son – is to be the successor to the Poon business empire. Even before Mr Poon's death the female family members, the amahs and the children have placed the mantle of the patriarch on the outsider son-in-law's shoulders. In Mo's vision of the family, the men may be the patriarchs but they can only rule with the assent of the ruled, the women. The family that Nolasco wishes to be aloof from has consumed him and made him their own. The metaphorical concept is driven home in a less than subtle manner in a nightmare in which Nolasco sees himself presiding over a banquet where a chained live monkey is brought in. He realises that he is about to partake of a grotesque ritual meal of live monkey brain. Although a participant in the feast, he also identifies with the monkey. In the folktales of the Monkey King, however, the Monkey makes many escapes through transformation but Nolasco's monkey appears to be finally trapped. There is no escape for either of them. The Poon family has triumphed over the barbarian outsider in their midst and moulded him to suit their needs.

The theme of the family as an 'amoeba-like' entity that accommodates obstacles by enveloping and incorporating them is one that Mo pursues again in *Sour Sweet*.[11] The clannish Poon household of Hong Kong is worlds away from the Chen family of London in *Sour Sweet*. Whereas the Poons maintain their position in Hong Kong society through social exclusiveness, the Chen family as immigrants to Britain are among the excluded. Both families are inwardly oriented and self-reliant and both are also forced by circumstance to accommodate change.

Lily and her husband Chen (we never learn his given name), live in London with their son Man Kee, Lily's sister Mui and, later on, Chen's father. The Chens have no illusions about their status in life, they had little in China and they have less in England. But Lily, the heart of the exiled family, has ambitions for the future. She harbours an idealised almost social Darwinian philosophy of family life. 'In her experience there was no standstill in life. Families rose and fell ... If one generation didn't climb, then the next declined, or the one after that' (p. 7). Her ambitions focus on her infant son, Man Kee, who she has already determined will be the 'key brick in a planned and highly structured edifice'. Although strong-willed and independent, Lily, like the Poon women, plays out her role as dutiful daughter-in-law, sending regular remittances to Chen's parents in southern China. When Chen's mother dies she welcomes his father into their household even more wholeheartedly than Chen himself. Thanks to Lily's frugality, they are able to open their own Chinese takeaway in South London, the Dah Ling. The takeaway counter becomes the symbolic barrier between Lily and Chen and the alien world of the pink-faced consumers of their specially concocted Chinese dishes.

The three family members embody a range of attitudes towards the natives of their new home. While Lily, certain of her superiority, tries to run her world as if they did not exist, Chen is intimidated by them. Though no one has assaulted or insulted him, Chen felt 'like a gatecrasher who had stayed too long and been identified' (p. 1). The role of cultural mediator is left to Lily's sister Mui who learns about many of the idiosyncrasies of British life through television. Mui is the one who delivers the orders to the lorry drivers at the neighbouring garage, who negotiates for a standing order of drinks that have 'fallen off the back of a lorry' and talks to the tax man and school officials.

In the end Mui is also the one to break up the carefully prepared foundations of Lily's 'edifice' by giving birth to a baby of uncertain paternity and then marrying and settling down with 'Uncle Lo' – a most untraditional family arrangement. When Chen himself disappears, a victim of a Chinese triad gang, it seems that the disintegration of Lily's household is complete. But Lily finds to her own surprise that she does not really miss Chen, 'it was as if a stone had been taken off her and she had sprung to what her height should have been' (p. 278). Each sister finally finds freedom in different ways not *from* family but *with* family. Mui's family, like the menu of the Chinese takeaway, is neither recognisably English nor Chinese but a creation of her own. Lily, on the other hand, finds herself adapting to circumstances and accepting that her family will not be the 'edifice' she once planned.

Mo's counterpoint to Lily's household is found in the Hung family, one of the triad societies in London. While Lily and Mr Poon, the patriarch of *Monkey King*, may wish to uphold ideals about family life, in practice they have to adjust to the way things turn out, which is to say imperfectly. This is a world where only an authoritarian organisation like the triads can ensure that 'tradition' will be passed on intact from one generation to the next; those who challenge or disrupt their fraternal order are likely to be eliminated. Like other isolated and lonely Chinese immigrants, Chen is vulnerable to the triads who distort the symbols of 'tradition' and 'family' in order to exploit and control their members.

The machinations of the triads intrude awkwardly into the plot. The criminal characters remain two-dimensional, playing out their roles for us like characters from a Chinese opera or a pantomime; we recognise them but we do not know them. Despite the bibliographical citations for the arcane aspects of triad life, the Hung family serves not as a source of 'authenticity' in the novel but as a heavy-handed reminder that 'tradition' can be a source of oppression as well as security. Chen in the end sacrifices himself without complaint to the Hung family, leaving Lily and Mui free to invent their own version of a family in a new country.

Once more, Mo's female characters subvert the patriarchal intent of family life while maintaining its form. This vision of family life mirrors the Chinese vision of their own history stated explicitly by Mo when he compares Chen to 'a barbarian conqueror of a highly civilised people' who has 'an avuncular glow from the collective attainments of an apparently subjugated race, unaware all the time that the one who was being absorbed, subverted, changed, was himself' (p. 15). This is a reference to the successive 'barbarian' rulers of China, the Mongols and later the Manchus, who were eventually absorbed by China and became 'Chinese' rulers. Like the barbarian Emperors, the patriarchs of the Poon and Chen family have power only so long as their families acknowledge it; without the collaboration of their subjects in their own domination, they are merely figureheads.

In *An Insular Possession*,[12] history itself is under scrutiny. The story of the first Opium War and the British acquisition of Hong Kong is told through letters, journal entries and newspaper excerpts. The distance from the historical past and the genre of historical fiction is conveyed by a present-tense narrative, and, in a parody of a 'real' history, a couple of realistic appendices containing 'references' to the historical as well as the fictional characters who appear in the book. Mo's many-layered narrative appears to be a reversal of the technique of the historian which is to transform the chaos of conflicting accounts and multiple sources into the smooth order of a narrative, what Hans Kellner has called 'an aesthetic beautification of chaotic mere existence'.[13] Mo the post-colonial writer resorts to a post-modern deconstruction of the seamless historical narrative into some of its component parts. The effect of reading this collage of sources and narrative is to see colonialism reconstituted as chaotic, disruptive and more often than not an improvisation in the face of unexpected events rather than the orderly march of progress.

Once again the plot focuses on a group of people living far from home among faceless strangers, but this time, in a reversal of the plot of *Sour Sweet*, the fortune-seekers are Americans and Europeans. Southern China in the period leading up to the Opium Wars serves as the backdrop for two enterprising Americans, Gideon Chase and Walter Eastman, who struggle to comprehend the Chinese 'natives' – as anonymous as Lily's pink-faced English customers. With the help of a cynical Irish artist named Harry O'Rourke (a thinly fictionalised George Chinnery, the Irish artist who lived in Macao in the early nineteenth century), the two men leave the security of an American trading house for the capricious world of publishing. Their newspaper, *The Lin Tin Bulletin and River Bee* competes with the *Canton Monitor* for the attention of the expatriate community of traders, soldiers, diplomats and adventurers. The rival papers chronicle the events of the period such as the arrivals of Commissioner Lin and Captain Elliott and the destruction of the Bogue Forts.

Eastman and Chase use the *Bulletin* not only as a mouthpiece of opposition to the *Canton Monitor* and a chronicle of the times they are living in, but also as an outlet for their own quirky interests. Eastman expounds on the new daguerreotype technology and Chase, who is learning Chinese, makes earnest attempts to enlighten his fellow expatriates about the 'subterranean life' of those *whom they have regarded but never seen*. Under his pen name 'Pursuer', he relates anecdotal stories that claim to be illustrative of the Chinese character and customs such as the Chinese sense of time, their 'contradictory nature' and their cruelty. He also comments on the differences between the Chinese and the western novel; the latter, he explains, progresses in a linear fashion but the 'native' novel, 'moves in a path which is altogether circular' (p. 316). Gideon Chase, alias 'Pursuer', is the perfect orientalist, labouring away to establish cultural differences and to construct a notion of 'Chineseness' that would lay the foundations of the western discourse on China over the next century of colonial intervention. Eastman, on the other hand, has a fascination with the new technology of the daguerreotype which he promotes as 'a piece of the congealed substance of time, sliced out of the body of the changing world. It is an instant frozen, purloined. It is the river of time arrested in its flow' (p. 524). Chase attempts to understand and interpret the events around him, Eastman is interested only in the surface, the image – and even that can be arranged. At the end of the novel he identifies their differences, telling Chase that he belongs to the category 'which will have things in the round, which does love an end, causes, the balance sheet drawn and equalled. But, by dear Gid, the world is not like that – it is untidy, there are no reasons, the final sum never balances' (p. 575).

Similarly, as an *Insular Possession* is set among real events, there can be no real closure to the story; history is untidy, reasons are obscured by politics and the sum never balances evenly. By telling the story through the experiences of foreigners, Mo makes it clear that the events which led up to the Opium War and the long history of foreign intervention in southern China are not a Chinese story but a western one. Unlike the Chinese characters of his other novels, the Chinese in this story hardly even figure as passive victims of history, they are props rather than actors in a human melodrama of historical significance.

The bachelor male, unencumbered by the obligations of family, is once more the protagonist in Mo's most recent novel, *The Redundancy of Courage*.[14] While Chase and Eastman are placed at the margins of the grand games of colonial appropriation and empire-building, Adolph Ng is a participant in the mess of post-colonial disorder. Mo again makes use of real events, this time the invasion and occupation of East Timor, a former Portuguese colony, by the Indonesians; events that caused scarcely a ripple in the western media. The island of Danu is a thinly fictionalised East Timor, its 'history' could in fact be the history of any number of small nations. In the wake of the revolution in Portugal, Danu is given instant independence. There follows a period of open free-for-all where everyone (except the local Chinese) quarrel over the political spoils. The story of the struggle for autonomy by this unfortunate nation is narrated by one of its citizens, Adolph Ng, who has his own personal conflict over identity. The exigencies of independence, civil

New Nations, New Selves

war and finally exile lead him to try out one identity after another;
Ng the cosmopolitan intellectual, Ng the Chinaman, Ng the
Danuese freedom fighter and finally Ng the homosexual. The cynical and not very likeable voice that he assumes throughout the
narrative comes from his position as the perpetual outsider. He
survives but not in very admirable ways, a double bind that is the
burden of many survivors.

This novel, more than its predecessors, focuses critically on the
meaning of being Chinese in a non-Chinese nation. As a member
of the Chinese community on Danu, Ng is part of the Chinese
diaspora scattered throughout Southeast Asia – a successful but
often persecuted minority. At the outset, Ng rejects this part of
himself, wavering in his choice of pronouns as he takes up the
Danuese view of the Chinese community:

They – we – had been the ones who'd had the most to lose by
Independence. Most Chinese didn't give a damn about politics,
independence or dependency, it was all one and the same to
them ... Exploitation was the name of the game. We'd always
done it and were cheerfully continuing the tradition of our
ancestors. (p. 7)

Ng considers himself to be more than an ethnic or national category, he has travelled to the West and received an education. He
considers himself to be a man of the world but in reality is a man of
many worlds: 'The world of television, of universities, of advertising,
of instant communications, made me what I am. It made me a
citizen of the great world and it made me a misfit for ever' (p. 24).

Back in Danu, he tries to be as much 'a man of the world' as
the place will allow. He eschews the company of Chinese traders
and businessmen for the company of other misfits of the colonial
world: the self-appointed intellectuals, the educated *mestizos* and
assorted radicals. When he decides to make a living by opening a
hotel, he suddenly finds the mantle of Chinaman falling on his
shoulders with all its connotations but decides that it is not all
bad: 'I was a Chinese entrepreneur with capital. I was an ex-
ploiter. I was a provider of work ... I was vulnerable. I was powerful. This was interesting' (p. 51).

The era of post-independence nationalism is rudely interrupted
by the neighbouring *malais* who invade Danu on a flimsy pretext.
Thus life begins to change for Ng in unpredictable ways, for
though the Chinese are no more loved by the *malais* than by the
Danuese, they are still needed for their business skills to adminis-
ter the fortunes acquired through force and corruption. Ng is

allowed to manage the very hotel he used to own for the general who has expropriated it from him. His role as a quasi comprador is rudely interrupted when he is forcefully recruited by a guerrilla band. Not surprisingly, Ng the Danuese 'freedom fighter' turns out to be no fighter but instead finds his metier among the guerrillas as a designer of booby-traps. With a logic that reveals the depth of his self-loathing, Ng attributes the skill with which he executes his deadly new craft to a cultural inheritance: 'It was a craft – mining, booby-trapping – that was peculiarly Chinese. I mean in its low small-mindedness, its attention to detail, its pettifogging neatness. At that kind of handiwork the Chinese traditionally excelled' (p. 168). His talent for blowing up people and equipment makes him into a hero among the guerrillas but Ng 'the Chinaman' knows that, for the Danuese, he will always be an outsider and not quite Danuese.

When recaptured by the *malais* army, Ng changes coat once more, surviving as a 'half-slave, half-best friend and confidant' to the wife of a *malais* army officer. It is a position that he is entrusted with only because his homosexuality renders him sexually unthreatening to the woman's husband. Ironically, the key to his survival throughout the vicious civil war has lain in his despised identities both as a Chinese man and as a homosexual. In the end Ng realises that his efforts to escape his role as 'Chinaman' through his worldliness and education are doomed to failure in the post-colonial politics of his island nation. He is seeking freedom but not the freedom of the liberation fighters whose discomforts he knows well. 'I'd rather be a slave in comfort than endure those conditions of freedom', he says sardonically. Finally Ng escapes his war-torn homeland and chooses Brazil as his destination for self-liberation.

There, he once more tries to cast off the burden of his Chinese identity, refusing to disappear into 'that petty Diaspora of restaurateurs and storekeepers'. He chooses instead the 'nobler' identity of Mr Kawasaki, the Japanese hotelier, with all its connotations of ethnic success. But even in the new world, shorn of his personal history, he finds that he cannot terminate Adolph Ng: 'I was trying to accomplish within my own small person what the *malais* hadn't been able to do to a nation. An identity and a history cannot be obliterated with a switch of a name or the stroke of a pen' (p. 406).

Ng in his new life realises that it is as difficult to make away with his 'self', as it is for the *malais* to obliterate a whole nation. The Danuese citizen, the Chinese man, the cosmopolitan and homosexual, always there beneath the surface, can coexist. His sexuality, which he as narrator keeps closeted, can now express itself more openly in the ambience of Rio where he becomes part of 'that special freemasonry of glances'. For Ng, freedom and identity are tied together; when he has the freedom to be who he wants, it does not matter who or what he is. His choice of Brazil with its image of racial and sexual tolerance is therefore a natural one. While he considers and rejects the former colonial motherland of Portugal, the idea of 'returning' to China does not even enter into his calculations. Ng's new homeland has been determined not by birth or blood or colonial connection but, in the ultimate act of liberation, by choice.

Whether the setting for Mo's novels is the diaspora or the peculiarly hybrid outpost of Hong Kong, the ghost of a 'real' China somewhere pulls at his characters. This is a China that is re-imagined and reproduced with each generation as a *leitmotif* for the actions of the next one. Mo's China is an invention of both westerners and Chinese. The China of tradition invoked by Lily Chen and the Poons pragmatically serves the purpose of justifying their present actions. The China of the *Lin Tin Bulletin* is an ossified relic that will be enshrined by the orientalists. The China of Adolph Ng is a burden of blood and community that both imprison and liberate him.

* * *

Unlike Hong Kong, Mo's place of origin, Japan has never been a subject of colonial domination, except perhaps for the post-war years of military occupation. Rather, Japan itself has been a colonial power in China and throughout Southeast Asia for a brief period up to the end of the Second World War. Since then, Japan's expansion has been an economic one, and the members of the tiny Japanese community who live in Britain are more likely to be expatriate employees of Japanese corporations than immigrants.

Kazuo Ishiguro, for his part, was born in Nagasaki, Japan, and at the age of five came to Britain with his parents where he has remained. Ishiguro himself has commented on the effects that this literary and personal 'homelessness' has had on his writing: 'I wasn't a very English Englishman and I wasn't a very Japanese Japanese either. And so I had no clear role, no society or country to speak for or write about. Nobody's history seemed to be my history.'[15] The novels of Kazuo Ishiguro take place within quite specific historical settings, namely pre- and post-war Japan and Britain.

The question of conflicting loyalties to nations, to higher moral values and to human dignity in a world of transition and change is the territory explored by Ishiguro. His first novel, *A Pale View of Hills* (1982), deals with guilt and loyalty in a Japanese woman as she negotiates two cultures, Japanese and British. *An Artist of the Floating World* (1986) is set in pre- and post-war Japan in a family that must come to terms with the consequences of the wartime activities of the patriarch. *The Remains of the Day* (1989) takes place in the same time period but this time in an English country house with an English cast of characters. It is the story of a man who serves power but has none himself.

Ishiguro masters a range of voices, taking up in turn the identity of a Japanese housewife, a retired Japanese master artist and an ageing English butler. Each of the three first-person narrators looks back on the decisions that they made at critical points in their lives with varying degrees of regret. Through these disparate individuals Ishiguro reflects on the nature of character, not necessarily Japanese or English character, but the character that emerges in times of personal and national crisis.

A Pale View of Hills,[16] is narrated by Etsuko, the Japanese widow of an Englishman, now living in England. The story weaves back and forth from the immediate present of the recent suicide of her Japanese-born daughter Keiko to her past in post-war Nagasaki, a city whose name is forever associated with nuclear devastation. But Ishiguro's Nagasaki, with its new concrete apartment blocks rising out of mosquito-infested wastelands and occupying American troops, is also a site of flux and transience. It is a deliberate contrast to the unchanging rhythms of life in the English village where Etsuko lives. In a reversal of stereotypes of East and West, England is stability and security while Japan in the throes of modernisation represents uncertainty and change.

Etsuko's younger daughter, Niki, comes down from London to be with her mother after her half-sister's suicide. Recollections of the past nag at the present as she pieces together the summer that she was pregnant with Keiko and still with her first husband Jiro. Etsuko tries to reconcile the world-views of her past life with the present one. The old world is exemplified by the opinions of her benevolent former father-in-law, Ogata-San, who denounces the changes in post-war Japanese society:

> Discipline, loyalty, such things held Japan together once ... People were bound by a sense of duty. Towards one's family, towards superiors, towards the country. But now instead there's all this talk of democracy. You hear it whenever people want to be selfish, whenever they want to forget obligations. (p. 65)

By these standards, Etsuko's conduct in leaving her husband for another man could only be considered as an abandonment of duty and an act of selfishness. However, a continent away and a generation later, Niki, who has embarked on her own adventure of independence in London, interprets her mother's past quite differently:

> In recent years she has taken it upon herself to admire certain aspects of my past, and she had come prepared to tell me things were no different now, that I should have no regrets for those choices I once made. In short to reassure me I was not responsible for Keiko's death. (p. 11)

The differences are not so much those of culture as of generation, for Ogata-San drew little sympathy for his view even from his own son who ridiculed his father's idealisation of the old school syllabus.

Etsuko's memories are drawn back to a brief friendship she had with a woman named Sachiko during the summer that she was pregnant with Keiko. Their lives have obvious parallels in retrospect. Sachiko was involved with an American and planned to move to America despite the rebellious resistance of her young daughter, Mariko. Her desperation and determination to move to America over her daughter's objections foreshadow the struggle that Etsuko has later with Keiko when she chooses to leave Jiro and move to England with an Englishman.

As Etsuko recalls the end of that summer with Sachiko, the line between the lives of Sachiko and Mariko and her own and Keiko blur together. The image of a girl's body hanging from a tree haunts Etsuko in England as she reconstructs those past events which, with hindsight, now seem to have been a premonition. She voices a theme that recurs in all Ishiguro's novels, that memory can be an unreliable thing: 'often it is heavily coloured by the circumstances in which one remembers, and no doubt this applies to certain of the recollections I have gathered here' (p. 156). In the light of Keiko's suicide, she lives with the guilt of having chosen self-fulfilment over loyalty to her husband and her life in Japan. She retrieves her half-forgotten past for the signs that she should have seen and heeded: the warnings of Mrs Fujiwara to keep her mind on happy things during her pregnancy, the mysterious deaths of children in the city that summer and finally the death of the child Mariko.

Etsuko's assumption of responsibility for Keiko's life and death lies in contrast to her father-in-law's refusal to evaluate his own small role in Japan's militaristic past. They both remember the past selectively, Ogata-San remembers only a life of discipline, loyalty and duty and not its consequences, Etsuko as the self-abnegating mother can only read the past events as signposts missed on the way to sad present. Ogata-San, who preaches loyalty to family, superiors and country, is obsessed with an ex-student who chose morality over loyalty when he wrote an article critical of the unethical acts of his former teachers. Etsuko has taken the risk of changing her life and her loyalties and has to live with the consequences of that decision. As a woman born into a time and place of pre-feminist consciousness, the reader can sympathise with Etsuko whose act of disloyalty and abandonment of duty are reinterpreted for us as a risk she had to take by her English-born daughter. Her anachronistic father-in-law, on the other hand, has no voice to support him in the new world. The concept of absolute loyalty to nation is revealed here as a false god by Ishiguro and even more so in his next two novels.

The man who acts out of the highest principles of patriotism only to find his work no longer appreciated, is developed in more detail by Ishiguro in *An Artist of the Floating World*.[17] The story narrated by Masuji Ono ostensibly concerns the marriage negotiations for his youngest daughter Noriko, but in pondering the nuances of the negotiations, he must also reconsider his past. Ono, who constantly seeks recognition of his past prestige and status, begins by recalling how he acquired his house in an 'auction of prestige' which, though an unusual procedure, he considered to be not unlike marriage negotiations. Gradually it becomes clear that the marriage negotiations are not progressing as fast as they should because Ono's prestige has fallen since the end of the war. His rise had been based on his 'patriotic' style of painting that depicted the 'real' world, a style that had found political favour with the militarists in pre-war Japan. In adopting this new style he had rejected the style of his old master who encouraged his pupils to depict images from the 'floating world' of the women from the pleasure district. The cycle is repeated when one of Ono's best pupils, Kuroda, turns out to harbour 'unpatriotic' thoughts during the war. Ono, an adviser to the Committee of Unpatriotic Activities, betrays Kuroda to the committee, an act which leads to Kuroda's imprisonment. Through Ono's narrative, it becomes clear that he was not 'simply a painter', during the former era of militarism, but a very active participant in the patriotic movement.

The reader is taken by Ono through the 'new' militarised Japan of the pre-war and wartime years as well as the post-war 'new' Japan. Ono deplores the new climate in Japan, particularly the Americanisation of Japanese culture. The country, he tells his son-in-law, 'has come to look like a small child learning from a strange adult' (p. 185). But as a doting grandfather, he finds himself indulging his grandson's passion for American icons of entertainment such as the Lone Ranger and Popeye and listening to his daughter Setsuko praise cowboys as more appropriate models for children than samurai. The American victory is indeed complete.

Setsuko urges Ono to ensure that 'misunderstandings' about the past do not upset the marriage negotiations with the family of her sister's suitors. Thus he seeks out Kuroda to make amends but Kuroda, who has suffered greatly because of Ono's actions, wants nothing to do with him. He also visits a former colleague, Matsuda, who he fears might speak indiscreetly. Matsuda who once encouraged him in the patriotic movement now explains that their contributions were in fact marginal: 'No one cares now what the likes of you and me did ... When we look back over our lives and see they were flawed, we're the only ones who care now' (p. 201). The irony is that in the end even his pretence at making amends and confessing his past, an activity that enables him to boast of his former 'prestige', appears to make no difference to his daughters or to the new in-laws who brush off his former activities as insignificant.

While Ono carefully preserves memories of his former prestige, his daughters have scrupulously reconstructed their memories to render those same activities as trivial. When he declares with false humility that he was 'a man of some influence, who used that influence towards a disastrous end', Setsuko insists that 'Father was simply a painter. He must stop believing he has done some great wrong' (pp. 192–3). In refusing to let go of his prestigious past, the master artist bears witness to his own small part in the mistakes of his generation, whereas his daughters and colleagues, who either wish to diminish or forget the past, contribute to the denial of history. Ishiguro's constant comment on the art of memory still has significance in contemporary Japan where school textbooks have repeatedly failed to refer to the atrocities committed in China and the government has been reluctant to acknowledge the claims of the 'comfort women' forced to prostitute themselves for the Japanese army.

Questions of loyalty and betrayal, both the public and the private kind, resurface in all of Ishiguro's novels. As a 'patriotic' artist, Ono has been loyal to his country and so betrayed his pupil who is labelled a traitor. But in the reconstructed Japan, Ono is the traitor. Though we are almost moved to be sympathetic to an old man who finds himself out of sync with the times and with his family, Ishiguro gives us a sharp reminder of the ultimate horror behind banalities such as an art campaign when Matsuda reassures Ono that,

> There's no need to blame ourselves unduly ... We at least acted on what we believed and did our utmost. It's just that in the end we turned out to be ordinary men. Ordinary men with no special gifts of insight. It was simply our misfortune to have been ordinary men during such times. (pp. 200–201)

The words appear modest until one realises that they are discussing their inadequacies, not in contemporary terms, but in the terms of their shared past – the New Japan campaign that they conducted and Matsuda's manifesto for the 'China crisis campaign'. They do not mention that the 'China crisis' involved unspeakable crimes against humanity. Just as the Nazi party members 'were only following orders', Matsuda considers the two of them to have been 'ordinary men' who should bear no burden of blame.

Ishiguro presents us with the uncomfortable irony that in order to honour and understand the tragic events of the past, we have to listen not only to the voices of the victims but also to the self-serving revelations of men such as Ono. In *An Artist of the Floating World*, Ishiguro recognises that if individuals cannot remember the past with all its problems, then how much more difficult must it be for a nation to account for itself.

In *The Remains of the Day*,[18] Ishiguro's study of a period of changing moral values, 'when the very things that had been thought of as the highest patriotic achievements suddenly turned out to be something dreadful',[19] is brought closer to home, to the dalliance with fascism among the upper classes of Britain. The butler of Darlington Hall, Stevens, narrates another tale of loyalty and deference but from a servant's point of view. He is not as sophisticated as Ono and his ambitions are more modest; he delves into the past not to review a life of 'prestige' but to reassure himself that his life of service had 'dignity'. Stevens the loyal servant becomes an apologist for the late Lord Darlington who is only remembered in the post-war England for his associations with Sir Oswald Mosley's fascist organisation. With the defeat of fascism in Europe, Darlington is pilloried in the press and shunned by society; slowly the moral worth of his employer begins to crumble and along with it the 'dignity' of Stevens.

Ishiguro masterfully controls two concurrent story lines in two different time frames but, as the narrative progresses, it becomes evident that they are not separate stories, but braided together as

New Nations, New Selves

a whole in the life of the butler. Like Ono and Etsuko, Stevens'
reflection is precipitated by a crisis. In this case, two incidents
have coincided, the arrival of the new owner of Darlington Hall,
an American who unnerves his butler with his bantering familiarity, and the arrival of a letter from Miss Kenton, the former
housekeeper.

Stevens interprets the letter as a desire by Miss Kenton to
return to her old job. As he drives across the countryside, ostensibly on a mission to recruit Miss Kenton and solve the 'staffing
problem', Stevens meditates on the question of *what* is a great
butler?' – a question with few apparent cosmic implications but
Ishiguro teases out the issue through the dissimulations of the
butler until the question can be seen as a mask for the real
questions of a nation. What makes a great leader? Who is deserv-
ing of loyalty? How can one have dignity without autonomy? It
becomes evident that the feudal values of unquestioning service
to a master are not conducive to democratic society nor to per
sonal fulfilment and that what makes a great butler may not make
a very complete man.

Stevens the great butler has maintained his 'dignity' at the
expense of his private and personal life. While he ensures the
smooth running of Darlington's conference of world statesmen
who want to treat Germany like gentlemen, his father, an ex-
butler, is drawing his last breath. As he attends to the Prime
Minister and the German ambassador on the eve of war, he
ignores the signs of Miss Kenton's love for him and loses her to
another man. Stevens is not a cruel man, but the belief in his
duty to his employer has outweighed all personal considerations.
His journey is a chance to make amends for the past, but when
Miss Kenton tells him that it is 'too late to turn the clock back',
he confesses that his 'heart was breaking' – it is the first expression of emotion he allows himself, albeit too late.

As Stevens ventures into the real world beyond Darlington, it
has become more and more apparent that he is something of an
anachronism, for the class that he was born into has become
redundant in post-war Britain. The aristocracy and landed gentry
are closing their homes or selling them to Americans to pay estate
taxes and the army of men and women born into service as
maids, cooks and butlers are no longer needed. In presenting us
with an England that is as foreign to a native as it would be to an
outsider like Etsuko, Ishiguro waves an optimistic farewell to the
structured class society of pre-war Britain. The values of the new
England are voiced by a villager, Harry Smith, who boldly tells
Stevens that, 'you can't have dignity if you're a slave'. It is a

sentiment that Stevens has no sympathy with until the end of his journey when he is able to reflect that 'Lord Darlington ... had the privilege of being able to say at the end of his life that he made his own mistakes ... I can't even say I made my own mistakes. Really ... what dignity is there in that?' (p. 243).

This comment on personal autonomy is also a comment on democracy which the paternalistic Darlingtons of the world see as a dangerous tool in the hands of 'the common man' or the subjects of the empire. The fear is that 'they', the people, might not make the 'right' choices. But Stevens does not have the luxury of choice in his private life that the masters of servants do and so he vows to 'try to make the best of what remains of my day' – that is, the day of a butler.

Questions of loyalty and betrayal, both the public and the private kind, are common to all three of Ishiguro's novels. As a 'patriotic' artist, Ono has been loyal to his country and so betrayed his pupil who is labelled a traitor. But in the reconstructed Japan, Ono is the traitor. Stevens' loyalty goes to his employer whose judgement he defers to on all occasions, secure in the knowledge that his actions are in the 'best interests of his country'. Thus, unquestioning loyalty to the Emperor and country has its corollary in the loyalty of servants to employers; Ono defers to the might of Japanese militarism and the honour of the Emperor, Stevens defers to the better judgement of Lord Darlington. This is how empires are sustained; the difference is in the price that is paid. Ono and Darlington lose only prestige, whereas Stevens has lost his dignity and the possibility of any kind of personal life. Similarly, Etsuko also grapples with divided loyalties at the private level of family loyalty – the loyalties of wife to husband, and mother to child.

All the characters claim that the critical decisions of their lives were motivated not out of self-interest. There is an element of post-facto self-justification in the recollections of all three. Ishiguro uses the device of memory in each story to alert us to the fact that the recollection is always tempered by the moment when one decides to draw upon it. The experience is not unfamiliar to the author who has related his own experience of 'remembering' a Japan in adulthood that he had only known as a child:

> I think when I reached the age of perhaps twenty-three or twenty-four I realised that this Japan, which was very precious to me, actually existed only in my own imagination ... I realised that it was a place of my own childhood, and I could never return to this particular Japan.[20]

In Ishiguro's novels the distinction between what 'actually exist-ed' and what is 'imagination' becomes a question of a changing consciousness rather than changing realities.

* * *

A cultural critic recently suggested that the meaning of 'being Chinese' is increasingly being redefined and transformed not from the 'centre' of the Middle Kingdom, but at the periphery, in the numerous Chinese communities around the world, especially Southeast Asia.[21] The same could be said for the meaning of being British, but the process is reversed as those from the periphery transform the centre. In the works of both authors, post-colonial insecurity brings with it various degrees of freedom as well as burdens. Some are burdened by their memories, others would like to insulate themselves from the challenges of these new worlds. Yet others want the freedom to forget the past and to create new selves in a new nation. Identities which were once invented and imposed by the politics of colonialism, nationalism and migration are now re-imagined and re-invented by those same post-colonial selves and the national self becomes subject to a fresh negotiation.

Notes

1. Homi K. Bhabha, 'DissemiNation: Time, Narrative, and the Margins of the Modern Nation', In Homi K. Bhabha (ed), *Nation and Narra-tion* (London: Routledge, 1990), p. 291.
2. Ibid., p. 318.
3. Bill Ashcroft, Gareth Griffiths and Helen Tiffin (eds), *The Empire Writes Back: Theory and Practice in Post-colonial Literatures* (London and New York: Routledge, 1989) p. 196.
4. This discourse has been impressively described by Edward Said in *Orientalism* (New York: Random House, 1978).
5. Rey Chow, *Woman and Chinese Modernity: The Politics of Reading between East and West* (University of Minnesota Press, 1991) p. 28.
6. Ibid., p. 32.
7. Ashcroft et al. (eds), *The Empire Writes Back*, p. 195.
8. Michael Neve, 'The Hong Kong Beat', *The Times Literary Supplement*, 7 July 1978, p. 757.
9. Gabriele Annan, 'On the High Wire', *New York Review of Books*, vol. 36, no. 19, 7 December 1989, pp. 3–4.
10. Timothy Mo, *The Monkey King* (New York: William Morrow, 1978).
11. Timothy Mo, *Sour Sweet* (New York: Vintage, 1985).

12. Timothy Mo, *An Insular Possession* (London: Chatto and Windus, 1986).
13. Hans Kellner, 'Beautifying the Nightmare: The Aesthetics of Postmodern History', in *Strategies*, 4/5 (1991), pp. 289–313.
14. Timothy Mo, *The Redundancy of Courage* (London: Vintage, 1992).
15. Oe Kenzaburo and Kazuo Ishiguro, 'The Novelist in Today's World: A Conversation', *Boundary 2*, vol. 18, no. 3 (Fall 1991), pp. 109–22.
16. Kazuo Ishiguro, *A Pale View of Hills* (New York: Vintage, 1982).
17. Kazuo Ishiguro, *An Artist of the Floating World* (New York: Putnams, 1986).
18. Kazuo Ishiguro, *The Remains of the Day* (New York: Knopf, 1989).
19. Christopher Bigsby, 'An Interview with Kazuo Ishiguro', *The European English Messenger* (Autumn 1990), pp. 26–9.
20. Kenzaburo and Ishiguro, 'The Novelist in Today's World'.
21. Tu Wei-ming, 'Cultural China: The Periphery as the Center', in *Daedalus* (Spring 1991), pp. 1–32.

7. Long Day's Journey: The Novels of Abdulrazak Gurnah

A. Robert Lee

I was interested in exploring what happens to people who are in every respect part of a place, but who neither feel part of a place, nor are regarded as being part of a place.

Abdulrazak Gurnah (1992)[1]

Pilgrimage, as no doubt befits a novelist with a university base in Canterbury, supplies a ready configuration in all of Abdulrazak Gurnah's fiction. This is hardly surprising, given Gurnah's personal circuit of displacement from Zanzibar to Tanzania, Tanzania to England, together with a writer's subsequent research and conferencings across Europe, America, Canada and, by way of return, East Africa as just one of a variety of continuing African venues. Such the life such the art may not cover all the bases in his specific case, but it comes fairly close.

If, too, almost two decades on, Gurnah finds himself speaking warmly of his entry into a 'permissive' and 'hospitable' British academia, on more than a few occasions he has referred to the irony of an arrival in England in 1968 which happened to coincide with Enoch Powell's 'rivers of blood' harangue.[2] So contrary, and memorable, an overlap has had every reason to leave its mark.

Contrariety, however, has been nothing if not symptomatic for Gurnah. The historical ancestry which arose out of Somali and Gulf slave-venturing into coastal, 'Indian Ocean' Africa, and Tanzania/Zanzibar in particular, was, and continues to be, prone to its own reverses of status. The residual Islam, African tribal belief and Christianity, and the use of a Kiswahili uneasily at odds with the imported colonial English of secondary school and administration, he equally remembers as a jostle of claims and loyalties. From a present vantage-point, if he looks to a settled-in 'English' marriage, and a next Gurnah generation, he has no choice but to be mindful of the dislocations which lie behind so post-colonial a turn.

Leavetakings and homecomings, then, and even more the crossings in between, have understandably played a determining part in each of the four novels he has published to date. For pilgrimage, 'journey', lies at the heart of things, its resonances at once African and European, the footfall, say, of Achebe as much as of Conrad, of Ngugi as much as of Chaucer. Nor, however distinctive his own imaginative direction, has he shown any wish to disallow the affinities seen by many readers with fellow diasporist storytellers from V.S. Naipaul to Salman Rushdie, Timothy Mo to Buchi Emecheta.

In *Memory of Departure* (1987), Hassan Omar travels from village to city, and then beyond both, a promissory moving-on from Africa and yet always present is the resort to memory, the residual imprint of origins. For Daud, in *Pilgrims Way* (1988), the journey requires the negotiation of an English homeland, a Canterbury, interwovenly ancient and modern, genteel and yet brutal. In *Dottie* (1990), the excavation of the names which make up Dottie Badoura Fatma Balfour, black Londoner, becomes a pathway both into past dynasty and into the terms of her future. Latterly, the densely imagised (and Booker-nominated) *Paradise* (1994) uses the several journeys of its boy-hero Yusuf, as in the Koranic/Biblical parable it echoes, to explore in his coming-of-age the larger paradigms behind the mutual journey-encounters of Islam, 'traditional' Africa, India and Europe.[3]

Looking back on the crossplies in his history, Gurnah has spoken of what he has come to regard as 'the magnitude of his expedition', his autobiographical enactment of 'a kind of migrant paradigm'.[4] Few could do so with a better claim, given, precisely, the different tensions and transitions involved: the Zanzibari Arab/African who once departed Tanzania as much in dismay at graft and provincial nit-picking as at colonial legacy; the make-do hospital orderly eventually to study English at London University and take up his own lecturing career; and, above all, the now long British-based novelist imaginatively out to reclaim not only Africa, but also England, from, as he has observed in connection with *Paradise*, 'the colonisers' stories of us'.[5]

Little wonder, in turn, that 'journey' both within Africa (with the historic north-to-south migration of his ancestors always a reference) and, in a celebrated phrase, 'out of Africa', so recurs in

Gurnah's novel-writing. As a theme, a shaping design, it affords an almost irresistible means of entry into a body of work which, however perfectly ongoing, has from the outset laid its own insistent claims to recognition.

* * *

'What about England? Godless country, but there are opportunities there.' So, in *Memory of Departure*, and with a teasing slap of irreverence, Hassan Omar's teacher dangles before him the prospect of escape, transformation, journey.

An English overseas is offered to counter, in one of the novel's recurring *mots clé*, the African 'coastal' terms of his everyday existence, a future 'there' to escape a seemingly intractable and all-too-present 'here'. The appeal, for sure, catches perfectly at Hassan's own doubly felt need, the deepening sense of self-incarceration on the one hand, the will to self-extrication on the other.

For in no uncertain terms he finds himself held within a circle, a corridor, of hell. 'Family' may well call up Somali-conqueror antecedents, symbolic access to one-time Omani or Zanzibari power. It may look back to a sumptuous Islam not only of belief, but of learning, philosophy and mathematics – much of it passed on largely unacknowledged to the West. Islam's great mosques and walled-gardens and other mosaical architecture may bespeak a classical heritage along with storytelling ranging from the Koran and Prophet's life to *Alfu Leila u Leila* to whose heroine he ironically likens his 'grey', 'reproachful' mother. But these, in Hassan's life, and in 'coastal' East Africa, have given way to a world turned upside-down, a kind of diminished counter-face or residue.

In the immediate realm, the legacy has evolved into his paedophilic father-drunk who invokes the Koran as mere punitive writ, his put-upon, fatalistic mother, his prostitute sister Zakiya, his sodomite brother, Said, harrowingly burned to death in boyhood and for which Hassan himself is blamed, and his dying and ever accusatory grandmother, Bi Mkubwa, the Elder Mistress. Around them, Hassan inhabits a village whose no more than makings-do, beatings and drinking, and (especially to a vulnerable adolescent) threats of sexual rape, deplete as much as the often oppressively tropical climate. Even Hassan's dream of redemption at the behest of a rich Nairobi kinsman proves illusory, the near-indigent's perennial dream of gold. Life, on these terms, reduces to virtual contingency, sparseness, relieved only by his own gathering prompts to imagining and fabulation.

Little wonder, too, in rueful contemplation of his remnant dynasty, he observes: 'We had strutted our miscegenated way through centuries.' No romance of Mother Africa, then, for Hassan as boy-neophyte. No fantasy of either pre-colonial grandeur (he perfectly acknowledges the slave-venturing which brought his ancestors south), nor, for all his indictments of the intruding power-play of British Empire, no undue alibi for the grim 'African' regime which has followed. These, for him, refract into an immediate personal realm of aloneness, a general lack of childhood warmth and intimacy, vistas of street dirt and defecation, and, as always, likely sodomy.

The temptation, thus, might have been to use the novel as mere Cautionary Tale, 'Third World' Africa as a latest Anatomy of Melancholy. A far savvier storyteller, Gurnah, however, invests Hassan and his world (whatever its ongoing dispossession) with anything but simple *tristesse*. For *Memory of Departure* also portrays, at every turn, the writer-in-waiting, Hassan's story as equally a making-over, a reflexive possession, not only of the 'history' which has made him but of the powers of word whereby to speak, to write, that history. The upshot is that the 'history' in question, and the world in which it has been played out, comes over as at once narrow and yet expansive, depleted and yet rich. Only a storyteller's art, Hassan's eventually, can best mediate.

Each weigh-station en route bears out the point. If this, indeed, is not only a 'coastal region' but a 'dry season' of history as much as climate, the memorialisation involves an idiom of always implied first-hand sensation:

> The clearing round the mzambarau tree was empty so early in the day. From the green mosque came the hum of prayer, the faithful clustered in a saving huddle. In the distance a cock crowed. Jagged ends of rock had thrust through the earth in the square, a peril for unwary feet. With the rains, the earth would turn into fields of sprouting grass, but it was now the middle of the dry season ... Clouds of dust rising and rising ... Trees glare hard-headed at the noon sun. Tortured by the power of the heat, the sea turns and turns. (pp. 5–6)

The note registered is nothing if not figural, a time and place encapsulated not so much as 'event' as personally stored sensory and visual memory. Hassan's life, throughout, is thus told as much for its gathering inner resonance as for its outward rite-of-passage. Both come together, too, in the prospect of likely other journeys, not least when the boy contemplates an arriving vessel stirringly 'carrying its shipload of Greek sailors and Thai rice'.

114

This inlaying of the one journey inside the other is kept up to good purpose. If the novel draws on a contour of 'real' components – the expulsion of the British some years earlier, say, or the 1967 Arab–Israeli War, or a political outfit like the 'People's Progressive Party' with its catch-phrase of FREEDOM NOW and 'large photograph of our Leader, embarrassingly fat and with eyes hooded with malice and booze, standing next to the Queen of England' – it also invites a sense of history as at the same time always reiteration, the one process, however obliquely, replayed as another.

Hassan's father, for instance, fantasises a Koranic paradise and yet hellfires for his son, having himself been imprisoned for the sodomy (in his view for the love?) of a child. If Moses Mwinyi poses as a literary student on Hassan's train-journey to Nairobi, he, also, as befits a hustler-middleman, speaks the language of a credibly unliterary politics ('If we have to kill those who are holding us back or exploiting us, then I say let's do it ... And if it's only a Stalin who can do that, then I say let's have him').

Paradox resonates in Hassan's mind. At each turn, accordingly, he finds himself drawn towards 'story', 'metaphor', 'image' as a language to hold, if not necessarily to dissolve, contradiction. Koran School, for instance, stirs him as much by its allusions to desert odyssey and adventure as by its calls to worship and submission. A Jane Austen vernacularly mocked by his teacher as 'hoity-toity big nose and a little mouth' none the less elicits a necessary, imagined 'England'. If on the journey to Nairobi, Moses Mwinyi derides literature as an unaffordable luxury in 'developing' Africa, this veteran of street and big city makes his entrance accompanied by a copy of Peter Abrahams' *Mine Boy*. The well-named Bwana Ahmed bin Khalifa, kinsman-patron yet not, businessman yet wife-abuser, may betray Hassan. But through Ahmed's daughter Salma, and her student friend Mariam, Hassan enters a world of bookshops, music and art (Mariam's canvas, 'Betrayal', suitably, almost Magritte-like, features 'a leaking fountain-pen').

Journeying as both a life-passage and a 'passage' out of silence or marginality into word assumes its final, suitably inscriptive, form for him in the letter he writes to Salma, at once full of regret yet love, at once a journey-log yet a confession of homesickness. Composed, appropriately, in *media res*, from a cargo ship 'between Bombay and Madras', it underlines almost all the linked, overlapping implications of 'journey' for the novel. Not the least of these is that, as the bearer of his own freight of experience and custom, he assumes but the one place alongside the ship's other journeying human cargo.

But Gurnah's well-chosen allusions in the letter, his text-within-the-text, are also to the Middle Passage, to Conrad's Lord Jim, perhaps above all to dreams of yet other literal–emblematic voyaging – southwards down the Nile, eastwards to Macao. Hassan himself speaks of crossing a sea variously, and indicatively, 'hostile' and yet 'beautifully bright', 'solid-seeming' and yet 'treacherous'.

It is, indissolubly, actual, historic, voyaging, from Africa to India, or, more precisely, from one 'coastal' India to another. Yet at the same time there inheres within it a poet's voyaging, the call of, and the necessary answering to, the journeys, and in surest likelihood the journeys-to-be, within his own newly awakened imagination.

* * *

In *Pilgrims Way* 'journey' lies both behind and at the same time underway, Daud's arrival from Tanzania at England's premier cathedral city where, for five years, he has worked as an orderly in the local hospital. To the one side stands Canterbury's medieval house of worship, stately, Gothic, flag-bedecked, with, at least in appearance, a township to match. To the other, he finds himself cleaning the muck and mire of the operating theatre, living in a rented, shabby–genteel terrace house, and at almost every pub and other encounter exposed to a litany of racist resentment or patronage.

Cathedral towers may bespeak high iconography, a heart-of-the-nation sublimity underwritten by Chaucerian and other literary–cultural associations. 'Street' Canterbury, however, registers something else: threat, contempt, the all too often unleavened boast and bullying of what once was empire. Daud's own pilgrim's way is to negotiate, somehow to broker, both.

Pilgrimage again shapes the novel in interacting ways. The references-back to Augustine, Becket, Chaucer, Marlowe, Conrad, even to Canterbury-educated David Gower, supply one kind of allusive texture. Herein lies a roll-call, a prompt (whatever the origins of Augustine or Conrad) to thoughts of Englishness, the nature, be it selective or not, of Anglo-Saxon heritage. The 'journey' of nationhood lies enseamed, too, as Gurnah leaves little doubt, in the very street-names of Canterbury, a geography whose every mention amounts to history-by-association, typically Kingsmead, St George's Tower or Palace Street.

These 'journeyings' the novel adroitly also links to the colonial journeyers who brought Bible, gun and, always crucial, the English language itself, to Africa. Each of these, however, has a returning face, a secret sharer, not only in Daud but in his African student friend, Karta Benso, about to finish a degree at the newly created university. They, as others, import a kind of returning-pilgrim 'afri-

116

canisation' to the very England which once sought to 'anglicise' Africa.

The televised Test Cricket (the year is 1967), with England in Daud's phrase led by 'the boer', Tony Greig, and the West Indies by a serene Clive Lloyd, especially underscores the point. Daud and Karta, their partisanship rooted in feelings well beyond merest sport, cannot but recognise a latest 'game' of empire – albeit played under new gladiatorial colours (the West Indies for Africa), under, as it were, new home-and-away rules of engagement.

How, for Daud, to find, and maintain, bearings? One side of him is indeed drawn to the high-soaring cathedral whatever its triumphalist royal mortuary and typical 'grubby altar cloth'. He ponders, and is frequently enough moved by, the 'incredible grace of stone', the architectural 'vaulting', each a powerful marker to encode some rising-above of human spite. Yet at the same time, as he encounters each abuse, each insult, he finds himself obliged to think the English 'a gifted killer race that roamed the globe' and as prone as any to all of 'the racist confusions of the European mind'.

In Catherine, the English-born nurse he falls in love with, he can find balance yet the suspicion that even she can, or will, betray him for an all too English, almost hospital-romance, doctor. His heart's desire she may be, but between them, white Englishwoman with her African lover, they arouse a sexual–racial fury to call up all the ancient taboos of empire and Aryanism, 'colour' and mingling. In his English friend, David, he sees a kind of wounded liberal largesse, not least in his bags of food and general well-intendedness. Matters take a yet more serious turn in David's spats, and eventual fight, with Karta, the one the bearer of a liberal rubric, the other of an African nationalist implacability.

On meeting David's Empire Loyalist parents, Daud finds himself negotiating the continuance of British colonialism's assumption of itself as the agency of 'discovery' and/or of 'civilisation', but now displaced into an English suburban, a Canterbury, inflection. His response is to meet these assumptions with the fact and presence of his own 'journey': himself a maker as much as an object of definition, and that, whether of who he himself is, or of Africa, or (in a changed dispensation) of England.

Others add to this gallery of paradox. In the figure of the South African exile, Sam, he calls up a heroism sapped by drink and the impact of a daily toll of death and defeat, the litany one of Sharpeville or the townships, ANC losses or exile. At the hospital he sees in the (Jewish?) orderly, Mr Solomon, the West Indian-born Sister Wilhemena Shelton, and especially the pay-clerk, Mrs Coop, workers both exploited yet somehow willing to

play out a certain exploitation of those 'below' them, vintage
divide-and-rule along class lines.

Nor does he bring to a conflicted England anything but his own
sources of conflict. If outsiderness is pressed upon him in Canterbury, he is also haunted by having broken out of an earlier outsiderness in Africa – the latter tied in equal part to European colonialism
and to its successor African governments. A series of flashbacks
brings back to him the stain of regimes involving his murdered
friend Bossy, detention-camps, pillage and rape, and a genocidal Idi
Amin or ruinous Biafra war also there to pursue him.

He so vacillates between anger at the past and anger at the
present, an inescapable belonging to Africa and England, the wish
to have the best of both and yet the frequent wish to belong to
neither. His eventual beating-up in a local 'plantagenet' cemetery
perfectly underscores this legacy of mutually contesting paradox.
Thomas à Becket's Canterbury again calls up transcendence yet
the meanest everyday, a cathedral city at once 'something huge
and beautiful' and yet 'banal shrine'.

Even as he is set upon to cries of 'nigger spook' and 'wog', he
at the same time derides his white youth-attackers. 'I thank you,
Men of England', he says to this 'flower of England', literally
broken-armed yet full of mock high courtesy. The ambulance-
men, too, add their penny's worth. 'You some kind of royalty?'
one of them asks, a laconic synopsis of the myth and anti-myth of
'jungle' kingship.

A sacrificial Becket, however, Daud is not (at least not the
Daud who vows finally, euphorically, to 'release the bunched
pythons of his coiled psyche on an unsuspecting world'). Yet,
whatever the distance of time and origins between them, he
travels in his predecessor's company, nothing as Gurnah conceives
him if not a latest fellow-pilgrim, a catalyst, in the process
whereby England's Africa has become engaged in the making of
Africa's England – or at least in the emergent, and at its future
possible best, the enhancing dispensation to be shaped from both.

The novel thus casts Daud as a figure of more than usual midway: between the one and the mutual self, between the excluded
and the included. For *Pilgrims Way*, like its predecessor, tells of
overlapping journeys, Daud's Africa-to-England 'life' and the on
going push and pull, the post-colonialisation, of Englishness. This
very ambition in itself offers grounds for attention. But Gurnah's
storytelling, the imagination with which he localises the varying
cultural processes of displacement and adjustment, gives a confirm-
ing weight.

* * *

'Journey' in *Dottie* initially takes the form of a constellation of names:

> Dottie had been christened Dottie Badoura Fatma Balfour. They were names she relished, and she sometimes secretly smiled over them. When she was younger she used to imagine and fabricate around the names, making childish romances and warm tales of painless sacrifice and abundant affection. In her absorption, she sometimes played the games in a soft whisper and was mocked and told off for talking to herself. She persisted in her games despite the ill-tempered correction that was administered for her own good. They told her, those teachers or whoever they were, that all people were the same, and that she would do best to realize that she now lived in England, and she should determine to do what she could do to make herself acceptable. She could do more to help herself to that end than behave in such an obstinate and dreamy way. (pp. 11–12)

The story to follow can be thought a kind of unravelling, a de-encrypting, centred in its heroine, Dottie Balfour, but widening to take in the eclectic play of histories which have gone into the making of all three Balfours, herself, her slightly backward sister, Sophie, and their doomed street-boy brother, Hudson. The upshot is a novel full of event, episodicity, an unwillingness to wrap up or complete all plot-lines.

Reviewers had their doubts about *Dottie*. Did it not offer too unremitting a story of human set-back and affliction, a cast as one said, of the walking wounded?[6] Was Gurnah not over-indulgent in his story's pacing, its willingness to risk inertness or pursue too many minor byways and nooks in the Balfour saga? Why, indeed, no clear, everything-resolved ending?

A counter-view, however, would rightly insist that all of this comes close to missing the point. For even if one in fact acknowledges certain *longueurs*, does not the novel offer itself, in William Styron's still valuable formulation from *The Confessions of Nat Turner*, as 'less an "historical novel" than a meditation on history?'[7] *Dottie* operates accordingly as both event and contemplative pause, at one in pace with its central figure's uncertain rise to consciousness.

In a 'roots' sense the journey-back is indeed into the historicity of Dottie's names: the amalgam which, on her prostitute mother's side, led from the Pathans, through the Punjab, the Sind and the Arabian Gulf, into Cardiff and, under a betrayal of Islamic rules, Bilkisu/Sharon's 'arranged' marriage-rape; and on her likely father's side, from a Syrian–Jamaican line, with the addition, through the paternity of Hudson, of a possible African–American dynasty. Diaspora could not be more eclectically imaged: a human evolution compounded of Asia, Africa, America, Europe, the Antilles, Wales and England, of Islam and Christianity, and, eventually, with the three Balfours fostered out, and then uncertainly united, under Social Services, of the South London of Balham and Brixton and with Victoria and Tooting there to fill out the geography.

But if 'Badoura' calls up the Algerian–Islamic 'Ahoggars' in Dottie's make-up, 'Fatma' a possible daughter-of-the-prophet association, and 'Balfour' a revenge-name taken against the 'Araby' which ruined her mother, Dottie will also insist to Ken Dawes, her English first-lover, 'I am not a foreigner'. For indeed she is not. England, too, has been the making of her, whatever the sexual–racial mix of forebears and origins.

Her factory work, her relationship with the social worker Brenda Holly, her library reading of Jane Austen and Dickens, her witness to the sexual designs on Sophie of the Greek Cypriot landlord Andreas, her friendship with Estella Hogarth (herself an outcome of the French–Jewish diaspora), her house-buying and warm female Caribbean friendships in Brixton and elsewhere even as she negotiates male betrayal – all bespeak 'England', its competing pluses and minuses, perhaps above all its true and false 'parenting' of her and her Balfour siblings.

To this end, the novel weaves a precise trajectory around her: the abuse, prostitution in Carlyle and Leeds, and eventual horrific, poisoned death of her mother in run-down London; the 'care' of the three Balfour offspring – Dottie under her social worker, Sophie at 'special school', and Hudson in Dover; Sophie's young womanhood, relationship with her Jamaican lover-man, Jimmy, his successors, and eventual pregnancy; Hudson's decline into drugs and violence (and New York death in the very river for which he has been named); and Dottie's own passage from manual factory worker to office-skilled secretary.

If, too, Dottie plays custodian to others then that leads to eventual custodianship of her own needs. The point is again given specific form as the figure of the increasingly tyrannical Ghanaian man-about-the-house, Patterson, gives way to Michael Mann, her African–English likely lover and himself embarked upon a dynastic search of his African kinsman, the first-ever black GP, Dr Murray, who by chance and in silence Dottie has encountered in her library visits. The motion, appropriately, is again one of journey, itinerary chance and encounter.

Things, of necessity, 'end' in irresolution. A kind of implicit ongoingness holds Dottie's past which, even when fully excavated, will not explain everything; her present, which even if an improvement in her life, remains provisional. Gurnah's tactic in the novel is to depict Dottie's life as a journey of contributing parts and speeds, neither all victimry nor otherwise, neither all to be accounted for in the diaspora papers stored in her biscuit-tin ('half-made stories that gave their lives substance and significance') nor in the everyday of the London, the England, she has inherited.

The novel's point of arrival does matching duty, closure yet at the same time non-closure, more a kind of intermediary respite. Dottie and Michael look out upon 'The Common', with 'the immense city spread away into the dusk', comparing the journeys, the 'immense cities' indeed, which have brought them to where and what they are. Theirs, suggests the text, is 'a conversation that it would take many attempts to resolve'.

Exactly so. *Dottie* resists the pat ending to good purpose. No one journey's end, Gurnah implies, would ever be likely to resolve the contradictory histories, the human disjuncture, which have been the determinants in Dottie Balfour's life. She has, however, at least become conversant with them on her own terms. Equally, and in another of the novel's phrases, 'the nearby river' of 'Englishness' which Dottie so affectingly embodies requires its own new terms of negotiation – like her own journey never less than always both the one and the many.

* * *

That *Paradise* made the Whitbread as well as the Booker shortlist merely confirms a quite special virtuosity. For the memorability of the journeys it tells, boyhood to adulthood, coast to interior, Islam to animism, the shadow of a prior colonisation replayed in the arriving Germans and British, full of the spirit of ancientness yet set in the early years of the century, lies as much as anything in its telling: to be met in each often dazzling and fabular local effect as in the forward dynamic of Yusuf's story. It has to be Gurnah's most decisive effort to date.

The opening accent of *Paradise* has something of *Memories of Departure* about it, the suggestion of a Koranic or Biblical terrain. Omen, prophecy, even magic, immediately come into the imaginative reckoning:

The boy first. His name was Yusuf, and he left home suddenly during his twelfth year. He remembered it was the season of drought, when every day was the same as the last. Unexpected flowers bloomed and died. Strange insects scuttled from under rocks and writhed to their deaths in the burning light. The sun made distant trees tremble in the air and made the houses shudder and heave for breath. Clouds of dust puffed up at every trampling footfall and a hard-edged stillness lay over the daylight hours. Precise moments like that came back of the season. (p. 1)

Once Yusuf has been indentured out in payment of his father's debts to the merchant-trader *seyyid*, 'Uncle' Aziz, he journeys literally enough: to Aziz's compound at the coast with its 'Paradise' walled garden, hidden wife, and servant-girl Amina, the sister of the factotum Khalil; then to the inland store of Hamid Suleiman and beyond into 'the land of the warriors' in company with the irreverent Punjabi driver, Kalasingh, whose Sikh–Islam banter opens to Yusuf new vistas of piety and apostasy; and, eventually, to the heart-of-darkness kingdom of Chatu as part of Aziz's largest-ever caravan, alongside the harsh *mnyapara*, Mohammed Abdalla, and his orderly Simba Mwene, and where amid skirmish and capture a first tier of European colonialists also make their entrance.

But each of these adventurely, physical journeys also take up the cues of the novel's opening. Yusuf, apprentice *par excellence*, finds himself set to decipher the past lore and diasporas of Islam, the totem and taboo of African tribalism, terrains of desert and jungle which literally carry the impress of the fabulous. Gurnah works his material with a true insider's touch. Languages – Arabic, African, European – fuse into the single account. Private histories, that of Yusuf's father, Aziz's, the Mistress's, Amina's or Khalil's, are revealed to lie oddly both in and just out of view. Africa itself, Islamic Paradise or as Yusuf imagines himself saying to Amina *'the middle of nowhere'*, can be at once history and myth, the actual but also the oblique or fantasied.

For Yusuf, 'beautiful boy', human payment for his father's debt, designated lover in turn to the Chatu-African girl Bati, to Amina, even to the afflicted wife of Aziz, the journeys so constitute his heirship. At one level Mohammed Abdalla spells it out as a kind of Arab-trader predestination:

This is what we're on this earth to do ... To trade. We go to the driest deserts and darkest forests, and care nothing whether we trade with a king or savage, or whether we live or die ... There are no people more clever than traders, no calling more noble. It is what gives us life. (p. 119)

But Yusuf finds himself encountering other possibilities. Will he one day journey railroads beyond where he first sees the European couple and which takes him to Aziz's house? Will he move beyond Ramadan and the angels and *jihns* of Islam to other religious dispensations? Will he, can he, secure Amina for his own or are the duties of kinship with Aziz too forbidding? How, finally, will he come to regard the Islam bound up in Aziz's garden and its exquisite cultivation of fruit and terrace at the hands of the willing slave-gardener Mzee Hamdani – as an image of 'paradise' indeed or as an emblem to mock his own harsh destiny?

For, in a style suitably parabular, Gurnah tells in *Paradise* no one master-story, or again no one master-journey. Rather his is an Africa-novel of truly competing journeys, past into future, Islam into non-Islam, Europe into Africa, Aziz into Yusuf, with each delicately seamed and interwoven across the other. Only in one respect might equivocation be thought not to hold: that of the well-earned right of *Paradise* to prime status in the making of fiction's contemporary canon.

Notes

1. Transcript of 'Book Shelf', BBC Radio 4, November 1992.
2. Ibid.
3. *Memory of Departure* (London: Jonathan Cape, 1987); *Pilgrims Way* (London: Jonathan Cape, 1988); *Dottie* (London: Jonathan Cape, 1990); and *Paradise* (London: Hamish Hamilton, 1994).
4. Maya Jaggi, 'Glimpses of a Paradise Lost', *Guardian*, 24 September 1994.
5. Ibid.
6. *Literary Review*, June 1988.
7. William Styron, *The Confessions of Nat Turner* (London: Jonathan Cape, 1968).

8. Negotiating the Self: Jewish Fiction in Britain Since 1945

Michael Woolf

The British novel since 1945 has been characterised as provincial in its concerns, a parochial art-form that, since the great modernists of the first three decades of this century, has become unambitious and narrow.[1] Whatever the justice of this view, there have always been alternatives, other voices, that have challenged this orthodoxy. In many cases, this notion of provincialism has been countered by the influence of 'other' British writers whose origins are, in part only, British and who bring to their work a broader cultural dimension. In recent years, the work of the Japanese–English novelist, Kazuo Ishiguro and the Chinese, Timothy Mo, have with other ethnic writers moved the British novel beyond the perceived usual range of themes, forms and locations.

The one-time colonies in general have also, inevitably, produced writers with diverse backgrounds and alternative perspectives. The Anglo-Indian novelist Salman Rushdie has created large-scale novels that challenge the formal restraints of the genre. *Midnight's Children*, for example, develops a cacophony of conflicting voices cutting and intercutting across each other as if the author moved randomly among radio channels. *The Satanic Verses* especially signified the degree to which the British novel had moved outside national boundaries and into the world of international conflict itself. Rushdie himself, of course, became ominously embroiled in the religious politics the novel most sought to satirise.

Jewish fiction in Britain is part of this alternative history. The very nature of Jewish experience has placed these novelists in a particular kind of relationship to continental Europe. A history marked by a complex interaction with eastern and central Europe in the Ashkenazy tradition and southern Europe in the Sephardic tradition inevitably shifts the concerns of the writing beyond the limits of Britain. The Jews in Britain have, in many cases, a European consciousness shaped by ambiguity. Europe exists in many forms in these works and it is invented and re-invented throughout.

Two versions of Europe are exemplified in Elaine Feinstein's much underrated *Loving Brecht* (1992).[2] In this novel, Europe exists in one sense as an intellectual and artistic environment with which the novelist can assert a form of historical intimacy. The literary, cultural and intellectual environment of Europe is part of the claimed inheritance of much Jewish writing in a manner that is not emulated by the British and, particularly, the English novel. Another Europe is also, however, part of a Jewish inheritance and that is the decline into savagery and the failure of the rational world that was expressed in the Holocaust. Feinstein characterises that historical time as 'that terrifying human moment when Hitler and his triumphant troops were surveying the world about them with such lordly certainty of power' (p. 158).

In *The Border* (1984),[3] Feinstein creates a version of Henry James's *The Aspern Papers* against the background of Jewish displacement in the war. The locations of this short novel include Sydney, Vienna, Paris and Moscow. It tells of wartime traumas through the experiences of the Wendlers and a fictionalised Walter Benjamin. From Australia Inge Wendler, the surviving wife, recalls a Europe that was both 'a dungeon' (p. 51) and the heart of the intellectual and artistic world.

Both versions of Europe again reverberate in Clive Sinclair's novel *Blood Libels* (1985),[4] a key text in this discussion. His fiction locates itself in relation to Europe as intellectual tradition and, at the same time, to Europe as nightmare:

> Some people are up to their knees in gore ... we're up to our knees in history, which happens to be full of dead Jews. You're right, I'm a vampire, I suck stories from corpses. How else can a Jewish writer join the immortals? (p. 104)

In this kind of formulation, the Jewish writer has a relationship with Europe unlike that of his/her non-Jewish counterpart. This imposes a burden but offers subject-matter and imaginative opportunities of profound significance: a theme huge enough for the times. The relationship of the writer to this theme is somehow a morally obligated one. The Holocaust is a necessary presence in any Jewish view of recent history, whether explicitly or not.

While no great texts of Holocaust witness, along the lines of Primo Levi's work, have been produced in Britain, the experience exists repeatedly as an undercurrent. This is apparent even within the comic and ironic structure of Bernard Kops's novel of 1960s rebellion, *The Dissent of Dominick Shapiro* (1966):

> He had survived the Germans by a miracle; all the Jews of England were lucky, thirty miles of sea had saved them from the gas chambers. The only pounding on the door in the middle of the night was probably a teenage daughter coming home from a party. (p. 84)

The other necessary location is Israel. The relationship between the British–Jewish writer and Israel has rarely been untroubled and, typically, several layers of ambiguity accumulate around the subject. In the first place, the political nation of Israel is inextricably interwoven with the mythic Zion. The existence of Israel also has challenged an archetypal identity: the Jew as victim. While Jewish survival in the face of implacably hostile neighbours has been a cause for celebration, the military successes of Israel have caused simultaneously some moral unease. On the one hand, the situation has created the potential for Jewish writers to identify the Jews as the oppressors in an ironic and terrible inversion of history. The myth of a liberal humanist tradition is challenged by the *realpolitik* of Israel the nation. The myth of Zion, the dreamed world of Messianic significance, also contrasts with the flawed daily reality of a contemporary political environment. In short, the Jewish writer has felt the need in one way or another to address the confrontation between, and coexistence of, myths and realities, and the expression is for the most part ambiguous and uneasy.

There are then locations that pull the British–Jewish novel out of the parochial and, geographically, beyond the islands into various versions of Europe and towards the Middle East. These sites also offer large-scale subjects and themes, broad enough for cosmic tragedy and deep enough for moral comedy. The Jewish writer has been supplied with a field of subjects of greater significance than adultery in Hampstead or gin-drinking in Belgravia.

There is another sense in which the Jewish novelist has a further complexity to confront. For the most part, Britain has offered the Jewish writer a path towards comfort and success. Ralph Glasser's autobiography *Gorbals Boy at Oxford* (1988)[6] is, for example, a record of transformation from poverty to intellectual achievement, from belief to doubt, yet also from the world of the father to a quite different dispensation:

I knew that for him the parting was cataclysmic. He did not see
my going to Oxford ... as a romantic, heroic quest, but prosaically
as doing something 'to better myself'. In attempted stoicism ... he
did try to accept that I must follow my star, as he and others had
done long ago when they had left *der heim* to seek fulfilment in
the melting pot of another culture. For me, as it had been for
him, 'it was written' – *es shtayt geshreeben* – it had to be. He could
not have failed to see in my going a re-enactment, in reverse, of
that day when as a young man he had set out to meet the unknown. He divined, I think more clearly than I did, that I too
would journey to a world light years distant from these my roots,
as he had done from his. (p. 4)

A number of important dynamics emerge out of this situation.
Glasser firstly reminds the reader that the Jewish tradition is one of
movement both in myth, the Wandering Jew, and in historical reality. Few Jews in Britain can claim a very long line of British descent.
The physical mobility is enforced, in a sense, by the kind of social
mobility described by Glasser. For the novelist a consequent sense
of rootlessness can coexist with notions of Britishness in some form
of unresolved tension. British Jews are, by definition, citizens of
place and no-place, Britain and nowhere/everywhere.
Furthermore, Glasser's autobiography recalls a process of
secularisation that is highly important in British–Jewish culture.
Loss of faith raises more than questions of spiritual identity. It
signifies a basic challenge to the nature of Judaism. To discard
religion cannot simply lead to discarding an identity that asserts a
symbolic empathy with Jews as victims. Such moral continuity
cannot easily be sloughed off in response to contemporary
secularisation. The loss of belief inevitably, too, involves some
alienation from father and son, from past and present, from
Hebrew and Yiddish to English; all that cannot but be seen as
some kind of painful betrayal:

As a child I had learned to read and write Hebrew and Yiddish
fluently; now the knowledge was fading fast. soon it would be
irrevocable. There indeed was a reminder, like a wind from the
icy mountains, of how far I had fled. I was destroying all signs
of the way I had come! How many more fierce ironies were in
store? (p. 46)

The comment focuses a major question that reverberates
through the fiction, and that is how can a moral person cast off a
sense of historical continuity with persecuted Jews? Furthermore,

what can it mean, in that context, to be a Jew without religious belief? Within these 'fierce ironies', the Jewish novel in Britain has been formed.

The question of material improvement and upward mobility is also found in Emanuel Litvinoff's *Journey Through a Small Planet* (1972)[7] which records a world of poverty in London's East End that is, for the Jews of today, only memory (often clouded by nostalgia). What these narratives, and others like them including Bernard Kops's *The World is a Wedding* (1963), signify is that relative material and intellectual success is not an untroubled process. It contains within some sense of contradiction, even betrayal, of a mythic form of Jewish identity. Thus, in Kops's *The Dissent of Dominick Shapiro*, the young protagonist's comic rebellion gains momentum and form when he puts on the shabby fur coat of his Russian grandfather. Only in asserting some kind of historical continuity (in symbolic terms) can there be some reaffirmation of Jewish values. That these are now located only in symbol and myth is part of the predicament of the rootless and unfocused contemporary Jew.

Litvinoff defines precisely the fact that the past (be it the Gorbals or the Jewish East End) exists now as a memory belonging to history (or to fiction or community myth) rather than actuality:

> Until I was sixteen I lived in the East London borough of Bethnal Green, in a small street that is now just a name on the map. Almost every house in it has gone and it exists, if at all, only in the pages of this book. (p. 9)

Revisiting these roots is a profoundly painful matter: 'I felt indescribably bereaved, a ghost haunting the irrecoverable past' (p. 11). Present meets the past in uneasy ways. Comfort and security in the present, for example, contradict historical marginality and suffering in the past. In some degree, material success correlates to an uneasy sense of moral failure.

Recurrently, the tension between present and past is framed within the context of conflict between father and son. Secularised fathers are weakened without the authority invested in religious function and belief. They are rendered powerless in the secular present, as Dominick Shapiro recognises: 'I needed a Moses. A god of wrath to accept or reject. All I got was a jellyfish for a father' (p. 143).

Beyond the comedy of emasculated fathers, there exists a core of pain deriving, at least in some respects, from a sense of lost faith expressed as a kind of nostalgia for spiritual certainty:

If only he had given Dominick and the others something really tangible to believe in. Could he be blamed if that intangible substance called faith had never descended upon him? How could you pass on something you never had? Yet why was he torturing himself? What was this thing called faith, suddenly? Why was it nagging at him tonight of all nights? Wasn't a good home and good food and good education enough? Did he have to feel ashamed for giving his children the real basic essentials? Yet still there was something lacking. Something wasn't exactly perfect. You couldn't buy faith; that was lacking. If you could buy faith the house of Lew Shapiro would be stacked up to the ceiling with it. (pp. 64–5)

The relationship between father and son here reflects the conjunction of two processes: upward social mobility with secularisation. The price of prosperity is, in this context, a spiritual vacuum that cannot be filled by any of the prizes available in the materialistic present. The past exists only in the grandfather's coat around which the historical and religious past symbolically adheres: 'It belonged there in the dark with all the ghosts and the dreams of the past. It lived, it had a life of its own. How could he leave it in the gutter of the Finchley Road' (p. 165).

These concerns are not, of course, to be found in any homogenised form in the work of writers as diverse as Elaine Feinstein, Bernice Rubens, Clive Sinclair, Howard Jacobson, Bernard Kops or their contemporaries. Neither are they, necessarily, treated in all the various works. But they are present in an identity that has to be negotiated and defined in relation to those other factors, Englishness, Britishness, the feminine, the masculine and so on, that constitute the self. The Jewish writer is *not* particularly different, in this sense, from any other writer except in that the fate of the Jews has been exceptionally contradictory and has led to a fiction which seeks, in the profoundest sense, to reconcile the irreconcilable. The Jewish writer in Britain is thus called upon to draw from a rich vein of paradox and ambiguity out of which a field of meaning can be constructed in the fiction.

* * *

No other single body of work more exemplifies this kind of ambiguity, and the richness of its potential, than that created by Clive Sinclair. His writing has brought together a playfulness reminiscent of post-modernist writing in the USA with a mordant wit that draws also upon a close intimacy with Europe and its traditions. Like other writers in the post-modernist environment, Sinclair has employed the fable as a means of exploring contemporary reality in a profoundly serious manner. Laughter is, often, at the edge of the precipice.

Blood Libels is perhaps the most powerful expression of Sinclair's complex fiction. It is on one level an alternative history of Britain, a fable of the landscapes of danger in which assumptions of suburban security are shown to be largely illusory. Beneath the calm surfaces of contemporary life there exist forces of menace and danger framed by European history. The significance of Sinclair's history is that, as in Kops's view, British–Jewish communities are only marginally outside the whirlwind of recent history and safe, only, through accidents of geography. Smugness and self-satisfaction are an affront to that reality.

Sinclair's work takes a contrary line in another respect; it is willing to question many Jewish community values, a pressure, as he sees it, which works against originality and independence. The writer, exemplifying alternative sets of values, is subject to familial and community pressure to conform and to act in accordance with powerful pressures. This has long been true for Clive Sinclair (frequently attacked in the mainstream Jewish press) and for his protagonist, the author of *Rabbi Nathan's Folly* in *Blood Libels*:

'Are you satisfied?' asked my mother, pointing to an empty bottle of Valium, beside which was cast the offending manuscript, like a suicide note. 'Why don't you write something nice about the Jews,' she said, 'instead of *dreck* like this?' (p. 43)

As in Kops's *The Dissent of Dominick Shapiro*, the protagonists exist in a state of anxious tension with the Jews of suburbia, both part and yet apart. In essence what they struggle against are the forces of suburban conformity and the smugness of prosperity.

Sinclair's comic vision shifts contemporary reality just enough to reveal an ironic history in which Israeli Jews form death squads and, in North London, the Jews of suburbia are victims of a Nazi pogrom:

On the fourth morning I awake to a new world. Astral-tripping and ethereal whispering reveal that Golders Green and Hendon have been set alight by Gascoyne's antisemitic storm troopers: forty Jews have been murdered, another five hundred injured. Ten synagogues have been destroyed as well as two hundred houses. From Golders Green and Hendon the disturbances spread north, south, east and west, nor are they yet at an end. (pp. 186–7)

In this radically original novel, Sinclair translates anxieties and insecurities into historical realities, creating his own objective correlative for community neuroses. His fantasy thus brings the Jews of Britain into the mainstream of European Jewish experience:

No doubt in years to come, when historians begin to write objectively about the destruction of Anglo-Jewry they will delineate the 'remote origins' and 'immediate causes' without ever mentioning the events I have outlined in these pages. (p. 188)

Sinclair's creative imagination here owes perhaps more to Kafka than to any English tradition. It is certainly, at least, informed by the bleak wit of middle-European fiction. The significant places of his work include the Jewish suburbs of North London to which the impoverished Jews of Litvinoff's East End went when they could afford to move upwards from an inner city to suburban life. Two stories in the collection *Hearts of Gold*, 'The Promised Land' and 'A Moment of Happiness', however, reveal yet other significant places of Sinclair's imagination.

'The Promised Land' is a comedy of sexual failure set in Israel where what is 'promised' and not delivered is both carnal bliss and spiritual security. In an episode that draws upon Philip Roth's portrayal of Portnoy's erotic and spiritual bewilderment in Israel in *Portnoy's Complaint*, Sinclair translates the ambiguous relationship of the British Jew into a comic sexual and spiritual debacle:

I want to believe in miracles, in love-on-earth and life-after-death, but I turn all abstractions into flesh and stone. To tell you the truth, I want to fuck Israel. Okay, so Ahab was obsessed with Moby Dick; well, my Promised Land is only an Israeli cunt! (p. 29)[8]

Thus Israel belongs not in some earnest Zionist perspective but in the bathos of sexual disappointment. What the narrator's defeat reveals is the fact that Israel is an alien location for the diaspora Jew and that visions of a 'promised land' are bound to fail when the myth meets the flawed reality. For all that, the subject of Israel remains crucial; it is worried over, explored, re-explored, searched for meaning. The Jewish writer is required, in one way or another, to interpret this place which is both country and idea, state and dream.

The other key location is found in 'A Moment of Happiness'. It is, of course, Europe, and specifically in this story Czechoslovakia, a Europe of Kafka, of holocaust, of inexplicable violence and official repression. Here as elsewhere, Europe takes on a plural force, to be expressed in many forms as history, as intellectual tradition, as literature, fable or fantasy. For Sinclair, as for Elaine Feinstein, the cultural tradition that shapes the writing is as much central European as it is British.

Another source for Sinclair's imagination is America and particularly its contemporary literature. The influence of Philip Roth is both clear (as in 'The Promised Land') and playfully, obliquely recognised in the story 'The Luftmensch': 'What is Joshua Smolinsky, private eye, doing in Philip Roth's former room at a colony for writers? In New England, no less' (p. 51).[9]

What Sinclair's work signifies is that much British Jewish writing has existence only partly within an English or British tradition and, indeed, is only partly concerned with issues relating to these landscapes. The sources at work are national *and* international. Indeed, movement of location is symptomatic in Sinclair's work. Little, including meaning, stays still. Characters shift from place to place, precisely contemporary in their perpetual, restless, rootless motion. History itself shifts its meanings and remakes its events. Figures move, like Strindberg in *Augustus Rex* (1992), even from death back into life. The fiction becomes open in significance, transgressing, mocking boundaries. All of this is indeed a metaphor of the experience of Jews (and their intimacy with paradox) and, even beyond that, of all modern humanity. The self itself loses solidity and has to be defined by negotiation across nations, across myths, across history. The self seeks a form, a character, that can truly contain multiplicity.

The refugee in this century has emerged as the archetypal modern figure and Jewish experience has especially brought myth and history together. The Wandering Jew of Christian myth becomes the refugee from Nazi Europe. This is the subject-matter of Elaine Feinstein's *The Border* (1984). Karen Gershon's autobiographical novel *The Bread of Exile* (1985)[10] also explores this theme and describes the experience of a young girl, Inge, and her brother forced into exile in England to escape the Nazi menace in Germany. The England they come to is not so much hostile as profoundly alien. An English official's view is enforced by the experiences described in the novel: '"Don't kid yourself," the girl with the form said, "that you'll ever be anything but a foreigner to the English." They did not believe her' (p. 22).

Inge's separation from England and Englishness at first is only linguistic but is gradually revealed to be also profoundly cultural. The children are seen as strangers in a strange land without a sustaining point of contact. The condition of being a refugee thus becomes not so much a predicament but a defining characteristic so that an accident occurs to Inge because of 'her refugee clumsiness' (p. 94) and 'Being refugees, they were both discovering, was turning them into liars' (p. 29).

Inge Wendler's grandson in *The Border* sees his refugee grandmother in Australia as alien by association. She carries Europe within her:

> The boy marvelled at the way she had enclosed herself in a piece of Central Europe, as if she had conjured the walnut chest, inlaid tables, and curving velvet button-back chairs into place; or perhaps transported them with infinite care, to be reassembled in Australia, like the wooden house of the first Governor General in Melbourne. When she put a porcelain plate before him, with a plain yellow cake upon it, the aroma of nutmeg and cinnamon rose to his memory as if he had spent his own childhood in Vienna or Budapest. Which he had not. (p. 11)

Thus, she is more than of European origin. She physically contains and expresses a heritage that the young man shares without having experienced.

In this context, the figure of the refugee becomes central in that it reflects Jewish displacement and suffering and expresses a heritage that cannot be discarded or assimilated. The past is a painful burden that the writer inevitably carries into the present, into the future.

* * *

Gershon's subject is, like Feinstein's in *Loving Brecht* and *The Border*, shaped by great movements of European history. Both offer Jewish protagonists whose destiny has been made into tragedy by forces hostile to them and outside of them. The Jewish writer in Britain has also made material out of tension between the individual and those other pressures outside of themselves, frequently family or community, that restrain them. In this sense, the notion of constraint by forces outside of personal control has been given a domestic form more appropriate, frequently, to comic modes. Bernard Kops used youthful dissent from family and community as the subject for comedy in *The Dissent of Dominick Shapiro*. In *Settle Down Simon Katz* (1973),[11] Kops revisited the subject but through a protagonist at the opposite end of the age spectrum. Simon Katz is an elderly con-man and general reprobate who exploits the stereotypes of Jewish familial and community values to earn his dubious income. He is also used in a comic form to invert the traditional form of revolt. In this context, it is the dissenting father who confronts and upsets the conventional notions of the son. The despairing cry of the son 'Dad, just be quiet and behave yourself' (p. 74) runs like a tortured refrain through the novel.

Simon Katz refuses, like Dominick Shapiro, to belong to a community whose values are shaped by suburban conformity. In a court appearance, watched over by his anguished and shamed son, Simon articulates the view that shapes the comic structure of the novel:

> Today, Your Honour, it is the teenage this and the teenage that. It is the age of the angry young man. Well what about the angry old man? To hell with the teenage revolt. What about the old-age revolt? (p. 76)

That this is a cynical position designed to enrage his suffering son, does not diminish the impact of Kops's protagonist. At every stage, Simon is an affront to the Jews of suburbia, to the conformist and middle-class signified geographically by the suburb of Wembley Park and by the coded phrase 'settle down'.

Simon continues to live in the East End of London, no longer a Jewish area, and Kops uses the location in contrast to Wembley Park to signify separate spectrums of social and community values. The East End belongs to a past which, in this novel's myth, was grander, wilder and unrestrained by respectability:

> The Jews had moved away forever. But the ghosts were still clinging to the roofs of tenements; tenements that were no longer there. Faces stared, pressed against panes of glass from windows shattered and pulverised to dust ages ago. Faces from the past smiling, crying, calling. All without sounds. Faces merging together; faces flying out of time from between the never-ending wars of bombs, poverty and affluence. Gone faces. Faces belonging to people who were gone into the ground, or into Golders Green, Finchley, or Wembley Park, or Jerusalem.
>
> Simon laughed out loud but it didn't matter. In the East End, people were used to people. And people were very strange creatures. No one would take any notice. He would sooner settle in Jerusalem than Wembley Park, and he would never go to Jerusalem.
>
> Alan, his terrible son, lived at Wembley Park, with his terrible wife. (p. 14)

Bernard Kops's use of irony is pervasive and it encompasses both the conventional figures and the moral outlaws presented in the figures of Dominick Shapiro and Simon Katz. They undermine the stereotypical notion of Jewish 'family' and replace cohesiveness by division, responsibility and order by irresponsibility and chaos.

The family is, in many respects, an inevitable subject for the Jewish writer not least because so many moral values and ethical structures are presumed to adhere to it. In two of her novels, separated by almost a decade, Bernice Rubens explores 'family' from distinct perspectives but through a perception at least as irreverent as that of Bernard Kops.

Set on Edge (1960)[12] offers a family chronicle of grotesques dominated by a mother figure as monstrous and pervasive as any found in Philip Roth:

> Mrs Sperber always wanted to feel that her family wished her death, but she regarded herself, and so did they, as the survivor. She could envisage her reaction to a world from which any of her family or her friends were absent, but her own death was to her a ridiculous impossibility. (p. 48)

She exhibits many of the characteristics of the stereotypical figure, particularly a dramatic capacity for public suffering which parodies and devalues real suffering, as in this exchange with her daughter:

> 'Take the house, if that's what you're after, throw me into the street, let me go out and beg. Let them all see what you really think of your mother. Take the clothes off my back,' she added as an afterthought. Mrs Sperber had a real talent for organizing her own martyrdom. (p. 197)

The creation of this figure, recurrent in Jewish writing of the diaspora, reflects a comic transformation through which the family becomes, instead of the refuge of Jewish convention, a battleground of greater intensity. The notion of family as the centre of Jewish social and emotional stability is denied by hyperbole. In addition, the emergence of the mother as monster reflects an exaggerated distortion of a real transformation of Jewish life in the diaspora. The traditional structure of the religious family placed the father at the centre because of value given to his religious authority. Patriarchal power was once a consequence of spiritual function. With the process of secularisation, that authority in effect diminished to vanishing point and the vacuum was filled by the powerful figure of the emerging mother assuming domestic control. Out of that transformation, the stuff of comedy (and pain) has been made.

The comedy in Jewish writing is rarely light and simple. It assumes a bleakness that, at times, shifts between laughter and despair. *Set on Edge* is, in many respects, a dark portrait of isolation and alienation. This is enhanced by a small-town setting used to create a life of narrowed horizons and limited options. The location could be Rubens' native Wales or any other small town but it is, in any case, presented as featureless, a landscape offering no possibility of diversion. Thus, by the end of the novel, the daughter's horizon has narrowed further towards only a sense of loss, a few inanimate objects and a lonely communion with the unresponsive dead:

> The house was empty now, and Gladys alone, as she had so often wished. And the tea was there and the clock and the crumbs on the table: the wall of certificates, the dining room table and the three dolls on the sofa. It was all there. And every night she would sit on her mother's bed and curse her for not being in it, and every week for the rest of her life she visited the cemetery and built a pyramid of pebbles on her mother's grave. (p. 222)

Rubens' vision combines lacerating loneliness with a fine eye for comedy and a capacity to create forms reminiscent of the paintings of Francis Bacon and Lucien Freud: 'Her body was like a filleted kipper that had been oversmoked and dried. Her stomach hung like an unpressed curtain reaching down to her thighs on which the strains of her child-bearing were chalked up in mother-of-pearl' (pp. 218–19). The similes create a figure both recognisably elderly and female but also grotesquely distorted. This is a harsh and dark comic vision.

Set on Edge is, predominantly, focused on mother–daughter relationships. The primary focus in *The Elected Member* (1969)[13] is on father–son and father–daughter relationships and here the tone is consistently serious, the subject one of unremitting despair. The father, Rabbi Zweig, is a first-generation immigrant whose talented son is driven to mental breakdown and lunacy through drug addiction. On one level at least the subject of the novel is the terrible agony of family love. Love is, in these circumstances, a source of anguish and pain. Bella's love for her brother began in incest and exists in his insanity as a disabling anguish: 'Her mother was dead; she owed no more to that quarter, and Norman, well, he was away, and this love of hers for him, it had to stop, it had to stop, it was crippling both of them' (p. 85). Love is repeatedly associated with anxiety, sorrow, anguished imperatives.

The Rabbi is, in many respects, victimised by modernity, traumatised by the present:

> In his state of sadness and anxiety, it was imperative to escape into his past, for his present was unbearable. He gripped the rails tightly. He had to hang on to them until the cold steel was real under his hands. And when he felt it, cold and undeniable in his grip, he was safely wrapped in his twenty-three years, almost fifty years ago, in sight of a new and frightening land. (p. 44)

For all the uncertainty of the immigrant experience, the Rabbi then inhabited a known world. In the environment of the novel, he is assaulted by circumstances which are mysterious and menacing. The known world shatters into the chaotic shapes of madness and loss. Simultaneously he recognises a loss of religious authority and a creeping secularisation that threatens Judaism itself:

> For forty years he had served in that synagogue, first as a pupil Rabbi, then as a fully-fledged teacher and minister, and then later on, as the congregation fell off, doubling as a cantor. The Hebrew class was now only a trickle of children, and who knew who and where they would marry? (p. 48)

In this version of Jewish existence, the Rabbi is menaced by a world that he can no longer understand and, in a broader sense, by a Jewish community dwindling, through intermarriage and secularisation, towards vanishing point.

Rubens and Kops dissent from a comforting or conventional view of the family and reveal, in various forms, family life that is far indeed from a secure oasis in a menacing world. It is, itself, an expression of the relationship that the Jewish writer has with modern Britain. While Britain has undeniably offered relative safety and freedom from persecution, it has also destabilised traditional faith and traditional community cohesion. Out of that uneasy interaction, Kops and Rubens have created dissenting versions of the family where the marked characteristics are separation and, at root, anguish.

* * *

It is frequent in discussion of this kind to describe the fate of Jews in terms of pain and alienation. There exists, however, another version of the contemporary fate of the Jews in Britain in which that fate is shaped by absurdity. To be a Jew in this version, exemplified in Jacobson's *Coming From Behind* (1983),[14] is a comic fate, an absurd condition over which the protagonist–schlemiel has no control. Sefton Goldberg offers himself as an embodiment of a Jew, an archetypal figure defined by his discomfort with both self and environment:

> How could they know ... that Sefton had never in his life, not even in his dreams, been physically comfortable; had never been certain, from one moment to the next, that any particular part of his body was going to function? And for this reason had never once – not even *once* – turned a somersault! (p. 176)

Jacobson's novel offers a Jewish version of the campus novel in which Judaism is defined through a series of associations which combine to make the Jew alien from a Britain conceived of as both rural and athletic. Thus, 'being Jewish he was as uninformed about beer as he was about flowers and birds' (pp. 129–30). The Jew, in this equation, is thus remorselessly urban and lacking in the spirit of male camaraderie located in rituals associated with the English pub. The nature of Judaism inevitably, in these comic collocations, enforces an unease with the world at large and, for the protagonist in particular, with the world he is forced to endure in the bleak Midlands polytechnic in which he teaches.

As Lenny Bruce did in his comic routines, Jacobson creates a world divided between what is Jewish and what is gentile and the two areas are profoundly separate from each other:

> In the highly improbable event of his being asked to nominate the most un-Jewish thing he could think of, Sefton Goldberg would have been hard pressed to decide between Nature – that's to say birds, trees, flowers, and country walks – and football – that's to say beer, bikies, mud and physical pain. (p. 58)

The character's general sense of unease is heightened by the environment in which he finds himself. The fictional town of Wrottesley is characterised as cultureless, mean-spirited, and inhospitable. 'The wrung out despondency of Wrottesley' (p. 13) frames Goldberg's sense of discomfort. His condition is precisely indicated: 'Backward and short-sighted as well as Jewish and a failure, Sefton Goldberg peered into the gloom' (p. 138).

Goldberg's condition is presented not as simply a personal one but as a defining characteristic of what is Jewish. This comic fate is without religious or spiritual dimension and is defined only negatively. The novel offers in essence a version of the Jewish condition at the end of a spectrum of representation. The tragic fate, envisaged by Gershon for example, becomes in Jacobson a comic condition. Between and among the possibilities of representation encompassed here, with Gershon and Jacobson representing the extremities, the Jewish writer in Britain has invented versions of the self and the community which contains it. Jacobson's character is an amalgamation of stereotypes that combine to create a lurid portrait of the Jew which exploits anti-semitic stereotypes and through comedy subverts and transforms them into laughter. In an ending reminiscent of Amis's *Lucky Jim*, Goldberg despite his sweaty discomfort wins some version of the glittering prize with a job at a Cambridge college that is uncompromisingly Christian. Jacobson, thus, allows his character a life-affirming revenge on both Church and Establishment.

* * *

Inevitably in the secular world, the conventional notions of what constitutes Judaism will be subject to revision and fragmentation. No single version of Judaism can emerge out of the radical reformation of Jewish experience in modern history and in the relatively prosperous communities of Britain. This argument has of necessity therefore considered a multiplicity of forms and it is clear that Judaism has become a matter of re-invention, not a known or given form but another fictional construction to be negotiated and developed in relation to the various notions of Britain that are similarly a matter for invention. In this respect, it is another of the fictional elements that, like plot or character, have to be made and located in the structure of the novel.

From high tragedy to absurd comedy, Jewish writers in Britain have had to invent the Jewish self. The Britain that contains and shapes that self is at times alien and at times refuge, and at times both. The Jewish writer in Britain, thus, reflects and partakes of the troublesome uncertainties of contemporary experience.

Notes

1. This subject has inevitably a number of problematic terms related to it. The precise nature of Englishness as against Britishness and the relationship of those to the European, and the United Kingdom,

could be, and has been, the subject of many a wearisome thesis. For the purposes of this essay Britishness is to be seen as being part of the cosmopolitan world contained within the islands of the United Kingdom. Jewish writers, as this essay will demonstrate, are found more often geographically in England rather than Scotland or Wales but they are, by nature of their cosmopolitan sympathies, more British, more European, more citizens of everywhere and nowhere than the English novelist. Within such terminological inexactitude the author aims to formulate a discussion that recognises the problems of terminology without getting too depressed about them.

The view of the British novel as 'small in ambition' has become something of a critical orthodoxy. It was expressed succinctly, for example, by Gilbert Phelps in 'The Novel Today' in *The Pelican Guide to English Literature 7: The Modern Age*: 'The trend of the English novel since the war has, on the whole, been analogous to that of the poetry of the period – a turning aside from the mainstream of European literature, and a tendency to retreat into parochialism' (London: Penguin, 1969), p. 475.

Although he dissents from the view, Malcolm Bradbury summarises the orthodoxy that contrasts unfavourably the English novel with the American on similar grounds: 'It is the English novel only that bears the marks of exhaustion, of provincialism, of "reaction against experiment", a reversion to an outworn materiality or a traditional realism in a time of significant generic evolution. By contrast, in the United States the spirit of modern experiment in fiction survives, large aspiration persists, vigour of invention, plenitude of technique, and spirited aesthetic curiosity sustain the species as an art form.' From *Possibilities: Essays on the State of the Novel* (London: Oxford University Press, 1973), p. 167.

2. Elaine Feinstein, *Loving Brecht* (1992; London: Sceptre Books, 1993).
3. Elaine Feinstein, *The Border* (London: Hutchinson, 1984).
4. Clive Sinclair, *Blood Libels* (1984; London: Picador, 1986).
5. Bernard Kops, *The Dissent of Dominick Shapiro* (1966; London: Mayflower, 1969).
6. Ralph Glasser, *Gorbals Boy at Oxford* (London: Chatto and Windus, 1988).
7. Emanuel Litvinoff, *Journey Through a Small Planet* (1972; London: Robin Clark, 1993).
8. Clive Sinclair, 'The Promised Land' in *Hearts of Gold* (London: Allison and Busby, 1979).
9. Clive Sinclair, 'The Luftmensch' in *Hearts of Gold*. Sinclair's interest in Philip Roth's writing is also revealed in his contribution to A. Milbauer and D. Watson (eds), *Reading Philip Roth* (London: Mac-

millan, 1988), pp. 168–79. His essay, 'The Son is Father to the Man' discusses Roth's Zuckerman novels.

10. Karen Gershon, *Bread of Exile* (London: Victor Gollancz, 1985).
11. Bernard Kops, *Settle Down Simon Katz* (1973; London: New English Library, 1977).
12. Bernice Rubens, *Set on Edge* (1960; London: Abacus, 1991).
13. Bernice Rubens, *The Elected Member* (1969; London: Penguin, 1971).
14. Howard Jacobson, *Coming From Behind* (1983; London: Penguin, 1993).

9. 'Lancelot's Position': The Fiction of Irish-Britain

Eamonn Hughes

There is a semantic difficulty with the concept of Irish-Britain which derives from the history of the two places. The entity 'Britain' is by definition something which for all or part of its history has contained all or part of Ireland, as it contains England, Scotland and Wales; in consequence the relationship between Ireland and Britain is unlike other post-colonial relationships in that Ireland can be seen as a metropolitan colony:

> In the supposed age of the nation-state, from the end of the sixteenth century, Ireland was undergoing a process of conquest and colonization – which meant being technically subsumed into the theoretical borders of the British state, at a time when that state itself was in the process of formation and definition. This interaction made for a development different from that of other colonies ... this, after the great conflicts and dispossessions of the seventeenth century, made Ireland's position, as a kind of metropolitan colony, unique.[1]

In addition, there are also a number of people for whom the rather odd term Irish-Britain, if they allowed that it had any meaning at all, could only mean Northern Ireland. However, for present purposes I shall stand by the full constitutional title of the state (the United Kingdom of Great Britain and Northern Ireland) and take as my subject the relationship of Irish writers to that elastic structure 'Britain' with its inclusions and exclusions.[2] Even allowing for this there are certain difficulties when considering the phrase Irish-Britain, not least the sense that it must be either tautologous or oxymoronic. We can refer to Black-British or Asian-British writers and have a sense of what we mean; referring to

142

Irish-British writers is a more awkward affair. Because writers whose background is Asian or Afro-Caribbean appear to be less easily assimilable – due to factors such as race, social and kinship structures, language and culture and because they come from countries with a more conventionally colonial history – than writers whose background is Irish, there is a sense to using a hyphenated phrase which indicates the merging and/or yoking together of different social and cultural experiences in those cases. In the Irish case, merging seems, on the one hand, to be too weak a word – Irish society and culture have contributed for so long to the British sociocultural entity as to be a constitutive part of it (and vice versa) – and, on the other hand, is far too strong a word in suggesting that social and cultural experiences which have for so long been defined on both sides as irreconcilable could ever be brought together in any fruitful way.

In the relationship between Ireland and Britain these and other factors have led to a sense that 'Irish-Britain' is not and may never be a satisfactory label in the way that 'Black-British' or 'Asian-British' are, even if only for pragmatic reasons. The most uncomplicated of these other factors is geography. The geographical proximity of Ireland and Britain has made the dream of return, common to all migrant groups, appear to be more plausible for the Irish than for other migrant groups. As Liam Ryan puts it: 'The ability to delude oneself that emigration was temporary has been one of the most powerful features of Irish migration to Britain among all classes.'[3] Despite its apparent plausibility, however, return (in the sense of permanent return to one's homeland) is no greater among the Irish than among other groups but the dream does have the effect of making the establishment of an Irish-British identity seem less necessary than is the case for other migrant groups, who despite their own dream of return, are forced by distance from their homeland to recognise the dream for what it is.[4] This perhaps explains the comparative absence of a fiction about Irish-Britain in the sense of a located and, at some level, stable and secure, community which sees itself as Irish-British and which requires cultural articulation.

There is no equivalent to, say, George V. Higgins whose novels are securely rooted in an Irish-American setting. This is true even when they deal with Irish matters; in *The Patriot Game*,[5] for example, the hero, Pete Riordan, an FBI agent, has little difficulty in upholding American values which he and most other Irish-Americans in the novel endorse even though this requires that he oppose a form of Irish nationalism.[6] In this case a new, composite identity overrides the originary identity. The novels considered in this essay accordingly tend to be concerned with individual figures for whom either Ireland itself or the state of Britain and the British, rather than a recognisable Irish-British community, is the point of reference.

To understand the nature of contemporary writing about Irish-Britain we need to pay some attention to the nature and history of Irish emigration. We need, that is to say, to understand something of its causes and historical changes before we can locate contemporary writing within its context. The first puzzle that this will allow us to address is the comparative absence of an Irish-British writing – a writing founded on a stable, composite identity, a writing we would expect to find in abundance given the history and scale of Irish migration to Britain.

The phenomenon of Irish emigration is, despite its long history and wide scale, still somewhat under-researched. Although there have recently been a number of works which have focused on the various aspects of Irish migration[7] and although synoptic Irish histories now include reference to it[8] it has for a long time been a source of such shame for the Irish at home that it has not received the kind of attention it deserves. There are therefore certain stereotypes with which one has to deal before considering the cultural manifestations of recent migrations.

The Irish emigrant is usually seen as Catholic, male, illiterate or poorly-educated, and working in unskilled or labouring jobs; I have just described the archetypal or stereotypical navvy. But even in the late nineteenth century, as Colin Holmes has shown, the range of employment for the Irish in Britain was wide: women worked in textiles and domestic service while men were government employees, post office workers, police, soldiers, doctors, lawyers, rural labourers and harvesters.[9] There are, additionally, other features of Irish emigration which we need to recognise. Many Protestants have emigrated (folk parks around Northern Ireland make play of the fact that numerous American presidents are of Ulster–Scots Protestant descent), and Irish emigration is unusual in that, at most times, at least half of emigrants have been female and they in turn have usually been better educated than their male counterparts.[10] (In the twentieth century the Irish nurse while being almost as stereotypical as the Irish navvy is at least useful in indicating the different educational levels of male and female emigrants.) If migrants accorded to the stereotype then we might expect that their educational levels and economic circumstances militated against concerted cultural expression, but, as the evidence shows, this is not the case.

Furthermore, while over the last two centuries politicians, journalists and writers may not have had numerical significance on emigration they have had at least as great a socio-cultural impact as the more numerous navvies.[11] This last socio-economic category, indeed, seems in the last decade or so to have overtaken the more typical migrant as the emigration of the 1980s is widely acknowledged to have been of a different order from that of the 1950s (the last decade of high emigration from Ireland on a scale which finally gave rise to concern at official levels in Ireland itself about the rate of migration). Data for the emigration of the 1980s are still scarce but the nature of that emigration may perhaps be partially judged by a 1980s acronym (perhaps the major manufacture of the Lawson-boom); alongside the yuppies, dinks and buppies of the 1980s, then, we find the nippils (New Irish Professional People in London), denoting a wave of highly educated young emigrants from Ireland, both North and South, working in banking, finance, computing and the service industries which displaced manufacturing in the south-east of England in the 1980s. It is this last category of emigrant which has given rise to a sense of Irish emigration as being part of a post-modern toing and froing which accords with the post-national and post-colonial nature of the modern world.[12] 'But this post-sixties model of cultural migration differs from the inherited patterns of Irish migration in that it affirms the option, or at least the possibility, of return.'[13] It would seem then that the Irish-British have had every opportunity for cultural expression and yet remain, in comparison to more recent migrant groups, culturally reticent. As Joseph O'Connor puts it:

> Emigration is as Irish as Cathleen Ní Houlihan's harp, yet it is only since the sixties and the generation of Edna O'Brien that Irish writers have written about the subject at first hand ... At the heart of the Irish emigrant experience there is a caution, a refusal to speak, a fear of the word.[14]

We need then to consider two things. First, the motivations of migrants and then the nature of literary relationships between Ireland and Britain, to see if these can explain this cultural reticence.

Despite the recent work on emigration, the motivations of the migrant remain a matter of debate between those who advocate a 'push' model (in which migrants are forced out) and those who advocate a 'pull' model (in which migrants are attracted by possibilities elsewhere). Joseph Lee places the blame for post-independence emigration firmly with the policy-makers and consequently locates motive firmly in the economic sphere:

Many in Ireland had long persuaded themselves that emigration was normal, and adjusted without undue discomfort to the emigrant wave of the fifties. *The Leader* observed that many politicians were privately more relieved than disturbed by the post-war emigration because 'If emigration were to be stopped tomorrow conditions favourable to social revolution might easily arise' ... The blame lay accordingly with the emigrants themselves, not with the society they left ... The response arose from the need felt by many in [the farming, business, bureaucratic and professional] classes to explain emigration in a manner that exonerated them from responsibility. Emigration was not unique to Ireland. But the type of emigration, the scale of emigration, and the impact of emigration were. In no other European country was emigration so essential a prerequisite for the preservation of the nature of society.[15]

Instructive though it is to have a withering, even excoriating, attack such as this from an authoritative figure and although the attitudes he attacks are still to be found among politicians,[16] it must be said that the motives behind emigration can be seen to be more various than the merely economic. Even such an apparently documentary work as Patrick MacGill's *Children of the Dead End*,[17] with its harrowing descriptions of near slavery among the Irish (and others) in Britain, can be read not only as an account of a life lived in response to a direct economic imperative, but also as a quest narrative in which the central figure's dissatisfactions and desires can be seen as extending beyond the bounds of the very real economic determinants which drive him from home and country. In a contemporary setting the same mixture of responses – economic need and a sense of adventure – are present in, for example, Gerry Conlon's account of his response to England:

People where I came from don't think too much about the English, but England is another matter. England is where the wealth is. England is where you have to go to get a job. London's a place where you can have the crack ... My private idea of England always had this exciting side to it.[18]

While it is then necessary to remember that emigration is a tragedy, the blame for which must be laid squarely at the door of politicians and policy-makers, we must also remember that emigration can be voluntaristic, a matter of individual agency. Emigration in this sense can be thought of as a critique of Irish society, not least in being an assertion of an individualism denied by that society. As in all such cases the response by Irish society is to counter this critique and its attendant individualism with a reassertion of the traditional and the communal. As Kerby Miller puts it:

> ... the idea that emigration was communal necessity rather than say, individual opportunity for self-betterment perfectly reflected a prevalent tendency in the traditional Irish Catholic world view to devalue individual action, ambition, and the assumption of personal responsibility – especially when actions such as emigration, seemed innovative and threatening to customary patterns of behaviour and thought which enjoined, by example and precept, passive or communal values such as duty, continuity, and conformity.[19]

It is by recognising this individual, voluntaristic aspect of emigration that we may begin to establish the terms within which we can study contemporary fiction.

Before going on to consider some instances of the contemporary fiction of Irish-Britain it also becomes necessary to take an overview (though it will be far from comprehensive) of the literary relationship between the two islands and the ways in which that relationship has been represented. Arising from that overview we will consider what seem to me to be the key features of the fiction of Irish-Britain.

Thinking of Ireland from a British perspective (or vice versa) immediately launches one onto the waters of politics and how those politics in turn define Irish writing. Those writers who, like George Bernard Shaw, paid little seeming attention to Ireland in their work are outside the defining lines of 'the Irish writer'; so Shaw is said to have written only one Irish play, *John Bull's Other Island*, while Sean O'Casey, for example, a long-term resident of Britain who for long refused permission for his plays to be performed in Ireland, is unproblematically an Irish writer because so much of his subject-matter is clearly Irish. Again, writers like Louis MacNeice or George Buchanan tend to be seen as only ambivalently Irish because they are seen, through residence in Britain, to have at some level betrayed their Irishness. It is to this situation which Shaw refers when in the 'Preface' to *John Bull's Other Island* he alludes to Tennyson's lines: 'Every Irishman is in Lancelot's position: his honour rooted in dishonour stands; and faith unfaithful keeps him falsely true.'[20]

Shaw's words could be seen to be teasingly referring to the paradox that to be 'properly' Irish one should live outside Ireland;

after all in historical and numerical terms more Irish people have lived (for a period or for most of their lives) outside Ireland than in it. The idea that those who live in Ireland all their lives are not, in majoritarian terms, 'properly' Irish is a paradox that would have appealed to Oscar Wilde as well as Shaw. Both are writers whose status has suffered from the overly narrow terms of the definition of the Irish writer propounded by the Irish Literary Revival,[21] though neither has become an Irish-British writer. Something similar is taken up by Robert MacLiam Wilson in *Ripley Bogle* when he has his central character adopt the name 'Ripley British Irish Bogle'; this seems to the character to reflect his background in a balanced way, but is perceived by everyone else as a matter of betrayal.[22]

It is this background which we need to take into account when we consider the contemporary fiction of Irish-Britain. I want to stress at the outset that for contemporary writers improved transport and communications mean that location is more likely than ever before to be a contingent matter rather than a life-long choice, which means that writers' allegiances are also more than ever unstable.

I have already referred to the comparative absence of a fiction, or any writing, of Irish-Britain but that statement depends on the way in which the 'Irish writer' is defined. Given the long-standing relationship between the two countries and their geographical proximity one would expect that the fiction of Irish-Britain would be a rich seam. It is, however, difficult to think of writers who would fit the bill. This is not to say that such writers do not exist. From the Restoration and the drama of Farquhar, Sheridan and Goldsmith, through the domination of the Victorian stage by Dion Boucicault, the turn of the century successes of Wilde and Shaw, more recent writers such as Patrick MacGill, Elizabeth Bowen and Louis MacNeice, and into the present day with writers as diverse as Edna O'Brien, William Trevor, Robert MacLiam Wilson and Ronan Bennett, there are plenty of writers who have lived and written between the socio-cultural formations of both Ireland and Britain. Looking through the names listed here, however, one becomes aware of a particular problem. The writers listed fall into one of two categories: they are considered solely as Irish writers, or they have an anomalous socio-cultural status which has damaged their reputation (often to the point of obscurity) in both countries.

There is a powerful force in Irish culture, both North and South, which reclaims as its own those whom Irish society has expelled or who felt the need to leave, when they become, by its lights, worthy of reclamation. In this the geographical proximity of the two countries actually helps to lessen the sense of a coherent and stable grouping of Irish-in-Britain writers. For many writers, too, Ireland continues to exert a fascination such that they project themselves, regardless of location, as Irish writers. Indeed, given the dominance of the nationalist imperative in Ireland for much of this century, in many cases writers who have spent a long time in Britain may actively disguise that fact, giving the impression that their residence in Britain was of brief duration and of minimal importance.

Of these writers, W.B. Yeats is the prime example. In the oppositional pairing Yeats-and-Joyce it is Joyce whose identity as writer is predicated on exile while Yeats is the stay-at-home. The success with which Yeats represented himself as not-an-emigrant is in part dependent on the ways in which Irish culture (for all the ambivalence about Yeats within it) has colluded with his self-representation. It is worth also bearing in mind Stephen Dedalus' comment that the shortest way to Tara is via Holyhead, a comment which indicates the way in which migration is seen not as a modification of cultural identity, a taking on of a new, composite identity, but actually a reinforcement of one's original identity. This can be linked to the idea of a migrant mentality, arising from the long-standing tradition of migration from Ireland, in which migration reinforces, rather than weakens or modifies, one's originary identity since migration has become such a central factor in that identity. In other words, despite migration writers spend their time examining their original identity rather than constructing a new, composite identity. It is on this basis that they can then be reclaimed by Irish culture.

Writers such as Patrick MacGill and George Buchanan represent the fate of those writers who are not reclaimed for Ireland in that they are little considered today.[23] Of other writers in this category, Elizabeth Bowen and Louis MacNeice are of prime importance in that their reputations foundered for some time before they were reclaimed. Both became important for Ireland at that point when Ireland needed instances of cultural pluralism to endorse the political pluralism which has recently been seen as necessary in the face of the continuing crisis in the North. That pluralism, though it may take account of the connection with Britain, is more concerned to broaden the definition of Irishness and the 'Irish writer' than to establish a category of Irish-British writer.[24] This is one reason why if we look for the stable and coherent grouping of Irish-in-Britain writers which an essay like this requires we cannot find them in the critical literature.

Alongside this politically-generated magnetic force of Irish culture we should place the possibility that the Irish in Britain are themselves not a coherent and stable enough group to generate a need for literary articulation; given the often low educational standards of the (stereo)typical Irish immigrant, this may not be a surprise. The economic reasons which impel so many out of Ireland may mean that for most migrants the business of living is enough to keep one occupied and to leave little time for cultural activity reflecting on one's status. Such activity as does exist may well be more often directed towards expressing and reinforcing one's Irishness in traditional ways rather then inventing a cultural expression for one's Irish-in-Britainness.[25]

As if this combination of geographical proximity, reclamation and nostalgic traditionalism were not enough, a final point to consider is the idea that emigration to England was perceived as a servile failure:

Oddly enough movement to England, of which there was a great deal, was hardly seen as emigration at all, to Scotland, not at all. Perhaps England was too near for emigration to be seen as irrevocable (although for most it was) ... This [moving to North America] was the real emigration ... Going to England carried a stigma of failure that was not associated with America. The local paper often carried reports of magistrates giving petty offenders the option of a fine or prison, or going to England.[26]

Taken together, these factors have not only served consistently to destabilise any Irish-British communal cultural expression, but actually to provide reason for *not* producing an Irish-British identity.

It is in semi-autobiographical or autobiographical works that we find many of the records of the experience of being Irish in Britain. In the work of Patrick MacGill and Donall MacAmhlaigh,[27] for example, there is the experience of hard labour and oppression that we might expect to find in records of that experience.[28] In the contemporary period the texts to refer to for this kind of experience are those of Paul Hill[29] and Gerard Conlon. Such open and blatant oppression as is experienced by MacGill and latterly by Hill and Conlon may well be what we would expect to find in the cultural record of Irish-Britain and it does exist. However, what should also be registered in each case is the sense, however ironised by hindsight, that England is a place of liberation, a point common to much contemporary and earlier fiction. Open oppression and consequent alienation are, however, now also the subject of much parodic venom on the part of Robert Wilson whose Ripley Bogle makes great play of being the lowest of the low. Indeed, one way of considering *Ripley Bogle* would be as an equivalent to Flann O'Brien's *An Beal Bocht* (*The Poor Mouth*). The latter is a parody of a certain type of autobiography in Irish in which much stress is laid on the poverty of the protagonist and his/her family. In this light *Ripley Bogle* can be seen as a parody of a genre which, while it exists perhaps ought to have existed in much greater numbers – the Irish autobiography of oppression and economic privation in England. If Bogle's status as a tramp is a parody of the idea of the Irish in Britain as being at the bottom of the pile, there is also a recognition that this is not a fate reserved by Britain for the Irish; the closest Bogle has to a friend is Perry, a Polish tramp.

This mixing with other 'migrant' communities is often part of the experience of the Irish in Britain in fiction and while it can be seen as a form of solidarity in the face of alienation it must also be seen as an indication that 'Britishness' or 'Englishness' for the Irish is marked by its heterogeneity, a heterogeneity signalled most visibly by colour and which is in contrast with the homogeneity of Irish society. So in the passage I quoted earlier from *Proved Innocent* it is an encounter with a black man which signals to the young Gerry Conlon that England is an exciting place compared to Belfast. In Linda Anderson's *Cuckoo*[30] the heroine, Fran, has a child as the result of a brief affair with a black man and the child functions to anchor her more firmly in Britain to which she moved in the first place to have an abortion. One of William Trevor's novels which is about marginality – *Miss Gomez and the Brethren*[31] – takes as its central figure a black woman while *Elizabeth Alone*,[32] at first sight about white, middle-class England, features characters from at least eight national backgrounds. Perhaps the most telling comment on this aspect of Irish-British fiction is not the inter-racial solidarity of Joseph O'Connor's *Cowboys and Indians*[33] but the teasing comment made by Rudi, a black mini-cab driver to Hennessy, the central figure of J.M. O'Neill's *Open Cut*: 'Funny', Rudi said, 'You're the immigrant, not me.'[34] which neatly sums up the sense of alienation from a heterogeneous Britain that the Irish experience. Rudi's comment finds an echo in Maurice Leitch's *Burning Bridges* when Sonny confronts a black policeman: 'If there was a God anywhere and one with a sense of humour surely he must make this [police]man recognise the irony of the situation, someone white like [Sonny] about to be frisked by a black man here in Thatcher's England.'[35]

If alienation can be defined as the wrong kind of visibility in a society, we must recognise the possibility of a kind of invisibility available to the Irish, particularly when economic circumstances do not set them apart. A writer such as William Trevor, in whose apparently genteel fictions a particular English middle-class accent is often expertly ventriloquised, would be by now all but invisible as an Irish-in-Britain writer were it not for his forays back into recognisably Irish subject-matter; he exists that is to say as both an Irish writer ('The Ballroom of Romance'; *Mrs Eckdorf in O'Neill's Hotel*; *The News from Ireland*) or as a British, even English, writer (*Elizabeth Alone*; *The Love Department*; *The Children of Dynmouth*) but he seemingly never functions as an Irish-in-Britain writer, at least not if we assume that in that instance his subject-matter would be explicitly about the dialogue set up between one's socio-cultural formation and one's different socio-cultural experience. Trevor's work provides a good example of the effects of displacement. He is perhaps best known (usually via television adaptations) for his elegiac representations of semi-rural Irish life which alongside his decorously middle-class subject-matter and attitudes may seem to some to disqualify him from centrality in the Irish-in-Britain experience. However, I would want to argue that while writers such as MacAmhlaigh and MacGill present us with valuable accounts of working-class Irish life in Britain, they do so at the expense of registering certain features of the British landscape as experienced and represented by the Irish. In their narratives the concern with work precludes reflection on the life around them, at least in regard to certain of its features. Trevor on the other hand writes about middle-class life and seems to benefit thereby. His style, unshowily influenced by Joyce, has developed into a medium for registering a polite surrealism; the overall emotional tone of the work is of amiable bewilderment rather than resented alienation.

It should also be said that Trevor's invisibility may also be due to his definition as an Irish writer who happens to live in Britain rather than as an Irish-in-Britain writer. In this he fits with what is surprisingly the dominant line of Irish-in-Britain writing. This is the line which can be said to stretch back to Goldsmith and Sheridan, to take in Sterne, Boucicault, Wilde, Shaw and even Samuel Beckett, whose *Murphy* is London-set. As has often been remarked, the work of all of these writers is characterised by paradox, inversion, contradiction and irony. It has also been said that these are features of some supposed Irish mentality; it seems to me to make much more sense to say that these features arise from, or are at least reinforced by, the experience of being Irish-in-Britain, of being in Lancelot's position. At one extreme this position may involve alienation and oppression, but for most, at least as far as the fiction is concerned, it more often involves a sense of displacement.

Burning Bridges with its journey through a 'deep England' of teashops and tourist traps, operates, like the work of Trevor, on the level of displacement. The narrative makes clear that for its two central figures – Sonny and Hazel – their journey is a journey into deep England. They travel south west from London, encountering Stonehenge and the Cerne Abbas giant along the way and in so doing it is evident that they are encountering the hollow heart of England. This *is* an England of alienation and latent violence but these are seen as endemic features of a society and a culture at the end of its tether in which 'people awoke each morning, seemingly a fraction crazier than the day before' (*BB* p. 232) rather than being exclusively directed at the Irish characters. Indeed, in one incident in a bar it is English commuters who are subject to taunts and humiliation by the Irish regulars (*BB*, p. 42). It is also obvious that for Sonny at least it is preferable to Ireland if only because it still allows for his dreams – he does not have to follow his mother's aspirations and take a job in the Metal Box Factory on the Derry Road (*BB*, p. 41). Country-and-western music in the novel shows that even 'deep England' is subject to the same ersatz culture as everywhere else.

Here, antagonism and alienation are not overriding factors (which is not to say that they do not exist); rather, we are confronted with characters whose experience is more prosaic and more private. This is not the world of open aggression which has to be openly confronted and dealt with; it is instead a world in which the continuously jarring effects of living in, or more accurately living a culture like and yet unlike one's own have to be internalised. It is not a question of having occasionally, or even often, to adopt an aggressively defensive stance against blatant attack; it is instead the feeling of being continuously off-balance, out of true: 'Something about older people made them that way, Sonny had noticed. No matter how long they had been away from the old country they couldn't adapt to the geography of the new' (*BB*, p. 6).

In these circumstances the world, even as you see it being treated as normal by those around you, is made strange. I would argue that to gain a true picture of Irish-Britain we have to take into account both the public stance of being Irish-in-Britain and the private consciousness; the feeling that one lives in an out-of-kilter world.

Writers such as Trevor and Leitch register not the irreconcilability of Irish and British culture but rather the sense that there are only minimal, but still significant, differences between Irish and British society. To move from Ireland (whether from North or South) to Britain is like walking into the house next door. Its layout, its style of furnishing, its rituals and its prevailing mores may all seem the same as your own house, you may know the people, they may know you, and if you are just visiting no harm will ensue; but act as if you belong there and mutual bafflement will be the result. If this seems too homely an image for what has been an often openly antagonistic relationship on both sides, that is because we are accustomed to thinking of immigrant groups as belonging at the bottom of a society where the friction and ensuing antagonism are most keenly felt. It seems to me, however, that those invasions of households by people who are not quite what they seem in the drama of Goldsmith, Boucicault and Wilde may be read as images of precisely the experience that I am discussing.

Even in such a brutal play as Tom Murphy's *A Whistle in the Dark*[36] which is set at the bottom end of society, it is the domesticity of Michael, a sign of his aspiration to be at least lower middle class, which is what we see being disrupted by his father and brothers. From Murphy's drama to Trevor's fiction may seem like a long haul but there is in both the sense that it is in the apparently slightest and least spectacular details that we can trace the disruptions of migrant experience and consciousness, rather than at the level of the state and legislation. As Colin Holmes puts it in another context: 'The Irish who had firm initial ideas on such matters [as politics and religion] did not always retain that reassuring certainty in their new environment. The process of immigration exerted its own effects upon perceptions and horizons.'[37] In this it seems to me that Trevor, for all his apparent decorum, which *could* be read as a form of compliance to the mores and ideology of middle England, registers the effects of migration at the level of consciousness. This is why I used the term 'surrealism' earlier. It is not only in the aggressively dark, London streets of Ronan Bennett's *The Second Prison*,[38] nor in the world of distrust, unachievable yearnings, unfulfillable ambitions and criminality of J.M. O'Neill's *Open Cut*, nor in the rather glib inter-cultural solidarity of Joseph O'Connor's *Cowboys and Indians* that we can find images of the experience of being Irish in Britain. While those works represent important, public aspects of that experience, they do so at the expense of recording the consequences of that experience at the level of consciousness and at the level of the idea of that most private of spaces, 'home'.

The contemporary fiction of Irish-Britain is, indeed, obsessed with ideas of home. Linda Anderson's *Cuckoo*, from its title onwards, is concerned with the temporary, often unsatisfactory nature of home and the consequences of that on the mentality of the heroine who comes from a middle-class Protestant background in Belfast. On the birth of her daughter she moves from a bedsit to a middle-class household in which she lives as a nanny-cum-house-keeper and in which she and her daughter are the 'cuckoo and the cuckoo's mother' (C, p. 27) and where she is 'still essentially home-less. A lodger' (C, p. 29). She is eventually most at home in the necessarily temporary and unstable home of the Women's Camp at Greenham Common with its constant evictions and upheavals (C, p. 142). But overall she is eventually forced to realise that 'the home in my mind was not one I had ever known' (C, p. 152). *Ripley Bogle* relies for much of its effect on the contrast between the richness of its language and the socio-economic privations of its eponymous central figure as he tramps, homeless, round London meditating on the unsatisfactory nature of his original home in Belfast's Turf Lodge. Maurice Leitch's *Burning Bridges* starts in a London of bedsits and shared flats but pursues its characters' dreams of England in a journey in a mobile home through a 'deep England' in which home cannot be found by anyone. Towards the end of the novel Sonny looks over the English landscape:

> Sonny ached at the beauty of this country. All of it. It was a hurt he could never, ever put into words just as, in the same way, he and his kind would never be able to make an impact, or imprint, on any part of it. (*BB*, p. 271)

But if this suggests a peculiarly Irish alienation from England and the English landscape, Sonny's memory at this point signifi-cantly broadens his own emotions and sense of homelessness to a symbolic universality:

> He thought of that final thing he'd done after he'd closed the door of the flat in London for the last time, all his bridges burned at his back. He'd prised off the painted-over *mezuza* from the jamb just to see what was inside, hoping for some clue to all those generations who'd gone before ... And when he'd got it away from the wood, what did he find there? Noth-ing but an empty socket. (*BB*, p. 271)

If this tracelessness seems to apply only to 'those other outsid-ers' like Sonny, then we must remember that the central English character in the novel, at whose house Sonny and Hazel stay, is the country-and-western-loving Pilgrim. England in this perspec-tive lacks an organic culture which can allow its own citizens to feel at home.

155

Even when we encounter a fiction, such as William Trevor's *Elizabeth Alone*, in which the home in question is a solid, middle-class nest, there is no escaping from the sense of unease and disquiet. It is not just that Elizabeth Aidallbery's suburban home is under threat from the external world, but also that the novel, for all the solidity and continuity of the home at its centre, displays an enormous range of real and symbolic homes. Elizabeth is alone for a number of reasons, one of which is that she is the only character to have experience only of a stable home. Other characters have been raised in orphanages, live in bedsits, nurses' homes and nursing homes, and communes, or inhabit homes which are versions of hell. Henry's house may stand for all of these:

> The house smelt of the beer and the organic matter, and everywhere rubbish had accumulated ... There was a feeling in the house of everything coming apart at once, not just a marriage, but all the possessions that hire-purchase had obtained to set the marriage up. Henry himself, accident-prone and luckless in adult life, had the same kind of built-in obsolescence about him. (*EA*, p. 30)

Even when Henry has cleared up the house he can find no ease, dying, as he does, in an accident more comic than tragic. Additionally, much of the action of the novel takes place in a women's hospital, in the wards of which people are brought accidentally together and as accidentally are torn apart again.

Two further features of these works need to be considered. The first of these goes back to the idea of reclamation which I discussed earlier and is concerned with a perennial problem for the Irish writer: audience. For whom are these fictions written? Some are Irish-published, some British-published, others again are jointly published in Ireland and Britain. Regardless of that, all are distributed in both countries but all may be said to have concerns which, from an Irish perspective, seem to be British or English. The centrality of Greenham Common and of a particular type of feminism in *Cuckoo*, the issue of homelessness in 1980s London in *Ripley Bogle*, the specificity of middle-class English life in *Elizabeth Alone*, and the concern with the deep England of Stonehenge and the Cerne Abbas giant in *Burning Bridges* may all indicate a desire to speak to an English audience. That all of these concerns are articulated in an Irish voice may cause them to be unheard in England while their subject-matter may make them unpopular in Ireland, as if Irish subjects were being betrayed. This leads to the second issue (on which I wish to conclude) which brings me back to the motives of the migrant. In all the cases that I have considered (and I have tried to cover a broad range), the concerns of the novels can be seen as a refusal to deal with Irish subjects and particularly with Irish or Irish in Britain communities. Alienation, insofar as it exists in these novels, is not only from British or English society, but also from Irish society. The desire in *Cuckoo* to fight against a mentality in which 'conformity and obedience are never taken to task' (*C*, p. 86); the refusal of community in *Ripley Bogle*; the isolation of the middle-class home in *Elizabeth Alone*; the desire to construct one's own transnational community based on country-and-western music in *Burning Bridges* are all indications not so much of alienation but of an almost desperate need to break from community, to be an individual, to escape the conformity of which Kerby Miller has written. In all of these novels perhaps the most heartfelt compliment to the 'dingy pleasures of England' comes from *Ripley Bogle*:

> The nicest thing about London is that London doesn't care. In Belfast I was fettered like all the Irish by the soft mastery of my country ... London will play ball if you make the effort but the city will leave you mostly unmolested. It provokes the pleasant spur of loneliness yet populates your dreams, despair or solitude ... London remains polite but distant. This is admirable behaviour on the part of any city and should be loudly commended. (*RB*, p. 271)

In all of this there is an indication that perhaps there can be no fiction of Irish-Britain, but only a fiction, set in Britain, in which Irish writers attempt to construct that which is severely lacking in Ireland: a non-communal, individual identity.

Notes

1. R.F. Foster, 'Knowing Your Place: Words and Boundaries in Anglo-Irish Relations', in his *Paddy and Mr Punch: Connections in Irish and English History* (London: Allen Lane, 1993), p. 86.
2. A growing awareness of the complexity of 'Britain' and 'Britishness' can be found in, for example, D.G. Boyce, '"The Marginal Britons": The Irish', in Robert Colls and Philip Dodd (eds), *Englishness: Politics and Culture, 1880–1920* (London: Croom Helm, 1986) pp. 230–53; Linda Colley, *Britons: Forging the Nation, 1707–1837* (New Haven and London: Yale University Press, 1992); Hugh Kearney, *The British Isles: A History of Four Nations* (Cambridge University Press, 1989).

3. Liam Ryan, 'Irish Emigration to Britain since World War II', in Richard Kearney (ed.), *Migrations: The Irish At Home and Abroad* (Dublin: Wolfhound, 1990) p. 48.
4. For a consideration of this 'bad dream' from a Caribbean perspective, see E.A. Markham, 'Random Thoughts', *Hinterland: Caribbean Poetry from the West Indies and Britain* (Newcastle: Bloodaxe, 1989), pp. 16–17.
5. George V. Higgins, *The Patriot Game* (1982; London: Robinson, 1985).
6. On Irish-American writing see Peggy O'Brien, 'The Irish-American Literary Connection', in David Noel Doyle and Owen Dudley Edwards (eds), *America and Ireland, 1776–1976: The American Identity and the Irish Connection*, Proceedings of the United States Bicentennial Conference of Cumann Merriman, Ennis, August 1976 (Westpoint, Connecticut: Greenwood Press, 1980), pp. 261–78; Carl Wittke, *The Irish in America* (New York: Russell and Russell, 1956), pp. 241–63; William V. Shannon, *The American Irish* (1963; rev. edn, New York and London: Macmillan, 1966). pp. 233–94.
7. See Patrick O'Sullivan (ed.), *The Irish World Wide: History, Heritage, Identity* 6 vols (Leicester University Press, 1991– ; Roger Swift and Sheridan Gilley (eds), *The Irish in Britain, 1815–1939* (London: Pinter, 1989); Kerby A. Miller, *Emigrants and Exiles: Ireland and the Irish Exodus to North America* (London: Oxford University Press, 1985); Kearney (ed.), *Migrations*, to all of which this chapter is indebted.
8. J.J. Lee, *Ireland 1912–1985: Politics and Society* (Cambridge University Press, 1989), pp. 374–87; R.F. Foster, *Modern Ireland, 1600–1972* (London: Allen Lane, 1988), pp. 345–72.
9. Colin Holmes, *John Bull's Island: Immigration and British Society, 1871–1971* (Basingstoke: Macmillan Education, 1988), pp. 36–8.
10. Jenny Beale, *Women in Ireland: Voices of Change* (London: Macmillan Education, 1986), pp. 33–5; Janet Nolan, *Ourselves Alone: Women's Emigration from Ireland, 1885–1920* (Lexington, KY: University Press of Kentucky, 1989), p. 43; Lee, *Ireland 1912–1985* p. 376.
11. R.F. Foster, 'Marginal Men and Micks on the Make: the Uses of Irish Exile, c. 1840–1922,' in his *Paddy and Mr Punch*, pp. 281–305.
12. Homi K. Bhabha, 'DissemiNation: Time, Narrative and the Margins of the Modern Nation', in Homi K. Bhabha (ed.), *Nation and Narration* (London: Routledge, 1990), pp. 291–322.
13. Richard Kearney, 'Migrant Minds', in Richard Kearney (ed.), *Across the Frontiers: Ireland in the 1990s* (Dublin: Wolfhound, 1988), p. 185.
14. Joseph O'Connor, 'Introduction', in Dermot Bolger (ed.), *Ireland in Exile: Irish Writers Abroad* (Dublin: New Island Books, 1993), p. 16.

15. Lee, *Ireland 1912–1985*, p. 374.
16. See the comments by Charles Haughey when he was still Taoiseach in an RTE interview on 22 September 1991, as reported in the *Irish Times* (23 September 1991): 'There had been an increase in unemployment *because of the fall-off in emigration* and difficulties in the international economy have led to lower spending which hit taxes on consumer spending' (emphasis added).
17. Patrick MacGill, *Children of the Dead End* (1914; Dingle, Co. Kerry: Brandon, 1982).
18. Gerry Conlon, *Proved Innocent* (London: Penguin, 1991), pp. 40–2. Significantly, Conlon's sense of England as 'exciting' derives from a childhood visit during which he first encountered a black man.
19. Kerby A. Miller, 'Emigration, Capitalism, and Ideology in Post-Famine Ireland', in Kearney (ed.) *Migrations*, p. 93. I would want to add that while Miller refers specifically to Irish Catholicism, the forms of Irish Protestantism, it seems to me, can also be best described as communal and conformist rather than individualistic and innovative.
20. George Bernard Shaw, 'Preface for Politicians', *John Bull's Other Island* (1906) in *The Field Day Anthology of Irish Writing* vol. 2. General editor Seamus Deane (Derry: Field Day Publications, 1991), p. 486.
21. On this see Declan Kiberd (ed.), 'The London Exiles: Wilde and Shaw', in *The Field Day Anthology of Irish Writing* vol. 2, pp. 372–6.
22. Robert MacLiam Wilson, *Ripley Bogle* (Belfast: Blackstaff, 1989), p. 14. Hereafter in the text as *RB*.
23. MacGill, in particular is an interesting case. His initial status as a best-seller in England gave way to almost complete obscurity until Irish Studies scholars such as Bernard Canavan, Owen Dudley Edwards and Patrick O'Sullivan rediscovered him and, although he is still relatively unknown, he now has a Summer School dedicated to him. The continuing re-establishment of his reputation has therefore relied on him being metaphorically brought back to Ireland, despite the joy with which he left it.
24. On Elizabeth Bowen see R.F. Foster, 'The Irishness of Elizabeth Bowen', in his *Paddy and Mr Punch* pp. 102–22; on Louis MacNeice see Edna Longley, 'The Room Where MacNeice Wrote "Snow"', which begins 'Louis MacNeice has influenced redefinitions of Irish poetry and Irish identity', in her *The Living Stream: Literature and Revisionism in Ireland* (Newcastle-upon-Tyne: Bloodaxe, 1994), pp. 252–70.
25. I have written elsewhere about the separation of culture and tradition implied by this statement. In this circumstance it is useful to think of 'tradition' as the passing on of increasingly ossified behaviours and practices such as can be seen represented in the pages of

the *Irish Post*, the main newspaper for the Irish in Britain; 'culture' can then be thought of as the area in which adjustment to changed circumstances and, consequently, innovation in behaviour and practice is carried out. See Eamonn Hughes, 'Art, Exiles, Ireland and Icons', *Fortnight* (Supplement: Voyages of Discovery), 295 (May 1991), pp. 9–11.

26. Maurice Hayes '"Migratory Birds and Roundy Heads" Chairman's Introduction', in Kearney (ed.) *Migrations*, pp. 15–16; and see also Maurice Goldring, *Pleasant the Scholar's Life: Irish Intellectuals and the Construction of the Nation State* (London: Serif, 1993), pp. 110–11.

27. Donall MacAmhlaigh, *An Irish Navvy: The Diary of an Exile*, trans. Valentine Iremonger (London: Routledge and Kegan Paul, 1964).

28. For an excellent account of such works see Bernard Canavan, 'Story-tellers and Writers: Irish Identity in Emigrant Labourers' Autobiographies, 1870–1970', in Patrick O'Sullivan (ed.), *The Creative Migrant*, vol. 3 of *The Irish World Wide: History, Heritage, Identity* (Leicester University Press, 1994), pp. 154–69.

29. Paul Hill with Ronan Bennett, *Stolen Years: Before and After Guildford* (1990; London: Corgi, 1991).

30. Linda Anderson, *Cuckoo* (1986; Dingle, Co. Kerry: Brandon, 1988). Hereafter in the text as *C*.

31. William Trevor, *Miss Gomez and the Brethren* (1971; London: Triad/Panther, 1978).

32. William Trevor, *Elizabeth Alone* (1973; St Albans: Triad/Panther, 1977). Hereafter in the text as *EA*.

33. Joseph O'Connor, *Cowboys and Indians* (1991; London: Flamingo, 1992).

34. J.M. O'Neill, *Open Cut* (London: Sceptre, 1987), p. 62.

35. Maurice Leitch, *Burning Bridges* (London: Hutchinson, 1989), p. 261. Hereafter in the text as *BB*.

36. Tom Murphy, *A Whistle in the Dark and Other Plays*. Preface by Fintan O'Toole (London: Methuen, 1989).

37. Holmes, *John Bull's Island* p. 42.

38. Ronan Bennett, *The Second Prison* (London: Hamish Hamilton, 1991).

10. 'In Search of the Lost Tribe': Janet Frame's England

Rod Edmond

In 1840 Macaulay imagined a future time when 'some traveller from New Zealand shall ... take his stand on a broken arch of London Bridge to sketch the ruins of St. Paul's.'[1] One hundred and fifty years later many New Zealand writers are reluctant even to visit the wreckage. Recently there has been furious debate in New Zealand literary circles, which spilled into the correspondence columns of the *The Times Literary Supplement,* over the New Zealand Ministry of Art's purchase of a flat in Bloomsbury for visiting New Zealand writers. A group of writers put up an alternative proposal for a house on an island off Whakatane, on the east coast of New Zealand's North Island, and won strong support for their idea. The argument even provided a question in a national examination paper ('Discuss the pros and cons of London and Whakatane').

Behind this argument is a perennial subject of cultural debate in New Zealand: What is the source of the national culture? Are New Zealand writers still, as Ian Wedde has put it, 'operating at a frontier where you have to carry a life-supporting canteen from some distantly located spring', or, as he would prefer, are they part of a confident national culture able to give and receive on equal terms?[2] In fact, both sides of the 'writers' house' argument confirmed the lingering importance of London as New Zealand's metropolitan centre and Britain as its cultural source. Both were locked into the same set of terms, either asserting or refuting London's centrality. No space was left for writers who might have preferred some other option altogether (San Francisco, Kingston, New Delhi ...).

For many New Zealand writers earlier in the century, there was no argument. You needed to escape New Zealand in order to write, even if having escaped you then wrote about home. Katherine Mansfield is the obvious point of reference here, and her journey to London to examine her place of departure was repeated by later New Zealand writers; for example, Robin Hyde (1906–39), John Mulgan (1911–45), James Courage (1905–63), Dan Davin (1913–90). Like Mansfield, these writers stayed away and their single ticket seemed to confirm the need for New Zealand writing to be validated from the imperial centre. In the period following the Second World War however, the *émigré* or expatriate writer became less common. This figure was replaced by a rather different one, the traveller, who came to look rather than to stay and who moved in worlds remote from Bloomsbury or Oxford. The most significant example of this figure is Janet Frame who lived in England for seven years from the late 1950s to the mid-1960s. Her third novel, *The Edge of the Alphabet* (1962), is concerned with a journey from New Zealand to London and with life on the margins of the city. Her third volume of autobiography, *The Envoy from Mirror City* (1985), reworks the same ground. In both these works new kinds of identification with other migrant figures and groups are hesitantly attempted. Together they give a very particular account of that new 'other Britain' that was forming in the 1950s and 1960s. In Frame's fifth novel, *The Adaptable Man* (1965), her picture of Britain three decades ago extends beyond London to the countryside, that *locus classicus* of the English novel. This novel of English rural life set in East Suffolk, together with *The Edge of the Alphabet* and *The Envoy from Mirror City*, provide an unusually comprehensive examination of Britain from the point of view of the New Zealand traveller–writer.

There were many reasons for the post-war experience of journeying to Britain and discovering that 'home' was no longer home at all. (Until quite recently older New Zealanders who might never have seen Britain commonly referred to it as home. 'Pommies' used to be called 'homeys'.) It was inevitable that as New Zealand's culture matured and its sense of identity deepened, relations with the 'home' culture would become more distant. New Zealand writer– travellers of the 1950s and 1960s were also part of that rolling back of empire, that migration of colonial writers from the imperial frontiers to the centre, and the anti- or post-imperialist works that resulted. And in the period immediately after the Second World War the United States filled many spaces previously occupied by Britain. Nowhere was this more so than in the Pacific. In this respect Britain's inability to defend Singapore in 1942 was crucial. After the war Australia and New

Zealand looked to the United States for their so-called security arrangements, and treaties such as ANZUS and SEATO resulted. All these factors contributed to a weakening of traditional ties between Britain and many of its former colonies in the 1940s and 1950s.

There were, however, aspects of this experience peculiar to the New Zealand writer which helped shape the images of Britain found in the writing of Janet Frame. New Zealand is predominantly 'western' but not European. In this it is different from Australia which was Europeanised by immigration in the 1950s and 1960s.[3] There were also special circumstances in its settlement, in particular its economic *raison d'être* as a provider of primary products for Britain, which meant that Britain's contraction of its imperial boundaries was more strongly felt in New Zealand than elsewhere. As Janet Frame says in *The Envoy from Mirror City*, New Zealand's imperative has always been 'export or die' (p. 46). (This phrase also appears in the final page of *The Edge of the Alphabet*.) If survival depended on the export of meat, wool and butter, then Britain's turning towards Europe after Suez, and its first application for Common Market membership in 1961 (which would have bound Britain into the Community's protectionist agricultural policy) threatened New Zealand's economic and cultural identity. As J.G.A. Pocock has put it, the rejection of the global capacity of British culture implicit in the end of empire also involved a rejection of the other nations of that culture. The advent of Europe cut New Zealand adrift from its British history and set it against those northern landmass cultures from which it in part derived.

Against this, Pocock has suggested a quite different way of thinking about New Zealand's identity. Ejection from Anglo-European history has encouraged a recognition of New Zealand as part of a Pacific world of small communities 'formed, separated and connected by voyagings over oceanic distances'. New Zealanders therefore, both Maori and Pakeha, are less *tangata whenua* (people of the land) than *tangata waka* (people of the ship), their histories shaped by voyaging, who continue to voyage in search of histories to which they remain distantly connected.

Both these elements of Pocock's analysis are helpful in approaching that voyage to England made by Frame's protagonists, travellers to a mother culture which fails to recognise them. In *The Edge of the Alphabet*, Toby Withers becomes a voyager, following his mother's advice to return to the home of his ancestors:

'If ever you go overseas, Toby, visit the places where your ancestors lived ... And, Toby, Toby, sit in the old churchyard where the yew trees grow and where are buried John Blaikie, Master of Model Training College, Evan Dunwoody, Minister to the King, Dr Charles Gibbs, F.R.C.S.' (p. 14)

There Toby will write his book about the Lost Tribe, the subject of his composition which had once been read to the class ('And his great great grandmother wrote a book of poems, signed by the Archbishop of Canterbury' p. 18). Toby is suffering 'an affliction of dream called Overseas' (p. 46), a myth of origin and return which his narrative is to dispel. First, however, he must become a Pacific voyager (*tangata waka*). Toby's ship stops at Pitcairn where the islanders invite him to stay, a standard invitation to all tourists which Toby misunderstands as sincerely meant. Perhaps, he wonders, he would find the Lost Tribe here. But the ship sails on across the Pacific into the old world of Europe. Toby disowns England on arrival. 'It's not *my* England', he says to two Dutchmen unimpressed by the view from the train taking them from the docks into London. But the train wheels sing 'higgledy-piggledy tribal higgledy-piggledy tribal' (p. 134).

Toby's antipodean vision of the unreal city is a place of freaks and nightmares. He visits a joke shop where he buys a cigarette lighter in the shape of a small pistol; the joke misfires when he produces it at a bank. He gets a job as a commissionaire at the Wonderland Cinema. Attracted to the Railway Lost Property Sale, 'saturated with a sense of poverty and loneliness' (p. 145), he has an epileptic fit. The woman living above his squalid basement flat, which he shares with two Irish street-sweepers, ekes out a living by painting faces on plastic dolls. Faceless dolls litter her flat. At Hyde Park a crowd gathers round an old woman who commands a set of paper dolls to dance on the pavement. And all this while Toby's swollen arm mysteriously continues to fester. These scenes and images of London crowd in on each other over a few pages. Their cumulative effect is of strangeness and dislocation, creating a bizarre dream world through which the misplaced aspiring author of The Lost Tribe wanders.

When, at the end of this sequence, Toby sits down to write his book he gets no further than the title. 'Then he had stopped, seized by fear. Perhaps that was his book, just that, three words, nothing else, no chapters or sections or descriptions of people' (p. 149). On one level Toby's book has been a lost cause from the start, a family myth invented by his mother to compensate for his epilepsy. But the title is resonant, and Toby's inability even to start the book is more than simply a matter of personal incapacity. The biggest trick London plays on its visitors is the language trick. The deceptions of language are manifold for a traveller from the South come to write the story of The Lost Tribe. Although the destinations displayed on the buses suggest that London is full of circuses these can never be reached. Arriving at Piccadilly Circus the sign mysteriously changes to 'Cricklewood': 'Words were running on and on in his head – laundries, lost property, circuses, buses and their destinations – High Wycombe, Peckham Rye, Tooting Bec and Tooting Bdy – did that mean Tooting Body? Tooting Body' (p. 162).

Another New Zealand London novel of this time, Marilyn Duckworth's *A Gap in the Spectrum* (1959) has an amnesic narrator lost in an *Alice Through the Looking Glass* world of language puzzles. Duckworth, like Frame, defamiliarises London place-names; an invitation to Covent Garden, for example, suggests an outdoor rather than an indoor performance to the narrator. London is no longer a refuge for the writer. Instead, the centre of empire, the source of language, has become the edge of the alphabet, an echo chamber of confusion.

The final London scene of *The Edge of the Alphabet* is set in a parlour of mirrors at a Pleasure Gardens. Toby is surrounded by distorted images of himself:

> One moment the mirrors transferred him into a dwarf with his legs too short, his face elongated, his hair like tussock overgrown. Then his body was a palace of width, a huge doorway of flesh and fat and the smile on his lips wound like a creek through his face ... his cheeks swung from their hooks, dripping with blood his legs were avenues, overhanging the lonely road out of town. (p. 217)

What he sees here are landscapes and images of New Zealand captured in his own body. The similes of 'hair like tussock' and 'smile ... like a creek' are from the geography of his childhood. The hooked cheeks and bleeding legs derive from his job in the meat works where he saved enough to pay for his trip overseas. And the lonely road out of town suggests the desolate exits of small New Zealand towns such as Toby's Waimaru. 'And suddenly he was thin, he was tissue-paper and distance ... The mirrors had stolen his very shape' (p. 217). The next morning Toby books a passage home. He travels back to the southern landscapes conjured up in the mirrors but there is no real sense of return. The last page of the novel asks:

Home?

The edge of the alphabet where words crumble and all forms of communication between the living are useless. (p. 224)

Toby's quest has petered out and the novel ends in silence.

* * *

Frame's account of her own passage to England in *The Envoy from Mirror City* opens in terms of narratives of quest. There is 'the perennial drama of the Arrival', the 'failed messenger', 'The Greeter who was also The Warner' and so on (pp. 10–12). The Envoy is the imagination of the writer. But these terms are soon discarded as the traditional elements of quest, whether of such narratives in general or those of antipodean travellers to the centre, are found to be inadequate. This voyager seems to have come to the wrong place; the land doesn't recognise her. Booked, as she thinks, into the Friends' Hostel in Euston Road, language and place let her down; the reception is unfriendly and unknowing. Her naively confident announcement, 'I'm Janet Frame from New Zealand', and her insistent 'I'm *all the way from New Zealand*' are years out of date. This is no longer (was it ever?) the England imagined by Janet Frame or by Toby's mother. Mrs Withers, for example, would have been surprised at the presence of black people in the 'home of her ancestors'. In *The Edge of the Alphabet* we are shown 'West Indians, stricken with cold, shrunk in their cheap baggy suits, standing on the grille above the Underground, warming their feet' (p. 155). Toby's Irish friend, Pat, blames the blacks for the moral decline of London. These are only passing references but they are a reminder that Frame's novel is contemporaneous with the London novels of Samuel Selvon and George Lamming.

In *The Envoy from Mirror City*, however, this aspect of Frame's London is enlarged. As she rewrites her years in London it is apparent that a good deal of her working and other life was spent with migrants from the 'New Commonwealth'. The world she moved in would have been unrecognisable to earlier New Zealand *émigrés*. And this has more than just sociological significance. Frame visits Hampstead Heath in search of Keats, and of course the sight of tall brown rushes at the edge of a pond suggests 'La Belle Dame Sans Merci'; 'The sedge has wither'd from the lake ...' But then turning to look down on London from the Heath she is oppressed by the weight of English literary tradition. In New Zealand, by contrast, nature still has its original voice. It follows, therefore, that the most exciting poetry and prose she meets in London is by West Indian writers whose work, she feels, is 'all charged with a morning vision of London and the United Kingdom' (p. 19). This was so much the case that she wrote a group of poems from the point of view of a newly arrived West Indian and sent it to the *London Magazine* with a covering letter testifying to her recent arrival from the Caribbean.[4] Frame's 'hoax' was partly an expression of her affinity with this new literature. It was also a result of feeling inadequate in her New Zealandness. Coming from a land 'more English than England', a British commonplace that deprived the New Zealand traveller–writer of her identity, 'my literary lie was an escape from a national lie that left a colonial New Zealander overseas without any real identity' (p. 20).

This forms an interesting contrast with the work of another New Zealand writer who was living in London at this time, C.K. Stead. In his long poem 'Pictures in a Gallery Undersea', written in the late 1950s, Stead calls up the ghosts of Pound, Eliot and their contemporaries. No matter how equivocal the poem is about the relation between the early modernist world of pre-1914 London and its own moment of 1958, it is able to establish a confident relationship with that masculine Anglo-American modernist tradition. The poem's style, a clever pastiche of Eliot, firmly establishes it within that world. The new writing from the Commonwealth with which Frame tentatively aligns herself is not even glimpsed in Stead's poem and appears to have been unknown to New Zealand readers of the time. In 1961 'Pictures in a Gallery Undersea' was voted the best poem published in the first 15 years of *Landfall*'s (New Zealand's main literary journal) existence. Like Stead, the readers of *Landfall* were still thinking in traditional ways about the relation between metropolitan centre and colonial outpost. Frame, by contrast, was alert to the new Britain of the 1950s and 1960s and the different kinds of cultural relationship it offered.

But this new identification could only be tentative and incomplete. Although she felt much in common with her Nigerian friend, Nigel – as colonials they had both had heavy doses of empire with lists of the good and bad, friends and enemies permanently identified – her ancestors, unlike Nigel's, were placed with the good and friendly. Hence the double disadvantage of the New Zealand traveller–writer, with her distinctive identity denied and no apparent basis for another. Earlier New Zealand writers might have gone to school in Harley Street or university at Oxford. Frame, on the other hand, cleans rooms at Battersea Technical College Hostel for students from Africa, India and the

Middle East. The exhausted wells of British literary culture peered into by Mansfield or Mulgan are no longer on the itinerary of the journey 'home'. As part of that movement back from the periphery to the metropolitan centre, Frame is closer to the world of Selvon and Lamming than of Murdoch or Spark. Her one meeting with a literary celebrity, Allen Sillitoe, has Frame looking on in wonder; 'I listened, quietly amazed, while Mrs. Goulden (the wife of her publisher) and the Sillitoes ranged from the servant problem to the au pair and back to the servant problem; there in the Mayfair apartment with its Persian rugs, Turkish cats, exquisite paintings, dark knobbly furniture' (p. 149).

There is, in *The Envoy from Mirror City*, a deeper, more personal level to all this. Frame had spent most of the decade before coming to Britain in mental hospitals in New Zealand. She arrived in London still diagnosed as a schizophrenic. The story of the patient investigation of her psychiatric history at the Maudsley, the discrediting of the diagnosis of schizophrenia, her 'poverty of being' once the by now reassuring label was removed, and her reconstruction of identity while writing novels in six-monthly cycles to fit in with the assured periods of National Assistance is mainly beyond the scope of this essay. However, this personal history can also be read as a version of that larger history of coming to London in search of the lost tribe of one's ancestors, discovering that the language has changed, and then beginning to rewrite oneself in the language and voices of London as it was being reconstructed in the 1950s and 1960s.

Frame's painful personal history is acutely her own and the insensitivity of reading it symptomatically is obvious. Yet there are significant parallels between the psychological and cultural levels of both *The Edge of the Alphabet* and *The Envoy from Mirror City*. The migrant or traveller is on a quest for identity. The place arrived at bears so little relation to the place expected that relocation becomes dislocation. The 'real thing' seems most unreal of all. Consequently the traveller continues to look back, examining not the place of arrival but the place of departure, clinging to an identity that no longer makes sense. Toby Withers remains caught, psychologically and culturally, at this point, unable to get beyond the title of his projected book. Frame, however, comes to find the strangeness and otherness of London hospitable. The discovery that she is not in the home of her ancestors allows her to settle and write. She completes three novels in eighteen months. She finds reassurance in the silent unknown company of other writers. When finally she leaves London after a residence of seven years it has become for her like living in the home of a

huge family even though she knows almost no one (and certainly
no one who is anyone). Britain has not proved to be a grandmother waiting to receive and inspect her, and to whom she is
answerable. It is no one she has ever seen before, and this has
allowed her to begin to construct new identities beyond the reach
of mother England and fledgeling colony. Towards the end of her
months in the Maudsley Frame changed her name and was issued
with a new passport. (I understand that her surname became
Clutha, the name of the largest river in New Zealand's South
Island.) The strangeness of London and its newly variegated
culture had helped to enable this reinvention of herself. New
possibilities had been opened up by that other Britain of the
1950s and 1960s.

The Adaptable Man had its genesis in time Frame spent in East
Suffolk as the caretaker of a thatched cottage.[5] This novel, however, is not as it seems. If London is no longer the imperial
centre validating the cultures of its far-flung outposts and authen-
ticating colonial identities, the English countryside has become
absurd and meaningless. *The Adaptable Man* is a post-colonial
full-stop to a tradition stretching from Austen through Hardy and
Powys to their latter-day imitators. Her mock setting of Little
Burgelstatham is less an attempt to expose the reality behind the
outward serenity of English village life, although it does this, than
to deconstruct a particular kind of novel which has been one of
the mainstays of English fiction. It can, I think, be read as a
further step in the process of Frame's decolonisation.

Although 'rooted' in the English countryside, *The Adaptable Man*
is full of travellers. The Prologue has the repeated sentence – 'The
thought that he is not a migrating bird might make a man mad' –
and this idea seems to power the novel. Characters announce themselves in terms of where they have recently come from: 'I, Vic
Baldry, farmer, returned from my honeymoon in Australia'; 'I, Botti
Julio, Italian farm worker, coming to Little Burgelstatham for six
weeks to help with the black-currant harvest.' Botti, gratuitously
murdered on the night he arrives, has travelled to England with an
image of the country as a nation of tailors, the streets full of people
in Sunday suits, and with meaningless tourist phrases learnt by rote:
'These photographs are under-exposed. Please will you intensify
them.' This is one of several recurring phrases which loop back into
the novel as a comment on its own procedures. Vic Baldry transforms his home into a replica of Australia with slide-shows and
pictures on the wall. In these and other ways a kind of mock-
rootedness is established, and with it the unreality of English country life and writing. There are some beautiful examples of dead-pan.

We are told of Russell Maude, old-fashioned dental surgeon: 'His reputation as a maker of teeth had extended as far as Tydd' (p. 193). As C.K. Stead has remarked, Frame 'planted landmines everywhere in those bogus English fields'.[6] This culminates at the end of the novel with the collapse of a huge chandelier which kills most of the main characters. It is also, however, played off against an East Suffolk past which is real enough. The renovation of a cottage in the village uncovers a poster advertising the slave sale of a negro woman for £5.00 at Tydd Market. This detonates romantic images of the past as well.

The novel's narrator, Unity Foreman, is a journalist writing 'first-hand' reports to her editor's specification on the life of a village she has never seen. Her recipe – one-third flora and fauna, one-third people, one-sixth old customs and one-sixth progress – is also Frame's. Unity, in turn, is mirrored by Alwyn, the novel's truly adaptable man (Botti's murderer, father of his mother's child) who ends up living in Spain writing for an English editor about places he has never seen. Behind these figures lie Frame and her editor at W.H. Allen, Mark Goulden. After publishing her fourth novel *Scented Gardens for the Blind* (1963), Goulden had set Frame up in a comfortable London flat in South Kensington to write a novel that would sell. Hence, it would seem, the pastiche; Frame is actually refusing to write the kind of novel her publisher has commissioned while seeming to do so, or rather, she is doing both at once. Even the novel's epigraph in which Mark Goulden is thanked for 'giving me a quiet place to write part of this novel' has been mined.[7]

The Adaptable Man is Frame's most explicit rebuttal of English culture and writing as it has commonly been understood. The 'green language' of pastoral (the phrase is Raymond Williams') traditionally used to celebrate an 'unchanging' countryside and, so often, the hierarchical social structure it supported, is wittily and systematically undermined. In this novel she writes ostensibly from within English culture. There is nothing, or little, to suggest that for narrator, or author, 'home' is elsewhere. She does record in *The Envoy from Mirror City* that a sharp-eyed reviewer noticed her un-English usage of Orwell River rather than River Orwell (New Zealand idiom has the name of the river first), and concludes from this that 'unless the writer embraces the language of the new land there are constant betrayals of language' (p. 153). But in *The Adaptable Man* Frame is only pretending to be an English writer. Her reviewer should have been more interested in why the untravelled and thoroughly English Greta Maude should, when thinking of the night sky, reflect: 'The heavens whirled, but the Southern Cross did not show' (p. 92).

* * *

Since the mid-1960s New Zealand writers have been no more likely to come to Britain than to go to New York or Sydney, or to stay at home. Frame's writing of the early 1960s demonstrated that all the old and particular reasons for journeying to Britain had gone. The recognition that New Zealand was being cut adrift from Britain led quickly to the development of a post-colonial mentality in literature as in other things. New Zealand writers have, of course, continued to see Britain as a possible setting for their fictions. Keith Ovenden's O.E. (1986) examines the cultural meaning for New Zealanders of overseas experience, and Marilyn Duckworth returns to an English setting in *Rest for the Wicked* (1986).[8] Most recently Barbara Anderson's *Portrait of the Artist's Wife* (1992) repeats the familiar journey in search of individual and cultural authentication. But for many writers, however, this narrative has lost its significance. England can still be visited, but the only real interest now in making the journey is to show how meaning has drained out of it.

A particularly good example of this is Bill Manhire's story 'South Pacific', collected in his volume *The New Land: A Picture Book* (1990). Its protagonist, Allen, comes to London from New Zealand to try and market a board game he has devised called *South Pacific*. It is the year of the Zebrugge ferry disaster. His visit to London is fleeting, almost subliminal. London in 1986 is a city of games – board games, sex games, fantasy games – and of bizarre heritage museums. The plague display at the London Dungeon has live rats behind the glass scurrying about a skull; on a grain-filled bowl beside the skull Allen can make out the lettering of the word DOG. This Pacific visitor pauses in front of Sawney Beane, the Scottish cannibal, a reversed and flattened re-enactment of European encounters with South Pacific cannibalism in previous centuries. 'I thought it would be *frightening*', remarks the disappointed eight-year-old daughter of a friend with whom he visits the London Dungeon. The language trick is, by now, played out. The signs of London are as obvious and banal as that word DOG on the side of the bowl. From Allen's hotel window in Bloomsbury (that place again) the signs read 'Prestige Office Space', 'Superior Office Space'. The unreality is still there – the view of roofs and chimney pots is 'Mary Poppins stuff' – but it is no longer disturbing or even interesting. Signs and images are more or less interchangeable. On the calendar above Allen's bed the legend reads, 'March – the Gardens at Crathes Castle, Grampian', but the picture is of snow-clad Ben Nevis against a background of cloud. Manhire's London is somewhere/nowhere, a city of images, a simulacrum of itself and of other world cities.

'South Pacific' is also a dialogue with Janet Frame. On leaving New Zealand Allen's wife has given him *The Envoy from Mirror City*, 'a suitable gift for travellers'. Waking early one morning he reads the section about Frame's stay in Andorra and her inadvertent engagement to an Italian fruit-picker, El Vici Mario, who lodged in the same house as she did. The autobiography tells how she escaped the engagement with a promise to return which she had no intention of keeping. Allen, asleep again, dreams that El Vici has pursued Frame to London where he discovers a display of her books in a shop behind New Zealand House in Haymarket. El Vici enters the shop holding Allen's *South Pacific* board game and asks: '"Dov'e Nuova Zelanda?" ... Another traveller lost in a foreign city.' (Frame's El Vici seems rather closely related to that other Italian Andorran fruit-picker Botti Julio who, in *The Adaptable Man*, fails to survive his first night in England.) In Manhire's story, however, Allen's dream of Frame, El Vici and lost travellers in a foreign city is of an earlier time. Allen's own visit to London has nothing to do with being lost or found. He is simply there to market his board game. His journey will not lead to residence, and nor has it anything to do with that 'affliction of dream called Overseas'. It will not result in the acquiring of knowledge as a preparation for returning home to know that place properly for the first time. These kinds of quest have become meaningless. Manhire's protagonist does not even finish *The Envoy from Mirror City*. Instead he leaves it behind in the house of a relative who lives directly beneath the flight-path of Gatwick. No longer 'a suitable gift for travellers', it can be discarded. On the flight back Allen acquires a guidebook to India in its place.

Unlike Toby Withers or Janet Frame, Allen has no firm point of origin or source of identity; nationality has become as fictional as any other idea of place. New Zealand is no longer somewhere to be set against everywhere else. It is just another counter in the board game of late-twentieth-century international culture. Auckland is a wall poster in New Zealand House, London: '"Auckland: City of Sails". The blue slashed with sheets of white.' The story's final section is headed, '*London – Bombay – Perth – Melbourne – Auckland*', Allen's flight route 'home', but the sequence is potentially endless. Unlike Eliot's litany – 'Jerusalem Athens Alexandria/Vienna London/Unreal' – Manhire's lacks historical depth. At the end of the story, mid-flight somewhere between Bombay and Perth, Allen has a second dream: 'he was in Auckland, clouds and sails. But it was London, and he was walking in the City ... Snow fell into the concrete moats of the Barbican. El Vici rode past on his bicycle waving slowly. "Dov'e Nuova Zelanda?"' It is a wave of farewell and a valedictory question. The old polarity of Britain and New Zealand within which one particular colonial identity was formed has been dissolved. The implicit defiance of Frame's post-colonial insistence that 'everyone comes from the other side of the world' (*The Edge of the Alphabet*, p. 104) has been given a post-modern inflexion in Manhire's version of this idea. At the end of the twentieth century everyone seems to come from more or less the same place. It is not that the margins have become the centre, but that centres can no longer hold; things fall together.

Notes

1. T.B. Macaulay, 'Von Ranke', *Critical and Historical Essays*, vol. 3 (London: Longman, 1862), p. 101.
2. Ian Wedde and Harvey McQueen (eds), *The Penguin Book of New Zealand Verse* (Auckland: Penguin, 1985), p. 25.
3. The immediately following discussion draws on J.G.A. Pocock's brilliant essay 'Deconstructing Europe', *London Review of Books*, 19 December 1991.
4. This repeated a previous hoax in which Frame had sent poems to the *London Magazine* from New Zealand claiming they were the work of a Pacific Island woman recently arrived in Auckland; see vol. 2 of Frame's autobiography *An Angel at My Table*, p. 161. In both cases the poems were said to be fresh and interesting but their standard of English was not quite up to scratch.
5. See *The Envoy from Mirror City*, ch. 20.
6. C.K. Stead, 'Janet Frame: Language is the Hawk', in Stead's *In the Glass Case: Essays on New Zealand Literature* (Auckland: AUP/OUP, 1981), p. 131.
7. See Stead, 'Janet Frame', pp. 131–2 for a fuller account of Frame and Goulden.
8. For an account of these and related novels see Lawrence Jones' essay 'The Novel', in Terry Sturm (ed.), *The Oxford History of New Zealand Literature in English* (Oxford University Press: 1991), pp. 179, 186–7.

11. England from the Antipodes: Images of England in Australian Fiction, 1960–88

Gay Raines

The record of changing images of England in Australian fiction is, at one and the same time, the record of the growing cultural confidence and independence of a 'new' literature. Australian literature, like its American counterpart, only gradually emerged from writing initially perceived as 'English', even though written in a different place. Two novels can be said to have marked the point of departure for the first phase of 'Australian' fiction. The first, and best known, is Marcus Clarke's *His Natural Life*,[1] first serialised in the *Australian Journal* in 1870–72. It opens with a splendidly evoked Dickensian England, full of darkness, doom, melodrama and Law Courts. The hero, transported as a convict, suffers dreadfully, escapes, becomes successful on the goldfields, and crosses Europe in an adventurous return to England. The initial mystery surrounding him is unfolded and he is exonerated. At the end he is an English aristocrat, safely home after adventures in the colonies. When the novel was edited for book publication, however, the return to England was dropped, allowing the major strength – the Australian convict sections – to have undiluted impact as the main drive and vision of the book.

A second marker came when Rolf Boldrewood attempted, in *Robbery Under Arms* (1888),[2] to do what Mark Twain had done for American literature in *Huckleberry Finn* (1884). Dick Marston, the narrator, is a bushranger, part of whose commentary is recorded in colloquial rhythms from which an Australian 'voice' frequently quite clearly emerges. Moreover, the most powerful character in the book, Marston's father, shows vividly that resistance to authority which even today is still sometimes seen as typically Australian. But the novelist does not manage the job quite thoroughly enough. The ethos which the book finally affirms is that of the English colonial gentleman, epitomised in the character of Falkland, the squatter. This character reflects the views of Boldrewood, the magistrate, and it is his values, and his polite prose, which the repentant Marston finally embraces.

By the 1890s, however, the journal, *The Bulletin*, had begun to encourage a much more determined local realism, giving rise to a self-consciously nationalist strain of writing, sometimes described as, precisely, 'the *Bulletin* school'. The bush stories of Henry Lawson and Barbara Baynton, for example, first published in its pages, show no trace of either English setting or ethos. Their vivid evocations of the land, the life lived on it, the experiences, social relations and morality derived from it, speak only of the Australian place. *Bulletin* writers were deliberately and consciously trying to create a national literature. Miles Franklin, one of the younger protégées of the school, almost aggressively hymns her Australia in the closing pages of *My Brilliant Career* (1901).[3] Just as Federation seemed to be preparing Australia for a degree of independent world citizenship, Australian fiction also seemed to be setting off to its own independent start.

Even so, the 'colonial mind' persisted, sowing in subsequent Australian authors and artists the pervasive suspicion that the centre of things really lay elsewhere, causing what A.A. Phillips described, in 1950, as a 'cultural cringe'.[4] The phrase elicited wide recognition on first publication and has had currency ever since. Even though Phillips himself argued, in 1983, that there was little justification for the continuing use of the phrase he had launched,[5] Chris Wallace-Crabbe, one of Australia's leading poets, could still, in 1990, be found questioning whether Australian writing can measure up with the best in the world.[6] In earlier decades, the need so many Australian authors felt, to get out of the provincialism which distance from England and Europe seemed to impose on them, led to a great deal of expatriation of talent – even as the Australian government was working overtime, by way of assisted passage schemes throughout the 1950s and 1960s, to attract immigrants travelling in the opposite direction.

Some notable expatriates, such as Clive James, Germaine Greer, Peter Porter and Janette Turner Hospital, did not return to settle permanently in Australia, but many more did, and it is in the images of England and the English recorded in their work that it is possible to observe a deeper and more pervasive reorientation taking place. It is a change which finally dissolved the umbilical relationship with the parent culture and set Australian fiction free within a more confident tradition than that first turn-of-the-century phase of nationalist literature. It is this change which the present discussion seeks to trace.

Henry Handel Richardson's trilogy, *The Fortunes of Richard Mahony* (1930), is an account of an emerging society which has, in Australian literature, a stature similar to that of George Eliot's *Middlemarch* in the English tradition. *Fortunes* is central in its tradition because, at its heart, however wide its scope, the trilogy grapples with the fundamental Australian experience – the disorientation caused by immigration trauma. Transmuted in subsequent generations into a persistent sense of being culturally misplaced on the globe, this disjunction lies behind all the later necessary processes of cultural adjustment.

Richardson herself, having left Australia, never returned, but the second volume of her trilogy, *The Way Home* (1925),[7] based on her own father's experience, records the restless movement back and forth which many an immigrant to Australia will recognise. Unable to settle down in Australia Richard Mahony goes back to England which, from the antipodes, had seemed a social and intellectual haven to which he thirsted to return. However, more Australianised than he had in fact realised, the English environment, in northern town or West Country village, now strikes him as claustrophobic, and the people as limited, rigid and insular. He sees them to be snobbish, incapable of appreciating the qualities of his wife's proudly Australian character and ways, and suspicious of his own medical skills, preferring ignorant or greedy practitioners to his own professionalism, simply because he had been to Australia. Frozen out, and bitterly disillusioned with his supposed homeland, he retreats south again. This early negative account of England is, in context, a reflection of the state of a sensitive mind suffering cultural dislocation, but it also appears to determine, being in a major and central work, the frequently antipathetic vision of England which later Australian writers would also be driven to record.

Better recognised in world letters is Christina Stead, whose *Cotter's England* (1967)[8] would provide her definitive account of the heart of England as she saw it. Her *For Love Alone* (1944)[9] – a largely autobiographical novel – is the forerunner of many another account of an Australian writer or artist who feels drawn to travel to England. The heroine, Teresa, overworks, almost starves herself, for four years to save money to go there but, ironically, the vividest parts of the novel lie in the Sydney sections before her departure. The detailed account of the young woman/incipient artist and her experience of London is introverted, rather than focusing on her environment. This heroine is far more interested in herself than in England. In Elizabeth Harrower's novel on a similar subject, *The Catherine Wheel* (1960),[10] issues generated by the place emerge more clearly. The protagonist, Clemency James, is described as, like Stead's Teresa, having worked hard to get to England, and also suffering disorientating personal relationships while there. But while Stead's Teresa loves a fellow-Australian, and then an American, Harrower's heroine is disturbed and undermined by her experience of different kinds of English people. This projects the author's perceptions of, and responses to, England and Englishness through more complicated frames than those established by her initial descriptions of place.

The vocabulary used to define the setting marks the faintly critical, distancing tension in the feelings of the Australian visitor. London in winter, 'the centre of the universe', is described as a place of steely dark sky and swirling smoke with enigmatic façades of semi-public buildings, bare black avenues and paths, and empty seats and grass. Snow lies untidily in drifts and camouflaged ice deceives on dark, apparently normal paths. A restaurant in Chelsea is plushy, stagey and hot. In spring, Richmond Park is palely green under a high, pale-blue sky, may trees are stiff with blossom, and the water glints grey and gold. In summer, there are blazing flowers in the parks, and sleazy blue blasts from the exhausts of snubby dark English cars. In either season, the house she lives in continually has the raw dank sooty smell of fog. Clearly rather out of tune with this environment, her difficulties do not surprise as they develop.

One problem in England, she finds, is people knowing who you are and how you make that clear. In her good-quality coat Clemency, a law student on a low budget, feels unintentionally deceitful, for it seems to disguise what she is. At home the aim was, whoever you were and if you could, to present a front of expensive elegance. But in the London of the late 1950s it was obligatory to show what one was and did: there was this uniform for socialists, or that for hereditary shoppers in Harrods. There, Clemency had no idea what the legitimate trappings for an Australian might be. She tried to articulate some kind of national identity for herself. Observing fellow-occupants in her house she thought: 'What a pity they [are] not happier, like me, not full of purpose, interest, affection, not born Australian and free, not less afraid of themselves and one another!' But there is irony in this for it is her own 'openness' which, becoming compulsive, brings about her downfall.

The English people who befriend her come from two poles of society: the self-destructive, self-indulgent cultural fringe epitomised by Christian Roland, with whom she becomes infatuated; and the calmly collected, faintly patronising brother and sister, Lewis and Helen, who watch kindly but with detachment as she falls apart under Roland's corrosive influence. The confident Australian self at the opening of the book loses command of her identity on extended exposure to the pressures of these kinds of people. Like Henry Handel Richardson, Harrower leaves us thinking that the weakness lies in the character of the protagonist, but there is no doubt that Harrower is depicting England and the English as contributing to the erosion of Australian composure.

Martin Boyd's slightly later *When Blackbirds Sing* (1962)[11] is set during the First World War. It was, by coincindence, published as the young Clive James arrived in England that very same year. Though among the best known of Australian commentators, James's continual tendency to neutralise or undercut his own opinions makes his autobiographical *Unreliable Memoirs* (1980, 1985, 1990) virtually useless for the present purpose. Nevertheless, in Volume 2, *Falling Towards England*,[12] he recalls his ambivalent feelings in 1962 while watching the Changing of the Guard at Buckingham Palace with a group of other Australians:

> Needless to say we did not regard ourselves as tourists. Whatever our convictions, we were children of the Empire. One of us rather embarrassingly stood to attention. It was not myself, since I was a radical socialist at the time, but I understood. It was something emotional that went back.

This duality, which at bottom, no doubt, also underlay the unease of Harrower's heroine, is also the basic subject of Martin Boyd in *Where Blackbirds Sing*. There he is able to project and distinguish its elements more clearly against the setting of the First World War. The England of that time is seen largely in terms of its aristocratic, town and country house dimension. The protagonist, Dominic, Australian-born of English parents, returns 'home' to fight both for his Australian farm and the English country estate he is to inherit. Staying with family friends at Dilton, on his way to the war, he sinks gracefully into the traditional way of life which is his heritage. But at the periphery of his consciousness lies his Australian farm where his wife can think of no better life than 'to live on their own land in this perfect climate' where 'human contacts were dictated by inclination and not by social compulsion'. That was far better than to 'live in a place which they had done nothing to make'.

In the early part of his visit to England, Dominic feels as much a part of the place as the oak trees and the bricks in old houses. It is his element. He lapses into the peacefulness of the past. But, gradually, the members of English society with whom he mixes (in particular the woman to whom he was once engaged, who attracts him again in the first glamour of his return) are revealed as spiritually bankrupt, altogether without the political will to end a war in which basic human values are being set at nought. He begins to see England as irresponsibly squandering its heritage. Estates similar to his own, for example, are vanishing under rapacious death duties as one son after another dies in the war. And yet it goes on. He finds he cannot understand what is inducing his supposed homeland to fling a whole generation into the jaws of Moloch. When compelled by tradition and convention to kill a young German boy at the very moment of human recognition between them, Dominic becomes finally disillusioned with his heritage. He no longer has any feelings about it. 'The traditional room in which he had lived [i.e. his concept of England] was stripped of its furnishings, hollow and dead.' On return to Australia he tosses his Military Cross, and the medal inscribed 'The War for Civilisation' into a deep pond, seeing his action as a repudiation of the social order which presented them, as well as of the war. It is ironic that his wife, whose basic instincts are pro-Australian, is unable to understand his disaffection. Colonial loyalty persists for her although she has not set foot in the old country.

Cotter's England (1967) was the last novel Christina Stead wrote before returning to live in Australia after many years in England, Europe and America. There are no Australian protagonists and therefore no distracting issues about uncertain Australian identity. This is, entirely, an Australian's objective view of England and the English, as seen at the fringe of metropolitan life in London's East End, and in the heart of the depressed industrial north of Durham and Newcastle, during the period of the Cold War. The main character, Nellie Cotter, a mediocre journalist, commutes between her work in London and family home in the north. The characters in the novel talk and argue continually, rather at the expense of anything like environmental and social content. Such images of England as appear, in the two main locations and a scattered handful of other places, are inclined to be bleak, in tune with the novelist's perception of both the country and its people. Stead chooses to describe the flint mines in Norfolk, where the heathland is especially desolate in winter (though occasionally it is lovely in summer); Stonehenge, where 'you can feel the people who were there thousands of years ago and you can't stand it'; the moors in Scotland, where the emptiness is frightening and stoats are threatening; and Newcastle, where 'the iron of its ribs and backbone stand out when you first look' and the people 'stand against the Scots, they stand against the southerners and midlanders: they don't even like their neighbours the Yorkshiremen; and yet they don't think much of themselves'. All these attributes of the people of Newcastle seem to sum up England and the English for this Australian commentator.

Nellie's husband, George, a once committed socialist, is disillusioned, saying that men have changed and the talk in pubs is no longer serious. Nellie argues with him but is not allowed to seem a sensible judge of such matters. Extravagant in her own sentimental socialism, an emotional bully wrapped up in her own feelings, she can be damaging to the other women and workers she encounters during their depressing bedsit life in London. Along with her brother, Tom, also eccentric and mercurial in temperament, she is summed up by their distorted and changing images in the fairground Palace of Mirrors. Nevertheless, the two of them remain profoundly connected to their home in Bridgehead, 'a bit of England with the lid off ... the furnace beneath the green moor'. That home, typical of the area, is poverty-stricken and depressed, inhabited by a senile mother, her crotchety and aged brother who keeps his savings in a tool-box under his bed, and Nellie's slightly mad sister who will rob her uncle and put him into the street when her mother dies. The family is a constant drain on Nellie who has sent money home all her working life. Tom sees that it is all dreadful, ruefully recalling the privations suffered in their childhood which, being widespread in the area, had resulted in a wizened, physically depleted population. The only glamour in their lives had been lent by the memory of their father, Pop Cotter, who, wrong-headed and self-destructive as he was, always proudly refused any pension or state handout on behalf of his undernourished family as well as himself.

But the connection remains passionate for Nellie. She protests when George wants to leave the country and live abroad: 'What's wrong with my England?' George replies that it is

The England of the depressed that starved you all to wraiths, gave Eliza TB, sent your sister into a Home, and your mother into bed with malnutrition ... I lived through the unemployment, the starvation, the war, I knocked out a few bloody eyes and I got me fists skinned a few times, that's all I ever got: and now I'm going to live for my country. You stay here and die in it.

Nellie does follow her husband when he goes but, ironically, George is killed in the privileged setting of a skiing accident on the continent where the foreign press write of him, not as the renegade he is, but as 'a great fighter for the British working class'. It is the unstable, garrulous Nellie who returns to 'Cotter's England' but she takes up the same ineffective life as before. There is no change, no escape. In this novel yet another Australian author projects England and the English as barren and self-destructive, lacking in principle and drive, and sluggish from the weight of the past.

If, in the 1960s, Boyd and Stead attempted an objective assessment of England and its people – instead of picturing Australian protagonists undermined by them as Richardson and Harrower had done – two novelists of the 1970s showed their characters as able to take the place, or leave it, confident enough to suffer and grow in their own way, neither conditioned nor warped by the environment in which they have happened to find themselves. Barbara Hanrahan's heroine, Virginia, in *Sea Green* (1974),[13] is a young artist who feels the perennial pull to be elsewhere, and sets out to study print-making in a college in Holborn. On the boat to England she has her first sexual experience with an Italian crewman who, being married, drops her at the end of the voyage. Later, in England, she has an affair with a heartless and self-centred South African, and undergoes an abortion. The novel closes with Virginia, having got through to the other side of these experiences and begun successfully to make her first screen print, content to stay in England for the time being, happy in a relationship with a fellow Australian, while others of their friends have been returning to Australia, unsatisfied with their experiences 'abroad'. The last page sums up her experience. She had crossed the sea, and she had suffered. Experience had ripped something away from her, but she had learned that for your life to come alive, and to grow, you had to be hurt. A seminal insight for her, as a person and an artist, it is something she has won from her private pain, and has nothing to do either with England (where most of her suffering took place) or with the English.

The England against which this experience unfolds is, for the most part, sympathetically rendered in language untouched by any hint of Australian resentment or tension of the kind which seems to mark descriptions in *The Catherine Wheel*. Living in Shepherds Bush 'she walked each day in a landscape which she loved – a gentle natural landscape of powder-blue and chalky-green built all over with grubby man-made grey'. The grubbiness, the flaws of age are what she likes best. The anonymous rows of weathered brick that leapt at the sky, the ragged privet and laurel and ivy that bloomed among the greyness – that had bloomed so long –

are beautiful to her: 'Somehow, in Adelaide age hadn't been poetic like this.' Bloomsbury squares, Drury Lane, the Strand, Fleet Street, Gamages and the jewellers' shops in Hatton Garden. So many old things – pendants and cameos, rings for mourning and golden chains ... even the ugliness seems beautiful because it is old.

Having grown up while the so-called 'White Australia' policy [14] was still in place, England, to her, occasionally seems strange: she buys lurid red meat in the 'Pak' butchers and looks at a window display of African cosmetics: La India Olive Oil, Pressing Oil Glosine, Florida Water and Liquid of Light. When, on low walls outside their houses people sat talking, lots of them were black – 'it was different from Australia'. But she soon identifies Kiwi Court and Kangaroo Valley, where other antipodeans hang out, and begins to get her bearings. In her dark times, however, she can feel imprisoned in a cage of loneliness, in a featureless, alien world. The language of her descriptions then becomes flatter, reflecting her state of mind. She goes to a Christmas party at a private house in Ealing which is 'stuccoed mock-Tudor, surrounded by balding lawns, sickly conifers, and shrivelled leaves that turned into delphiniums in summer'. Eric, who does something in computers, lets them in. He is wearing a fawn Acrilan jumper. They go into a front room where people 'sat in a glum circle about others more daring, who stood and chatted volubly ... Christmas cards yawned on a string, a nylon spruce bough wilted in the fireplace'.

This is more pathetic fallacy than a critique of the English, however, for it soon passes. By the end of the novel, her spirits improved, and with a fellow-Australian whom she loves, she leaves Fulham for Cornwall 'for sand that begins fine and white and crumbling, turns damp and cream as it meets water that changes from clear bottle-green to blue shot with purple'. Her house, among tubs of lobelias and marigolds outside the Swordfish Inn, overlooks a harbour that is sometimes blue, sometimes greyly muffled with fog, while a fishing fleet breathes softly before a pier. Throughout the novel, the English context is registered as by an artist's eye (Hanrahan was also a successful painter and print-maker with an international reputation) to reflect the feelings of the protagonist. It remains innocent of blame for her tribulations, and is barely analysed by the author. For this writer England is no more than a setting, little capable of influencing the character one way or another.

Norah Porteus, Jessica Anderson's heroine in *Tirra Lirra by the River* (1978),[15] is similarly indifferent to the England experience as such. After a painful marriage and divorce she goes to London 'not because I particularly wanted to, but as an affirmation of the wonderful discovery, that *nobody could stop me*'. To begin with she finds herself repelled by the stony look of London, and its chilly regularity. Though the soft green cumulus of English trees moves her to rapture, it is the rapture of an audience who intends soon to leave the theatre. She sympathises with fellow-Australians who think this a nasty, dank, unfriendly country and agrees when they say: 'If you stay more than five years you become a pommified Aussie, than which there is no more pitiful creature on God's earth. Unless it's an aussiefied Pom.'

Her first reaction gradually tones down, however, for she is also glad to be away for a time from the 'contradictions of our home society – its rawness and weak gentility, its innocence and deep deceptions'. Soon she loses her distaste for London – but this improvement has too little of the positive in it to affect her deeper underlying attachment to Sydney. Intending always to go home, she is kept in London accidentally at the outbreak of war after which, a lucky chance having opened for her a career as a theatrical designer, she stays all the time there is work of her chosen kind. Her memories of the Depression, when she was a young woman in Sydney, have led her not to turn down any chance of work. So, as the years pass, memories of her home blur. But by retirement her perceptions have changed. The London she had first learned to accept, made up of little villages, is no longer what it had been. Those villages 'were now meshed by the flow of traffic into one huge hard city, whose constant movement confused, whose noise beat upon the brain'. Rents, too, have become punitive, and the whole place seems to have lost any charm it might once have had.

She returns home to Sydney, suffering illness as she re-adapts and begins slowly to pick up the threads of her family and early life. She recalls, guiltily, the cat she had had put down before she left London – a poor reward for being one of the last ties she had there. But basically she doesn't care. As she watches television in Australia she muses on the way it reaches out to the rest of the world, but when it shows her familiar places in London she responds only with 'a detached interest that contains a touch of incredulity'. Even after all the years she has spent there the place has clearly made little impact on her. It is a graceful, complex novel, uncovering the multiple layers of one lonely woman's quiet and seemingly uneventful life, but both author and protagonist project the strength of self-confident Australian identity, which is able to be almost indifferent to England, pursuing private dramas undisturbed by the accident of the English environment.

At the end of the 1970s Patrick White, the Australian novelist with the strongest international reputation, was so far from any complicating emotional ties with England as to be able to use London simply as material to be manipulated for the melodramatic purposes of his art. *The Twyborn Affair* (1979)[16] is structured like a triptych, grouping in discrete artistic units different phases of one story. There is no evident plot connection between the parts, and no apparent rational explanation for any of the phases through which the main character passes. White's protagonist is a transsexual. In the first part of the book (s)he is living in France as the wife of a slightly mad, elderly Greek. In the second part the character returns to his native Australia to take work as a jackeroo, attempting to find himself by engaging in hard physical labour, in the landscape of his birth. Attracted to the men with whom he works he feels, for a while, as if he belongs. Soon involved in homosexual relationships he is equally at ease in either the male or female role. But, fundamentally, the character is hermaphrodite, including in his/her nature the many various aspects of human gender to such an extent that (s)he is almost depersonalised. Consequently, his/her name changes in every manifestation and (s)he feels more related to something impersonal. In the second section 'Eddie' concludes: 'It was not sexual ambivalence after all which prevented him identifying with other men. His true self responded more deeply to those natural phenomena [in the landscape] which were becoming his greatest source of solace.'

In the third part Eddie transmutes yet again, into 'Eadith Trist', a stylish 'Madam' running a fashionable London brothel at the time of the Second World War. Here London is simply a third setting, a useful contrast to the other settings in France and Australia. The background it is pictured as providing is one of the kind of corruption within which the protagonist of this stage of the novel naturally finds his/her place. The English in this London are depicted with a distaste which makes caricatures of them, and fleshes out the lurid picture required. In the same street as Mrs Trist's brothel live a 'detritus' of minor nobility and recently arrived Colonials. In some houses the vanishing race of servants is still to be found, whether the sad put-upon variety, or those who are doing an enormous favour before twisting the knife and giving notice. Eadith's house, No. 84, is fortunate in those protecting it. They 'cajoled the police, and introduced on a paying basis Cabinet Ministers, visiting Balkan royalty, even scions of the British monarchy'. The English are universally unpleasant. They 'break out' into discussion, 'quivering with daring, brandy and malice', and Eadith's would-be lover, Gravenor (of suitably deathly name), is an ignoble lord with 'squamous' skin, who provides the house she trades in. Eadith is converting it from a drab and musty barracks into a sequence of tantalising glimpses, perspectives opening through beckoning mirrors 'to seduce a society determined on its own downfall'.

That this is more a setting for a melodrama than an attempt to get England into an Australian focus is evident from the extraordinary nature of the central story and its deliberately stylised structure and design. The point is enforced by Eadith's own words when she says 'she accepted her own corruption along with everything else and started casting a play she had been engaged to direct by a management above or below Gravenor and his exalted friends'. Nevertheless, coming after the multiracial changes noted in London by Barbara Hanrahan, and the traffic strangled, economically punitive monster noted by Anderson, White's colourful picture of political and sexual corruption could be said to help fill out a multifaceted account of the changing English capital coming from Australian pens.

Among these later writers, Shirley Hazzard, author of *The Transit of Venus* (1980),[17] is the only one who has not returned to Australia permanently. A visit there in 1976 preceded the writing of this novel, however. Her heroine, Caro, suggests a latter-day Isabel Archer. She and her sister, being Australian, provide the English with something new. Christian Thrale notes their clear perception unmingled with suspiciousness, and felt that their distinction was 'a high humorous candour for which ... they would be willing to sacrifice'. The English aristocrat, Tertia Drage, like Christian Thrale before her, 'found them insufficiently conscious of their disadvantage [as Australians] and would have liked to bring it home to them'. Even so 'she could not manage to put them in the wrong or in the shade'. The girls seem to remain untouched by their environment, essentially above it. Beside them the English generally seem both more rigid and more insecure, but one Englishman (not of the upper classes) does become Caro's destiny and final touchstone of all that is loyal, able and good.

The book charts Caro's journey from the innocence which, like Isabel Archer's, fails to appreciate the love of the 'good' Englishman and favours the glamour of the selfish, Osmond-like Paul Ivory; through appreciation of, and by, an older American; and on to a final realisation of the qualities of faithful Edmund Tice. As this primary story-line is worked out the action moves through Sydney, London, New York and Stockholm. Reflecting on the things which have shaped her, Caro recalls the picture book history of England which had upstaged the 'shrivelled chronicle' of Australian history in her early schooling. During her stay in England she becomes aware of a different kind of history, that of the effete First World War poet (father of Paul Ivory) which is no more vital now than the flickers on the screen in the TV documentary about his work. The contemporary England shown is that of Peverel, the country house of the scientist Sefton Thrale, who had 'done his best work before the Great War', at the same time as the faded and unreal poet was doing his. His work and his ethos are outdated and yet Sefton Thrale is still allowed to wield an influence which overrides the greater scientific intelligence of Edmund Tice. In the London of the same time there are two new books and a musical on Burgess and Maclean, an anecdote which somehow sums up the general position; 'England is a dotard repeating a single anecdote', concludes the main narrative voice.

But this evaluation of England is placed in a larger perspective:

In America, a white man had been shot dead in a car ... In Russia, a novelist had emerged from hell ... Russian tanks rolled through Prague while America made war in Asia. In Greece the plays of Aristophanes were forbidden, in China the writings of Confucius. On the moon, the crepe souls of modern man impressed the Mare Tranquillitatis.

Throughout the book the movements of the characters are crafted to fit an overall planetary symbolism which further extends the novel's perspective. Caro thus lives out her life against a backdrop which includes England but is much larger than it. England shrinks, in this novel, into being no more than a small, even insignificant, limited part of the cosmos, with failings no better and no worse than the failings of many other countries on the globe.

In *Homesickness* (1980),[18] published in the same year as *The Transit of Venus*, Murray Bail makes the growing insignificance of England to Australians even more painfully clear. Bail writes about a group of Australians on a package-tour of Africa, England, South America, New York and Russia. The group is described as moving within a certain loosely defined shape, elastic yet definite, as if formed by the protoplasm of the individuals comprising it. Wherever they go they look and feel separate from the main population, to one side. Their first stop is in Africa, where they begin their habit of trying to get to the heart of a place by way of its museums. Such an institution in Africa they find quixotic and haphazardly conceived. Even the title over the museum door has not managed to hold its meaning together, proclaiming itself as a MUSEU, the last letter of the word having long ago dropped off. In comparison with the chaotic and rootless impressions which they take from Africa, they find that England 'has a heavy steadiness', an 'untidy stateliness', while the air seems old and oppressive.

After a quick trip round London and some of its environs the group bears down, as in Africa, on its museums – the National, the Portrait Gallery, the Hayward, the Tate and so on – but the 'museum' by which Bail and his characters are most powerfully impressed is the railway's Lost Property Office. There, they feel as if they are touching the heart of England. Most of the contents of the place have been there 'for donkeys' years' and they do, indeed, offer a museum-like insight into changing times. The man who runs it keeps losing track of time and memory. The place seems to act like a drain. 'Was time composed of broken fragments', wonders one Australian faced with this particular correlative of England and the English, 'before drifting into dots?' Others are more unnerved: 'I found that place spooky', 'I got frightened'. Another is reminded by it to take his quinine tablet, to counteract the condition of London's underground pipes: 'You can't tell me the place is clean', he says. That was the trouble, the further away from home. 'Some of these countries could do with a good scrub.' Only at Australia House, reading their own newspapers, do they feel at ease. To them, London, like everywhere else except Australia, is going down the drain. It is not a place where an Australian feels a kind of homecoming. It is a place where Australians suffer from homesickness.

While there they also visit a commercial genealogist who traces their respective family trees back to their early roots in England, making clear their historical, umbilical connection with the land they are travelling in. But this strikes no warmth of recognition in them – it is merely a slightly bemusing curiosity. Likewise, when they later visit a stately home, they see only a featureless mound. No feelings of connection with this place are generated such as those Dominic, in *Where Blackbirds Sing*, feels on his first return to England. As in every other country they visit, their purely touristic relation to their surroundings is emphasised by the constant taking of photographs. You *had* to visit these old places – people back home would ask. But they had to admit that they left them cold.

One (unlikely) museum in Yorkshire has the curious effect of reminding them of home, the museum of corrugated iron, which Australia uses more than any other land. There they see pictures

of their own country and its buildings which beget a chorus of
nationalistic self-approval: 'It's time people realised. At least we
get things done', says Hammersley. 'What we've seen', says Doug
'makes you realise how ruddy lucky we are.' And so they move
on, through more airports and other countries and, inevitably,
begin to make comparisons as the journey nears its end. When
they reflect on the English, among all the others, they have little
to say for them. 'They're alright', says Doug, but generally they
feel they can 'let em go'. Not the brightest of souls, on the whole,
and evidently meant to represent the average, these antipodean
tourists are depicted by Bail, in 1980, as having quite different
feelings about England from those Clive James had observed
among fellow-Australians outside Buckingham Palace, even as late
as 1962. Those young men had been sure that they were no mere
tourists in London town. Murray Bail's travellers are glad to think
that is all that they are in this gloomy place.

Elizabeth Jolley emigrated to Australia at the age of 35 in
1959. *Miss Peabody's Inheritance* (1983)[19] was published nearly 25
years later when she was already fully established as an Australian
writer. The text is an entertaining send-up of literary–critical
dilemmas, about the difference between text and reality, and
about the attribution of authorial genesis. It provides an apt conclusion to the development outlined above, as it sets out to invert
the usual cultural relation between the two countries situated on
different sides of the globe.

Miss Peabody is a colourless, middle-aged spinster, living in
suburban London, going up and down on daily trains, cowed by
an invalid mother at home, barely keeping her head up at work
where she makes countless typing errors as she slaves for Mr
Bains at Fortress Enterprises. Her life is 'a series of clichés and
platitudes'. Writing on impulse to an Australian author she
becomes the recipient of instalments of a novel currently being
written. The world of that novel becomes more real to her than
her own, she almost expects to meet the characters when they,
fictionally, set out for London. After the death of her mother, and
her own breakdown, precipitated by her passionate involvement
with the imaginative world reaching out to her from Australia,
Miss Peabody leaves England to go to her author friend.

On arrival in Australia, Miss Peabody finds that 'Diana' has
just died, and that she had not been at all what Miss Peabody
had imagined. That, however, is almost irrelevant in the urgency
of her new circumstance. Now she, who had been, heretofore, the
audience, the one who, in all her negative Englishness, had somehow been begetter/sayee of the text drawn out of the Australian

author, finds that she has to transmute into author herself. For someone has to carry the unfinished text, which almost has a life of its own, on to its next stage, and *she* is in the position to do it. The home she had lived in, in England, back in Kingston Avenue, is now, significantly, perceived by her to be just an 'empty' house. It is written off. She will stay in Australia.

So, in this instance, the draw of imaginative vitality and creative power comes, for once, from the Antipodes, pulling the provincial and marginalised spirit of England towards, and into, itself. There, Miss Peabody's writing powers, which have been steadily increasing throughout her correspondence with the Australian author, are ready at last to flourish. Becoming a vehicle for the Australian cultural vitality, which has finally brought her alive, she sets about getting a typewriter. Now 'all she really needed to enter into her inheritance was a title'. Thus, as the typical Englishwoman becomes subsumed in the Australian creative task, Jolley wittily demolishes any lingering vestige of cultural cringe.

With the approach of Australia's bicentennial in 1988 many Australian authors began instinctively to rewrite perceptions of their history.[20] Of those novels focusing on the English contribution to Australian culture, Thomas Keneally's *The Playmaker* (1987)[21] alone attempts to create a kindlier rapport with the 'mother' country, describing, instead of the harshest aspects of life in the Sydney Cove penal settlement of 1789, the way in which officers and administrators were under equal stress with the convicts, who themselves were, in fact, more comfortably placed there than they would have been at home. The main action is the attempt of one officer to help convicts stage a performance of Farquhar's *The Recruiting Officer* (1706), and the civilising care with which he ponders on and utilises the qualities of his cast, becoming thoroughly involved with them. Peter Carey's Booker Prize-winning *Oscar and Lucinda* (1988),[22] in contrast, pointedly begins from a rewriting of a famous passage in Victorian literature, the episode of the Christmas pudding in Edmund Gosse's *Father and Son* (1907). Carey's novel pictures the key figure of George Eliot as cold and distant, and unable to communicate fruitfully with the Australian heroine. It climaxes with the striking episode of an (Anglican) church, symbolically made of fragile glass, clumsily and inappropriately lugged into the bush, where it shatters and collapses about Oscar's ears on exposure to the treacherous forces of the new environment.

Kate Grenville's *Joan Makes History* (1988),[23] commissioned by the Bicentennial Committee, explores today's perceptions of what must have been the experience of a woman at different stages of

Australia's history. The main character is a grandmother born at the beginning of the twentieth century, an ordinary housewife, who likes to imagine her life as it would have been in earlier moments in history. The book starts with the conception of the earliest incarnation of Joan on one of the transport ships which brought 'muddles of mixed people' from the Thames or the Danube, in cabins which heard 'the roiling and difficult syllables, the guttural hawkings and strange sibilances of some of Europe's lesser-known languages' as well as the 'ingenious obscenities and sly, rude wit' of folk from Lambeth, Bow and Cheapside. Grenville, as author, 'gladly acknowledges the historical inaccuracies' but this 'muddle' is a 1988 Australian's perception of the degree of English input to her country's genesis, one which effectively cuts it down to smaller than the traditional size. English historical figures, like Captain Cook, are deliberately flat in characterisation, empty of sympathy or interest, and the main narrator, the representative twentieth-century Joan, is presented as being of second generation German–Australian extraction.

This handful of novels, seemingly begotten of a reflective point in a nation's history, could well be among the last in which England, or Englishness, figure as components with which Australian imaginations feel the need to get to grips, for, during the last half of the development which I have been describing, from 1979 to 1988, increasing numbers of Australia's best novels have been focusing on Asia.[24] England, so far away, on the other side of the world, is of fast decreasing interest in comparison with nearer neighbours. Almost in sympathy with this, the Australia Council's International Cultural Relations Budget is currently being redistributed in a way which reflects developments in Australian fiction. In 1990–91 12.5 per cent of the budget was allocated to Asian or Pacific-orientated projects. In 1991–92 this rose to 20.5 per cent. The target for 1992–93 is 50 per cent.[25]

In the spring of 1992, Australian, English and European academics gathered in Debrecen, Hungary, to launch, in two conferences, Australian Studies in its newly expanding academy. At Debrecen a Declaration was agreed upon by them, calling on the Australian government to improve funding levels to further cultural interchange with the old world. Government funds for this purpose in the UK, allotted to the Sir Robert Menzies Centre for Australian Studies,[26] have recently been directed to stretch to cover similar activities throughout Europe, in effect considerably cutting expenditure to be devoted in future to English–Australian cultural relations. If the findings of the present essay are valid, I fear that the Debrecen Declaration will be a cry in the wilderness. Political changes at national level usually ride on changes that have been gradually happening at the grass roots, which have already begun to find cultural expression. It has been suggested that England's membership of the European Community, loosening economic and, inevitably, political ties with Australia, was the trigger for Australian attention turning away from England and more towards Asia. But the changed attitude at government level no more than reflects, in administrative terms, changes in the perception of relations between England and Australia which Australian novelists have been exploring and expressing from the 1960s on. Not one of the novels discussed here appears, at any point, to attribute the changes in attitude which they reveal to the existence of the EC.

Though the implications for Australian Studies in England may well be regretted, steadily growing cultural independence is not. Requests for a change in the attitudes of governments, or even governmental decisions to increase funding, will make little difference to what has happened underneath. It is a long but valuable journey from Miles Franklin's rather shrill declaration in 1901:

> I am proud that I am an Australian, a daughter of the Southern Cross, a child of the mighty bush. I am thankful that I am a peasant, a part of the bone and muscle of my nation, and earn my bread by the sweat of my brow, as man was meant to do. I rejoice I was not born a parasite, one of the blood-suckers who loll on velvet and satin, crushed from the proceeds of human sweat and blood and souls. (p. 231)

to the kind of confidence expressed by Kate Grenville's Joan as she concludes her rewriting of Australian history (in *Joan Makes History*). There was a time when she would have raged at the idea that everything she has lived and felt had been experienced times over by others before her. But now she realises that in her ordinary life, as child, wife and grandmother in Australia, she has been part of all history:

> Around me in the mauve dusk, I can hear a child screeching at the idea of bedtime, a woman singing over the dishes clattering in the sink, and someone somewhere having a good sneeze. Long after I am dirt, there will still be such people screeching, singing and sneezing away, and I will always be a part of them. Stars blazed, protozoa coupled, apes levered themselves upright, generations of women and men lived and died, and like them all, I, Joan, have made history. (p. 285)

The author of these words thus places her Australian heroine's experience on an equal par with all human experience throughout time. She seems not to have heard of the 'cultural cringe' or, if she has, the phrase has left no impression on her at all.[27]

Notes

1. Marcus Clarke, *His Natural Life* (1870–2; Melbourn: George Robertson, 1874; London: Penguin, 1970).
2. Rolf Boldrewood, *Robbery Under Arms* (1882–3; London: Remington and Co., 1888).
3. Miles Franklin, *My Brilliant Career* (Edinburgh: Blackwood and Sons, 1901; London: Virago, 1980).
4. A.A. Phillips, 'The Cultural Cringe', *Meanjin* 9 (1950), pp. 299–302.
5. A.A. Phillips, 'Death to the Cringe!', *The Age Monthly Review* vol. 3, no. 2 (1983), pp. 16–17.
6. Chris Wallace-Crabbe, *Beyond the Fringe: Australian Cultural Over-Confidence?* (London: Sir Robert Menzies Centre for Australian Studies, 1990).
7. Henry Handel Richardson, *The Way Home* (London: Heinemann 1925).
8. Christina Stead, *Cotter's England* (London: Secker and Warburg, 1967).
9. Christina Stead, *For Love Alone* (New York: Harcourt Brace, 1944).
10. Elizabeth Harrower, *The Catherine Wheel* (London: Cassell, 1960).
11. Martin Boyd, *When Blackbirds Sing* (London: Abelard-Schuman. 1962).
12. Clive James, *Falling Towards England* (London: Jonathan Cape, 1985).
13. Barbara Hanrahan, *Sea Green* (London: Chatto and Windus, 1974).
14. The Immigration Restriction Act, drawn up at the time of Federation was, in effect, racist. It provided for a 'dictation test' to be used as a method of keeping Australia largely white European. The test was suspended in 1958 when it became possible for some non-white spouses of Australian or British citizens to enter the country. In 1966 further small changes allowed for a minimal number of highly skilled non-whites to enter, but it was not until 1973 that people of *any* colour could apply for entry as immigrants on an equal, non-selective basis. Until several years after that time the majority of urban Australians rarely saw a black face, unless it was an Aborigine's. And Aborigines had been written off as a race dying out, on the outskirts of society.

15. Jessica Anderson. *Tirra Lirra by the River* (Melbourne: Macmillan, 1978; New York: Penguin 1980).
16. Patrick White *The Twyborn Affair* (London: Jonathan Cape, 1979).
17. Shirley Hazzard, *The Transit of Venus* (London: Macmillan, 1980).
18. Murray Bail, *Homesickness* (London: Macmillan, 1980).
19. Elizabeth Jolley, *Miss Peabody's Inheritance* (St Lucia: University of Queensland Press, 1983; London: Penguin, 1984).
20. See Katerina Olijink Arthur's article 'Recasting History: Australian Bicentennial Writing', *Journal of Narrative Technique*, vol. 21, no. 1 (1991) pp. 52–9.
21. Thomas Keneally, *The Playmaker* (London: Hodder and Stoughton, 1987).
22. Peter Carey, *Oscar and Lucinda* (London: Faber, 1988).
23. Kate Grenville, *Joan Makes History* (St Lucia: University of Queensland Press, 1988).
24. Novels set in Asia by Australian authors are, for example: Robert Drewe's *A Cry in the Jungle Bar* (1979); C.J. Koch's *The Year of Living Dangerously* (1979); Blanche D'Alpuget's *Monkeys in the Dark* (1980) and *Turtle Beach* (1981); Ian Moffit's *The Retreat of Radiance* (1982); Margaret Jones's *The Smiling Buddha* (1985); Rod Jones's *Julia Paradise* (1986); R.F. Brissenden's *Poor Boy* (1987); Nicholas Jose's *Avenue of Eternal Peace* (1988); and Nancy Corbett's *Flouting* (1988). Helen Tiffin's 'Asia and the Contemporary Australian Novel' in *Australian Literary Studies* 11 (1984) pp. 468–79 examines the work of Patrick White, Randolph Stow, Robert Drewe, C.J. Koch, Blanche D'Alpuget, Janette Turner Hospital and Ian Moffit to reveal changing attitudes to Asia.
25. These figures are taken from the Minister for the Arts and Territories' reply to Senate Question No. 2018 placed by Senator Margaret Reynolds, one of the signatories of the Debrecen Declaration.
26. The Sir Robert Menzies Centre is situated in the Institute of Commonwealth Studies in the University of London.
27. For 'Images of Britain and the British' in Australian literature see Rudolph Bader, *The Visitable Past: Images of Europe in Anglo-Australian Literature* (Bern/Frankfurt/New York/Paris: Peter Lang, 1992).

Notes on Contributors

Rod Edmond is a Senior Lecturer in English at the University of Kent at Canterbury. His published work is mainly about Victorian Literature; *Affairs of The Hearth: Victorian Poetry and Domestic Ideology* appeared in 1988. He is currently writing a book about European representations of the Pacific from the time of Cook to the beginning of the twentieth century.

Abdulrazak Gurnah was born in Zanzibar/Tanzania. He was educated there and in England and now teaches literature at the University of Kent at Canterbury. He is the author of four novels, *Memory of Departure* (1987), *Pilgrims Way* (1988), *Dottie* (1990) and *Paradise* (1994), which was a finalist for the 1994 Booker Prize. He has edited *Essays on African Writing* (1993) and is an Associate Editor of the journal *Wasafari*.

Laura Hall has been a PhD candidate in the Department of Ethnic Studies at the University of California at Berkeley. She recently completed her dissertation on the Chinese community in Guyana.

Eamonn Hughes lectures in the School of English, Queen's University of Belfast. He is the editor of *Culture and Politics in Northern Ireland, 1960–1990* (1991) and has written numerous articles on Irish writing.

C.L. Innes is Professor of Post-Colonial Literatures at the University of Kent at Canterbury, where she teaches contemporary English literatures, including Irish, African and African-American. She is the author of *Chinua Achebe* (1990), *The Devil's Own Mirror: The African and the Irishman in Modern Literature* (1990) and *Woman and Nation in Irish Literature and Society, 1880–1935* (1993).

Louis James is Professor of Victorian and Modern Literature at the University of Kent at Canterbury. He taught at the University of the West Indies during the early 1960s, when the development of Caribbean writing was coming into being, and was involved in the ensuing Caribbean Artists Movement. He edited the first full-length study of Anglophone West Indian writing, *The Islands in Between* (1968) and wrote the first book on the Dominican-born Jean Rhys (1974). He has written and broadcast extensively on Caribbean literature.

A. Robert Lee is Reader in American Literature at the University of Kent at Canterbury. His publications include eleven volumes in the Vision Press Critical Series, *Black American Fiction Since Richard Wright* (1983), Everyman editions of Melville's *Typee* (1993), *Moby-Dick* (1973, 1993) and *Billy Budd* (1993), the essay-collection *A Permanent Etcetera: Cross-Cultural Perspectives on Post-War America* (1993), *Shadow Distance: A Gerald Vizenor Reader* (1994), and a wide range of essays on American and European multiculturalism.

Susheila Nasta lectures in the Department of English, Queen Mary and Westfield College, the University of London. She is founder editor of the literary journal *Wasafiri*, editor of *Critical Perspectives on Sam Selvon* (1986), and author of *Motherlands: Women's Writing from Africa, the Caribbean and South Asia* (1991).

Gay Raines is a Lecturer in English at the University of Kent at Canterbury where she has taught, and written about, Australian literature. She contributes the Australian report to *The Year's Work in English Studies*, is Secretary of the British Australian Studies Association, and organised the 1993 biennial conference, *Changing Courses: Australia Since the Forties*.

Michael Woolf is Director of the Council for International Exchange in London and wrote his PhD on contemporary Jewish–American literature at the University of Hull. He is the author of numerous articles on cultural matters and contributes regularly to BBC programmes.

Index

Index